LEVINAS
AND THE
CINEMA
OF
REDEMPTION

FILM AND CULTURE SERIES   *John Belton, General Editor*

FILM AND CULTURE
A series of Columbia University Press
EDITED BY JOHN BELTON

What Made Pistachio Nuts? Early Sound Comedy and the Vaudeville Aesthetic
HENRY JENKINS

Showstoppers: Busby Berkeley and the Tradition of Spectacle
MARTIN RUBIN

Projections of War: Hollywood, American Culture, and World War II
THOMAS DOHERTY

Laughing Screaming: Modern Hollywood Horror and Comedy
WILLIAM PAUL

Laughing Hysterically: American Screen Comedy of the 1950s
ED SIKOV

Primitive Passions: Visuality, Sexuality, Ethnography, and Contemporary Chinese Cinema
REY CHOW

The Cinema of Max Ophuls: Magisterial Vision and the Figure of Woman
SUSAN M. WHITE

Black Women as Cultural Readers
JACQUELINE BOBO

Picturing Japaneseness: Monumental Style, National Identity, Japanese Film
DARRELL WILLIAM DAVIS

Attack of the Leading Ladies: Gender, Sexuality, and Spectatorship in Classic Horror Cinema
RHONA J. BERENSTEIN

This Mad Masquerade: Stardom and Masculinity in the Jazz Age
GAYLYN STUDLAR

Sexual Politics and Narrative Film: Hollywood and Beyond
ROBIN WOOD

The Sounds of Commerce: Marketing Popular Film Music
JEFF SMITH

Orson Welles, Shakespeare, and Popular Culture
MICHAEL ANDEREGG

Pre-Code Hollywood: Sex, Immorality, and Insurrection in American Cinema, 1930–1934
THOMAS DOHERTY

Sound Technology and the American Cinema: Perception, Representation, Modernity
JAMES LASTRA

(continued page 257)

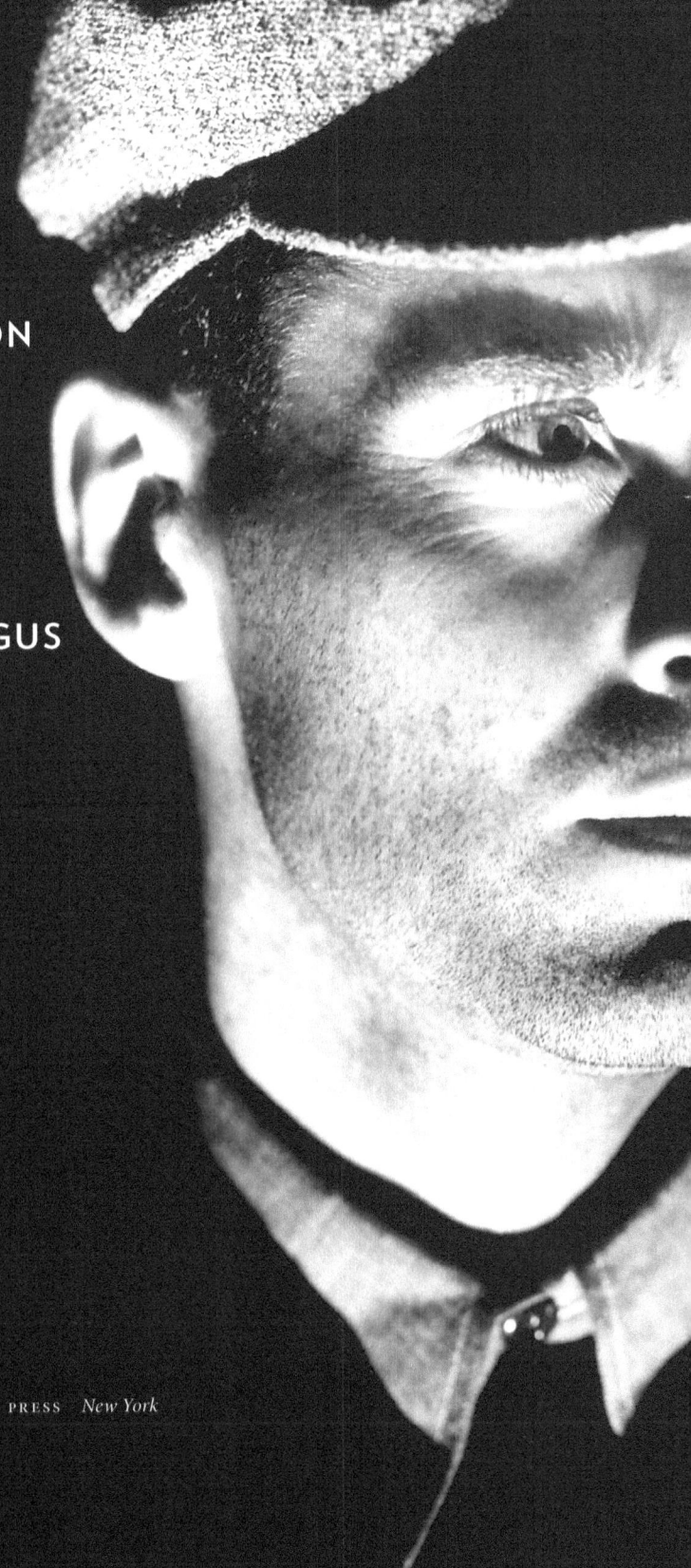

LEVINAS AND THE CINEMA OF REDEMPTION

TIME, ETHICS, AND THE FEMININE

SAM B. GIRGUS

COLUMBIA UNIVERSITY PRESS *New York*

COLUMBIA UNIVERSITY PRESS
Publishers Since 1893
New York   Chichester, West Sussex

COPYRIGHT © 2010 COLUMBIA UNIVERSITY PRESS
All rights reserved

Library of Congress Cataloging-in-Publication Data
Girgus, Sam B., 1941–
    Levinas and the cinema of redemption : time, ethics, and the feminine / Sam B. Girgus.
        p. cm. — (Film and culture)
    Includes bibliographical references and index.
    ISBN 978-0-231-14764-4 (cloth) — ISBN 978-0-231-14765-1 (pbk) — ISBN 978-0-231-51949-6 (e-book)
    1. Motion pictures—Moral and ethical aspects. 2. Motion pictures—Philosophy. 3. Redemption in motion pictures. 4. Lévinas, Emmanuel—Criticism and interpretation.
    I. Title. II. Series.
    PN1995.5.G57 2010
    791.43'684—dc22

                                                                2009045451

DESIGN BY **MARTIN N. HINZE**

To our grandchildren Arielle Gianni, Zachary Isaac (Ziggy), Mia Victoria, and Maxwell Scot-Smith; their parents, Katya and Jeff and Meighan and Ali; and Jennifer and Scottie

CONTENTS

ACKNOWLEDGMENTS IX

INTRODUCTION 1
TIME, FILM, AND THE ETHICAL VISION OF EMMANUEL LEVINAS

CHAPTER 1. 25
AMERICAN TRANSCENDENCE:
Levinas and a Short History of an American Idea in Film

CHAPTER 2. 49
FRANK CAPRA AND JAMES STEWART:
Time, Transcendence, and the Other

CHAPTER 3. 77
THE CHANGING FACE OF AMERICAN REDEMPTION:
Henry Fonda, Marilyn Monroe, Paul Newman, and Denzel Washington

CHAPTER 4. 113
SEX, ART, AND OEDIPUS:
The Unbearable Lightness of Being

CHAPTER 5. 144
FELLINI AND *LA DOLCE VITA*:
Documentary, Decadence, and Desire

CHAPTER 6. 168
ANTONIONI AND *L'AVVENTURA*:
Transcendence, the Body, and the Feminine

NOTES 219
INDEX 243

ACKNOWLEDGMENTS

For the past several years I have been fortunate to pursue a new area of study—the difficult ethical philosophy of Emmanuel Levinas—in the excellent company of outstanding Vanderbilt University students. Many of the ideas in this book grew out of those classroom encounters. I have cherished this learning experience and look forward to more. I am grateful to each and every student for the opportunity to study and learn together. I hope they also have gained from what my colleague Gregg Horowitz has called my "journey."

Indeed, as our work progressed, I came to realize that I was neighbors on campus with some of the leading philosophers in this new field for me of phenomenology and ethics. I am therefore especially appreciative for the support I received from David Wood and Kelly Oliver. Also in the Philosophy Department, I wish to thank Lisa Guenther, Katharine Loevy, J. Aaron Simmons, John Lachs, Charles Scott, and Gregg. A grant from Dan Cornfield's Vanderbilt Center for Nashville Studies, among other grants and funds, enabled other outstanding scholars in film, philosophy, and American studies to speak on campus. Their talks, conversation, and presence helped to create a special ambience on campus for students and colleagues with interests in these fields. Their work appears throughout this book. In philosophy these scholars include John Llewelyn, Tina Chanter, Simon Critchley, Ewa Ziarek, and Richard Cohen. In film I especially wish to thank John Belton, Anne Kern, Dudley Andrew, Peter Bailey, David Rodowick, and Rebecca Bell-Metereau. In American studies Thadious M. Davis, a special friend for years, returned to campus for a talk on ethics and race in America. Whether speaking on campus or writing about American studies, American literature, or Jewish studies, Sacvan Bercovitch remains a seminal influence.

Over several decades Emory Elliott's influence, friendship, and support pervaded American literary scholarship and American studies. He deeply touched the lives of an extraordinary number of people in these fields. His support and generosity proved crucial to many of us in all stages of our careers. As Michael Kreyling said about him after one of his visits, "Every time Emory comes here, he makes you feel better about yourself and your work." Emory's sudden death has been a devastating and unrecoverable loss to us as individuals and to the disciplines he inspired and led. His many visits to campus were vital events for American studies and American literature at Vanderbilt.

In the Department of English I wish to mention my colleagues, starting with three special chairs and friends. Jerry Christensen read an early version of an article that became the basis for this book. The acuity of his insights matched the brilliance of his continuing conversation with me over the years about film art and culture. I was fortunate that a colleague with such exciting ideas also became a close personal friend. Similarly, Jay Clayton and Leah Marcus have been steady sources of great personal and scholarly support. In addition, Carol Burke, Cecelia Tichi, Houston and Charlotte Baker, Jonathan Lamb, Bridget Orr, Michael Kreyling, Robert Barsky, and Kathryn Schwarz have been generously supportive of my work on this project. In American studies and film Teresa Goddu and Paul Young, as well as Vereen Bell, Dana Nelson, Colin Dayan, Hortense Spillers, and Ifeoma Nwankwo, have helped to make these growing university programs examples of outstanding scholarship and teaching. Kathy Conkwright's leadership in documentary filmmaking has been invaluable in developing that aspect of film production and study at Vanderbilt and in facilitating my role in it.

I gained enormously from readings of the manuscript by Sarah Cooper, who was among the first to encourage my work on Levinas, and by Cindy Lucia, who provides encouragement and inspiration for everything. Cindy epitomizes for me the perfect blending of professionalism and collegiality that makes a life in teaching and scholarship meaningful. In addition, Ronald Bogue provided helpful advice for strengthening the book's philosophical argument. An anonymous reader gave solid suggestions for improving two versions of the manuscript. Also, Robert Sklar, Cristina Giorcelli, Gilberto Perez, Lucy Fischer, Ina Rae Hark, Martina Urban, Stephen Prince, Christine Holmlund, James Naremore, Ray Carney, John Cawelti, and John Macready have been important sources of ideas and support. Associate Dean Martin Rapisarda, who has special interests in philosophy and educational innovation, has been especially encouraging. Thank you all.

I also wish to thank Sarah Childress for her help in and contribution to a great number of projects, including her assistance with this book and her work with me in the classroom. I learned much from her special insights into film art and criticism and her uniquely creative and informed close readings of cinetext, as mentioned in this book. Christian Long's help with research for the book proved invaluable. Also, Donald Jellerson and Valerie Sullivan in the Vanderbilt Department of English, Natalie Cisneros in the Philosophy Department, and Claire McKeever in the Department of Religious Studies have been of considerable help.

Friends have provided sustaining support for this work. I would like to thank Joel Jones, John Halperin, Robert Mack, David Marcus, Nadia Khromchenko Sikorsky, Dr. Eddie O'Neil, Carola and Christopher Chataway, Magda Zaborowska, Bill Tichi, Brian and Judy Jones, Beverly Moran, Keith and Carol Hagan, Cindy Lyle, Charles Walker, Trey Harwell, Ken Darling, Bill and Suzy Jones, Robyn Harris, Allen Weitsman, Samuele Pardini, Monica Osborne, Martha Matzke, Jim and Martha Bomboy, Trent and Jennifer McKenzie, Zsuzsa Nemeth, Chad Gervich, and Richard Hull.

I appreciate permission to use previously published work for this book from Sarah Cooper for "Beyond Ontology: Levinas and the Ethical Frame in Film," *Film-Philosophy* 11, no. 2 (2007): 88–107; and from Paul Cooke for "The Modernism of Frank Capra and European Ethical Thought," in *World Cinema's "Dialogues" with Hollywood*, ed. Paul Cooke (London: Palgrave/Macmillan, 2007), 86–102.

Some of the funding for the grants that helped pay for our visiting scholars also went into a program called "Re-facing High School," in which Vanderbilt students visited regional high schools to tutor, mentor, and make documentaries with high schoolers in the hope of putting Levinasian ethics of the other into practice. I would therefore like to thank those in education who made that two-year venture possible: Camille Holt, Andrew Davis, Susan Kessler, Melanie Faulkner Shepard, and Leslie Green.

The staffs of the Department of English—Janis May, Sara Corbitt, Donna Caplan, Margaret Quigley, and Susan Hilderbrand—and the Learning Research Center—Penny Peirce, Carol Beverly, Jamie Adams, Andy Snyder, and Jeff Baltz—and the various Vanderbilt centers and programs—Stephanie Pruitt, Erika Johnson, Barbara Kaeser, and Ashley Crownover—have been indispensable.

The administration and their staffs at Vanderbilt remain gracious in supporting scholarship and teaching, so I am happy to thank Chancellor Nicholas Zeppos, Provost Richard McCarty, Dean Carolyn Dever, and Associate Provost Lucius Outlaw.

I cannot adequately express my appreciation for the professionalism, editorial intelligence, and creative energy of the editors at Columbia University Press, led by Jennifer Crewe, with Anne McCoy, Afua Adusei-Gontarz, and Roy Thomas, along with my copyeditor Joe Abbott. It has been a wonderful experience to work with each of them. Thank you!

Finally the family! As distant as it must seem from their lives, this project in many ways was undertaken and pursued with our grandchildren and the whole family in mind. I think they understand the love, appreciation, and pride that go with it for Katya, Meighan, Jennifer, Jeff, and Ali. So thank you all, especially including Aida Scot-Smith, Audrey and Harris Shapiro, Danny and Emily Vafa, and Negi and Jean Darsess.

My greatest appreciation goes, of course, to my wife, Judith Ann Elizabeth Scot-Smith Girgus. This particular project began with her several years ago on a Saturday night at a Borders in Nashville, when I gathered all the books that the store had by Levinas and started reading. She has been with me on it ever since, as she has been over nearly five decades. She read and provided excellent advice for improving the initial manuscript, as well as portions of subsequent revisions of it. The completion of this work is another way of saying once again, thank you with love.

LEVINAS
AND THE
CINEMA
OF
REDEMPTION

INTRODUCTION
Time, Film, and the Ethical Vision of Emmanuel Levinas

TIME UNHINGED

At first, it could be argued that the philosopher Emmanuel Levinas was thinking primarily of himself when he wrote in 1947 that time had come "unhinged." Clearly, this statement, in his first important philosophical work, *Existence and Existents*, reflects the trauma of his experience as a Jew, a French soldier, and a prisoner of the Nazis during World War II. Levinas writes, "It is in times of misery and privation that the shadow of an ulterior finality which darkens the world is cast behind the object of desire. When one has to eat, drink and warm oneself in order not to die, when nourishment becomes fuel, as in certain kinds of hard labor, the world also seems to be at an end, turned upside down and absurd, needing to be renewed. Time becomes unhinged."[1]

Levinas's "telling observation," as Tina Chanter says, was "informed by his own imprisonment in a labor camp, and the death of many members of his Jewish family."[2] Perhaps his use of the pronoun *one* was Levinas's attempt to inject some objectivity into his account of this highly personal and traumatic experience. Nevertheless, the intensely personal tone of his statement indicates reflection on his own time of utter despair. The general trauma that the world suffered during the war and the Holocaust undoubtedly was internalized in Levinas's own thought and feelings and became a permanent part of his being, influencing all aspects of his experience.

A conscripted French soldier, Levinas was taken prisoner at the beginning of the war, in 1940. His status as a soldier in the West saved him from the death camps. While gentile friends in France hid his wife and daughter, most of the rest of his family in his native Lithuania died in the Holocaust. During this time of his imprisonment in Stalag XIB at Fallingbostel, situated between Bremen and Hannover, a number above the entrance, "1492," was filled with irony for him, not because of the discovery of America by

Christopher Columbus in that year but because, more significant for many Jews, it was the year of the expulsion of the Jews from Spain.[3]

Levinas recalls that the most humane occurrence during this long period of uncertainty about his own life and the future of his loved ones concerned a dog that has become somewhat legendary in modern philosophy, a stray dubbed "Bobby" by the Jewish prisoners. Bobby, according to Levinas, greeted the prisoners as men, "jumping up and down and barking in delight" when they appeared in the morning to go off into the forest to cut wood and when they returned to the prison at night, cold, hungry, and exhausted. In contrast, Levinas says, the German women and children, who observed the Jewish prisoners and invariably reminded the men of their own families, "passed by and sometimes raised their eyes—stripped us of our human skin. We were subhuman, a gang of apes." Bobby, Levinas says, had been given "an exotic name, as one does with a cherished dog," and was "the last Kantian in Nazi Germany."[4]

Indeed, then, time became unhinged for Emmanuel Levinas during this period of his life and this era of unprecedented death and human misery. His life up until that point had already acquired a remarkable quality, showing signs of great brilliance in the young philosopher and perhaps even genius. An emigrant from Jewish Lithuania, he studied philosophy in Strasburg and then moved to Freiburg to study with Edmund Husserl, the founder of modern phenomenology. Levinas's translation of Husserl's work into French helped introduce phenomenology to the French, most particularly to Jean-Paul Sartre, enabling Sartre to develop his own work on existentialism.

Levinas then turned to Martin Heidegger in Freiburg. Heidegger's influence on Levinas lasted throughout the latter's life, even in the face of his crushing disappointment over Heidegger's allegiance in the early 1930s to Nazism. Engaged intellectually and emotionally with Heidegger's work for his whole career, Levinas's break with him over politics and race marked the advent of his persistent philosophical challenge to Heidegger's thought by placing greater importance on ethics and the other than on the existential analytic of being and authenticity.

Accordingly, by the time of the war, Levinas, having been a French citizen for a decade and married to Raissa Levi, a childhood friend from Kovno, Lithuania, had become an important student of modern Continental philosophy with a promising future. So, for Levinas, calling time unhinged as a description of the ontic time of his lived experience of desperate loss during these years of imprisonment gains force for its understatement.

For Levinas, however, who wrote most of *Existence and Existents* during his imprisonment, the period of the unhinging of time inevitably extends beyond his own existential concerns. His time also refers to the condition of humanity and the Western mind. His idea of time unhinged resonates with Shakespearean overtones as developed, for example, in Jacques Derrida's expatiation on Hamlet's "The time is out of joint: Oh cursed spite, / That ever I was borne to set it right" (1.5.187–188). Hamlet's Denmark of murder, divided identities and loyalties, lust, and abuse becomes a metaphor for the brutality of the modern state and condition.

At the same time, double meaning and paradox imbue the notions of disjointed and unhinged time. For Derrida and Levinas unhinged time engenders disorder, but it also becomes the condition of possibility for the relationship of time to ethics and the other. Derrida even wonders if "this disjuncture" of time becomes "necessary for the good?" He also asks, "Is not disjuncture the very possibility of the other?"[5] For Derrida, then, "disjuncture" and "disadjustment" open the opportunity for the relation to the other. Time, indeed, relates to alterity or radical otherness. For Levinas also the introduction of time and the other, as in the title of another of his important early works, entails ethical encounter and the responsibility to the other.[6] Time establishes difference and distance to sever the circular solidity of sameness that can suffocate ethical responsibility in the enclosure of nontranscendent immanent being.

Derrida's discussion of Hamlet's disjointed time informs Levinas's meaning for unhinged time as part of Levinas's developing philosophy of time and ethics, which was in its formative stage in 1947. Derrida associates Hamlet's disjointed time with a conception he shared with Levinas of, in Derrida's words, "the infinite asymmetry of the relation to the other" (*Specters of Marx*, 26), a basic implication of Levinas's unhinged time in *Existence and Existents*. Derrida's phrase "infinite asymmetry" captures Levinas's idea throughout his ethical philosophy of the inequality of the ethical relationship that imposes infinite responsibility on the individual for the other. Thus, the philosopher Simon Critchley says that "for Levinas the relation to the other is asymmetrical. That is, the subject relates itself to something that exceeds its relational capacity."[7]

Levinas's body of work on time and ethics would be described by many contemporary philosophers as changing the landscape of modern Continental philosophy by making ethics first in philosophy, even before being and ontology and before the Western hegemony of knowledge as power. Levinas rethinks time to propose the primacy of ethics. Levinas's time unhinged, therefore, dramatically encapsulates a lifetime of work. Such time puts ethics first by dividing subjectivity with the imperative to act on the ethical priority of the infinite ethical demand of the other. This division of time and the subject for Levinas makes ethics possible in the first place. Ethics means breaking from the self for the other. The break makes ethics an infinite striving in the transcendent relationship to the other. Transcendence opens the time of the other for the ethical relationship. Levinas writes, "There is no model of transcendence outside of ethics." He challenges the temporal reduction of the human being to existence without ethical transcendence beyond inherent immanent being. He continues: "The sole manner by which an otherwise than being could signify is in the relationship with the neighbor—which the human sciences reduce to being."[8]

Thus, Levinas resists obeisance to a linear time that reduces the other to the same and entraps the self and the other in a temporality of fixed beginnings, middles, and endings. He questions a temporal paradigm that generates a Chaplinesque "modern times" of assembly-line morals, ethical uniformity, and social and political regimentation. Instead, Levinas, like Derrida, searches for the transcendent in immanent being that reaches beyond solipsistic subjectivity by placing ethical priority on the relationship to the other.

Levinas's work on time and ethics proposes breaking out of a closed circle of endless, repetitive representation. A temporality of disruption challenges the exclusive representation of time and reality by the spatial structuring of public clock time. For Levinas diachronic time, by which he means a time of disruption, counters the synchronic simultaneity of abstract clock time to place ethical responsibility for the other in an ethical dimension of a preoriginary time with an infinite future. Levinas's insight into time, therefore, presents an opportunity for regeneration. Rethinking time in terms of Levinasian ethical transcendence for the other can make time performative, a creative temporal event in itself. Levinasian thought itself, however, requires some redemption. Most important, it must answer for its position on the feminine. It also must rethink the relationship of ethics to aesthetics and politics.

In spite of such shortcomings it remains remarkable that after all Levinas suffered, his ethical philosophy works to justify, on modern philosophical grounds, the argument that humans are more than disposable bodies and meat. People are more than they appear to be, and life means more than can be seen, known, or understood. Levinas worked assiduously to keep his philosophy distinct from his Talmudic study and separate from any idea of God. Even so, a sense of spiritual transcendence, in the form of his argument for the ethical priority and the humanity of the other, certainly signals an inescapable connection between his philosophy and his religious faith.

Ethics cannot be reduced to clock time and calendar time and remain, for Levinas, ethics. In "God and Philosophy" he says, "Ethics is not a moment of being; it is otherwise and better than being, the very possibility of the beyond."[9] But ethics as a way of seeing and thinking, for him, overcomes death—death as annihilation, death as existential angst and fear, death as betrayal of the neighbor—and promises regeneration through access to "the very possibility of the beyond" in the relationship with the other. As Slavoj Žižek says, "For Levinas, ethics is not about life, but about something *more* than life."[10] Ethics in this light—the light of time and the other, the light of responsibility and transcendence—becomes for Levinas another word for the meaning of love in its promise of commitments greater than the self and the same and even life itself.[11]

THE CINEMA OF REDEMPTION: A NEW ETHICS OF FILM

Levinas's unhinged time includes the time of ethical challenge in what I call the cinema of redemption, a multinational body of films that enacts the struggle to achieve ethical transcendence by subordinating the self to the greater responsibility for the other, primarily as delineated in Levinas's ethical philosophy. I introduce this term, the cinema of redemption, to apply a Levinasian lens to the examination of the quest in film for a redeeming ethical experience that centers on the priority of the other. The journey transforms what Levinas, in "Substitution," terms the "ontological adventure" (*Emmanuel Levinas*, 86) of immediate, immanent experience into the "ethical adventure of the relationship to the other person" (Levinas, *Time and the Other*, 33). The films in the cinema of redemption dramatize the struggle for this transformation from being to ethics. They articulate a crisis of the change from ontological identity to ethical subjectivity.

The originality of this approach to film derives from its commitment to the ethical philosophy of Levinas and to the feminine engagement with and renewal of that philosophy. Levinasian thought and the feminine proffer a new means for examining a broad body of films, as well as the human experience on which these films are based. Levinasian thought provides a conceptual apparatus and governing theory of ethics and experience for structuring the elements of the cinema of redemption.

Along with the language of absolute, asymmetrical ethical priority, time plays a crucial role in the cinema of redemption, often presenting an alternative temporal dimension to challenge ethical relationships. Time becomes part of the very artistic structure of these films to present the ethical argument. This drama of time and ethics in the cinema of redemption occurs in very different films, ranging from classic American films such as *Mr. Smith Goes to Washington* (1939) and *On the Waterfront* (1954) to the Italian classic *L'avventura* (1960).

All the films in the cinema of redemption share in the search for redemption, but the nature of that search and its relationship to ethical transcendence and time vary. Ethical ambiguities and temporal disjuncture in the search for redemption pervade these films. While many classic American films focus on the ethical crisis of a time of transcendence, other films accentuate the tension between the desire for redemption and forms of radical immanence as manifested in wide-ranging aspects of modern life. For these other films—European films, American films, and other national cinemas—redemption becomes the object of troubled desire, a complex conflict between a yearning for transcendence and the enclosure of embedded immanence.

Occupying a foundational place in the cinema of redemption, some classic American films enact Levinas's project to make responsibility for the other the greatest priority in human relationships: Frank Capra's *Mr. Smith Goes to Washington* and *It's a Wonderful Life* (1946), John Ford's *The Grapes of Wrath* (1940) and *The Searchers* (1956), Michael Curtiz's *Casablanca* (1942), Robert Rossen's *Body and Soul* (1947) and *The Hustler* (1961), Abraham Polonsky's *Force of Evil* (1948), Elia Kazan's *On the Waterfront*, and John Huston's *The Misfits* (1961).

Faith in individual and national regeneration through transcendent, messianic time tends to drive classic American films of redemption. In contrast, other films in this cinema encounter perdurable obstacles in the struggle for redemption. In these films ethical transcendence through Levinas's priority of the transcendent humanity of "the face" of the other becomes stymied.[12] The search for belief continues in such films but often without the climactic sense of closure that usually occurs in the American classics. An ethical morass that for Levinas often defines much of modernity impedes transcendence in the relationship of responsibility for the other. A litany of doubts—such as disappointment, alienation, and nihilism—pervades these films of frustrated transcendence. For these films the impulse toward ethical transcendence frequently encounters what Critchley terms a condition of "radically immanent subjectivity" or "radical immanentism," a countermovement of immanent experiential forces that influences events along with transcendent forces of belief and action.[13] Films of such frustrated transcendence include Philip Kaufman's *The Unbearable Lightness of Being* (1988), Michelangelo Antonioni's *L'avventura* and *The Passenger* (1975), Federico Fellini's *La dolce vita* (1959), Ingmar Bergman's *The Seventh Seal* (1956), and Agnès Varda's *Cléo from 5 to 7* (1961). Martin Scorsese's *Raging Bull* (1980); Woody Allen's *Hannah and Her Sisters* (1986); and Clint Eastwood's *Unforgiven* (1992), *Mystic River* (2003), and *Million Dollar Baby* (2004) also fit this pattern, among many other films from the United States and other countries.

The traditional narrative of redemption predates film, of course, not only by centuries but millennia, reaching back to foundational narratives and beliefs in the Judeo-Christian tradition and in ancient literature and mythology. Even these traditions, however, do not have exclusive possession of the theme of redemption. The importance to these historic cultures of spiritual and psychological redemption parallels the centrality of such forces of renewal in other cultures throughout the world and throughout history. One need go no further than the accessible work of Joseph Campbell to see the universality of the search for rebirth for the self and culture. Campbell ranges widely over cultures and history in his study of the quest for transformation on journeys of initiation. He moves from the rituals of the Navajo and other Native Americans to cultures of Asia and Africa.[14]

The search for renewal in the cinema of redemption differs, however, from the classic journey of adventure and initiation that provides the basic frame for the quest motif that Campbell delineates. In the cinema of redemption the ethical engagement with the other, rather than the triumph of the self, provides the great challenge of the journey toward redemption. In these films it is not dragons, demons, monsters, maidens in distress, natural obstacles, or supernatural wonders that constitute the greatest dangers to the completion of the quest. Rather, in the cinema of redemption the greatest obstacles come from the subject's ethical encounter with the Levinasian other.

Like the broader redemption narrative itself, films from countries throughout the world exhibit the pattern of ethical struggle that Levinasian thought describes. Thus, directors such as Zhang Yimou, Abbas Kiarostami, and Akira Kurosawa and the cinemas of countries in Asia, the Middle East, Africa, and South America all contribute to the diversity of the cinema of redemption.[15] A Levinasian ethical analytic of transcendence, alterity, and time has great relevance to many cultures and cinemas of the world. Given such a broad spectrum of possibilities, this book follows Levinas and his feminist interpreters in a Eurocentric concentration on the Western intellectual tradition. The roots of this tradition go back to Plato through Descartes, Kant, Husserl, Rosenzweig, Heidegger, and many others. Thus, developing important connections in the cinema of redemption between this Western intellectual tradition and the thought and cultures of non-European countries remains outside the purview of this work yet needs to be done.

LEVINAS AND FILM

Although he often used the film term *mise-en-scène* to describe a philosophical point,[16] Levinas referred tangentially to film itself in his writings, and little evidence exists of any special passion on his part for cinema, even though he was living, teaching, and writing in Paris during the heady days of the New Wave movement, when the films of Jean-Luc Godard and Francois Truffaut, among others, were revolutionizing our understanding of the medium. This film movement belonged intellectually and emotionally to the popular philosophy of the time: Sartrean existentialism. In addition, little mention was made of Levinas by scholars interested in establishing a connection between film and philosophy. Such neglect reflected how Levinas for years was often overlooked, not just by scholars in the special field of philosophy and film but by philosophy itself. Thus, Levinas went unmentioned in major works of the 1990s in the field of film and philosophy.[17]

With Levinas's growing influence in continental philosophy, however, a dramatic rise has occurred during the past decade or more of academic interest in his ethical philosophy. This interest inevitably has directed attention to connections between Levinas and film. In 2007, for example, Sarah Cooper edited a special edition of *Film-Philosophy* entitled "The Occluded Relation: Levinas and Cinema," which included film scholars from several nations who wrote lengthy critical articles on Levinas and film on a variety of subjects, including representation, sexuality, time, and death. This volume followed Cooper's *Selfless Cinema? Ethics and French Documentary*, an important work on "Levinas's ethical vision" that focuses on the significance for film studies of the debate between phenomenology and ethics in Levinas as manifested in the difference between the physical face and the transcendent *"visage."*[18] In addition, Brian K. Bergen-Aurand's essay "Regarding Anna: Levinas, Antonioni and the Ethics of Film Absence" makes an important advance in Levinasian film studies with his focus on ethics, as opposed to Heideggerian ontology, in Michelangelo Antonioni's *L'avventura*.

Bergen-Aurand makes a crucial distinction between the "traditional" way of treating morality in film and the possible contribution that a Levinasian phenomenological perspective could make to representing ethics in film. He notes that "film and ethics have been coupled infrequently and film and Levinas have been connected even less." He says, "Traditional approaches to ethics and film have centered on mimesis and morality."[19] Indeed, many works deal with the history of morality, sexuality, religion, and censorship in film.[20] Bergen-Aurand suggests such studies of morality tend to be "concerned primarily with film language and ideological, political or religious representations" (109) rather than the philosophical or phenomenological analysis of film.

FILM AND A NEW TEMPORAL REGIME: *THE SEARCHERS* AND *LA DOLCE VITA*

Time, according to Levinas—ethical time—is a required element in the artistic construction of both the argument and the search for ethical transcendence in the cinema of redemption.[21] The Levinasian insistence on linking time and ethics to transcendence and infinity can transform ethical discussion in the film frame. The insinuation within filmic space of a relationship to a temporal dimension of infinite ethical responsibility creates a new mise-en-scène of ethics out of the ordinary design of the film scene. Also, the work of Paul Ricoeur and David Wood, who usually do not directly address film, and Gilles Deleuze and David Rodowick provides concepts and instruments that can help navigate the place of time in a Levinasian discourse on time and ethics in film.[22] They all seek a new time. Accordingly, Levinasian ethics suggests a potential for film that goes beyond the classic understanding of the ontology of the cinematic image to a transcendent ethical dimension in the relationship to the other.[23] As Levinas says, "Time is not the limitation of being but its relationship with infinity" (*God, Death, and Time*, 19).[24]

Examples abound of how time can operate in film to compel a vision of an ethical regime beyond being. Thus, much has been written about the opening scene of John Ford's *The Searchers*, with its shot from inside the entrance of a house on the Texas frontier. The camera is well behind Martha Edwards (Dorothy Jordan) as she opens the door to look out on the endless, open southwestern landscape. In retrospect we realize that Ethan Edwards (John Wayne), Martha's brother-in-law, approaches on horseback in the distance. The scene immediately conveys the mystery of Ethan's appearance from an unknown time and place, as well as the uncertainty of his ultimate purpose. While the deeply sexual and psychological implications of the shot have received considerable critical debate, the shot also dramatizes ethical tension and the encounter with the ethical in the context of a new temporal dimension.[25] With all of the meanings of this visual moment of inclusion and exclusion, belonging and alienation, shelter and estrangement, family and other, the shot resonates with ethical positioning and intrusion.

Ford's objective camera position from inside the house behind Martha contrasts with Martha's intense look from the doorway and the porch as Ethan comes ever closer. This contrast of shots suggests the construction of her subjective position. This unusual interior camera position gets repeated with a shot toward the end of the film from inside a cave when Ethan picks up and retrieves Debbie Edwards (Natalie Wood) and from inside the house again at the very end as Ethan stands outside alone, framed by the doorway. In the opening scene the pattern of shots projects a visual drama of the construction of the subject through time in the subject's relationship with the other.

Thus, the introduction of John Wayne's Ethan as the other in the long shot insinuates time, ethics, and the infinite into the scene, transforming the moment. The camera moves from the interior foyer of the frontier home and crosses the threshold to the outside with Martha. As Martha looks off into the distance toward Ethan, the scene suggests a transformation of time from the linearity of the progressive moments of physical movement through space to the potential of the infinite ethical relationship to the other. Martha's encounter with Ethan as the other vivifies subjectivity, time, and ethics.

This opening sequence of shots dramatizes Levinas's words in part 1 of *Time and the Other*: "time is not the achievement of an isolated and lone subject, but . . . it is the very relationship of the subject with the Other" (39). Ethan's arrival entails what David Ross Fryer describes as "the intervention of the other." Fryer writes, "Prior to the other, the self is not yet actualized, and not yet a subject."[26]

Kelly Oliver encapsulates the relationship of time, the subject, and the other to the Levinasian ethical project in a way that also helps describe the power of the opening moments of *The Searchers*. She says, "Only the relation with the other engenders time; and only where there is infinity is there time." Oliver develops her point by smartly playing on the crucial Levinasian argument that the relationship with the other inescapably means a "face-to-face" encounter with the humanity of the other that propels the relationship into the realm of infinite time and, for Levinas, infinite responsibility: "The relation between time and infinity is necessary not only in the simple sense that we cannot think of not-A without thinking of A or visa versa. Rather, it is the encounter with infinity through the face-to-face relationship that makes time possible. This encounter opens the subject onto itself and separates the subject from the world in a way that makes the counting necessary to time possible. The face-to-face relationship enables subjectivity, and there is no linear time without the subject."[27] Accordingly, the opening scene of *The Searchers* visually dramatizes a complex interaction of subjectivity, time, and the other as described by Oliver and Levinas to suggest a transcendent temporal and ethical dimension.

Equally important, the opening shot of interior space in *The Searchers* also visualizes a crucial theme in Levinas and his feminist interpreters of the woman as the embodiment of home. The scene articulates the role of the feminine as place, dwelling, and the condition of the ethical. This theme becomes a crisis of the feminine for Levinas but an opportunity for rethinking embodiment and the feminine for feminist writers. Significantly, at the end of *The Searchers* Ethan takes Debbie home but cannot enter there himself.

Another famous concluding scene in a very different film of redemption, Fellini's *La dolce vita*, also propounds an ethical dimension beyond being and conventional time. Fellini's conception of Marcello Mastroianni's sad character, Marcello Rubini, deals, however, with a moment of ethical encounter in a way that differs starkly from Ford's treatment of Wayne's character in *The Searchers*. In these films Ethan and Marcello each seek a form of redemption. By the end of *The Searchers* Ethan has fulfilled his journey and achieved a lonely, violent redemption. In contrast, Marcello, at the end of *La dolce vita*, faces frustration, doubt, and disappointment in his search for meaning, belief, and renewal.

In the concluding scene of *La dolce vita* a "monster" from the sea washes ashore to the amazement of giddy onlookers and exhausted partygoers, who stop to stare back at the dead fish's single grotesque eye. Marcello looks and moves away from the single eye to look across a small inlet to a beautiful gesturing figure, the girl from Perugia, Paola (Valeria Ciangottini), who has been the embodiment in the film of innocence. Connection between them proves impossible, however, because Marcello cannot bring himself to respond seriously to her gestures. In effect, Marcello resists the potential she offers of transcendence through a relationship with the other. He dismisses the ethical potential of the encounter to a failure to hear and understand. In fact, he really fails to see and believe. In both scenes—Mastroianni's in *La dolce vita* and Wayne's in *The Searchers*—the directors tend to idealize the alterity of the feminine in ways that problematize relationships, a theme to be pursued throughout this work.

Still, as in the opening scene of *The Searchers*, no verbal or discursive argument of ethics or responsibility transpires in the concluding scene of *La dolce vita*. Both scenes resist reducing ethics to narrative and character development based on the conventional organization of movement and linearity. Instead, time in the relationship to the other suggests an ethical responsibility beyond finite being.

In effect, Paola gestures to Marcello to have him accept a temporality that challenges his ordinary existence. She invites him to cross over the inlet, a symbolic act that suggests a new spiritual, transcendent view of life. Seeming to come from nowhere, like the fish, her presence introduces the other into the scene, challenging Marcello to create a new subjectivity. Her appearance means Marcello should move from a linear temporality of death to one of transcendence that recognizes her face as the face of humanity that touches infinity. It is time for Marcello to appreciate his own place in the world and his irreplaceable, irreducible responsibility in it to the other.

The suggestion of the possibility of transcendence through Paola in this closing scene contrasts with the film art, as well as the belief system, that tends to define *La dolce vita*. Fellini's long take and close-up of Paola, this lovely young woman from another time and place, constitutes a visual countermovement to his usual organization of time and space in the film in terms of the movement-images of montage. The time of the film in this concluding scene compels consideration of a new time for a new life. Film art endorses Paola's promise. This cohesion of visual art and spiritual vision makes Marcello's rejection even more painful.

In her innocence, charm, and beauty Paola reaches out to Marcello with what Levinas calls "the caress" that exceeds the tangible immediacy of immanence and that aspires to transcendence.[28] Fellini's long take of her effort signals the difference and significance of this special moment. As the face of the other, she introduces the possibility for Marcello of reinventing his own ethical subjectivity. But by turning away, Marcello rejects the visual proposition of her as the face of the other. He refuses the call from a time before linear time for him to acknowledge a transcendent responsibility beyond his own wishes. He walks away.

By leaving, Marcello takes the film with him. *La dolce vita* also leaves Paola behind for Marcello to resume his wasteful life without regeneration. A crucial significance of the film derives from its multilayered pessimism. The end of Marcello's search for redemption and the end of the film coincide with the suggestion of the coming end of hopeful time. In *The Searchers* the time of Ethan as the lone, alienated prophetic figure of redemption endures, but Marcello continues on a path of despair until eventual annihilation. When Marcello dismisses Paola's gesture of faith and love as irrelevant

FIGURE 1.1. Valeria Ciangottini, the girl from Perugia, beckons to Marcello Mastroianni in *La dolce vita* (1959).

to the ethical condition of humanity, he dismisses all hope for his own transcendence.

ETHICS AND POLITICS IN THE CINEMA OF REDEMPTION: *THE GRAPES OF WRATH*

The relationship between time and ethics in the cinema of redemption, as suggested in *The Searchers* and *La dolce vita*, has serious political implications. The search for redemption in these films demands consideration of a politics of redemption. Significantly, the relationship between time and ethics in the films becomes a sign of a politics that can go in very different directions. Much of the cinema of redemption, especially the American version exemplified by *The Searchers*, suggests a kind of messianic temporality and politics. The politics of ethical transcendence can espouse democracy and at the same time proclaim a superior force beyond history and politics. In contrast, in *La dolce vita* the search for redemption encounters a level of despair that vitiates the possibility of the transcendence the film desires as an ideal. Accordingly, the political implications of the relationship of time and ethics in the cinema of redemption entail a wide range of ideological positions.

A brilliant sequence in another Ford film, *The Grapes of Wrath*, suggests a time of redemption that espouses a democratic politics of responsibility based on the ethical relationship between self and other. The sequence provides a poignant illustration of how time in film brings together the relationship of ethics and politics. In the scene chronological, linear time is transformed into a powerful moment of ethical renewal. The sequence demonstrates how cinematographic techniques of shots, images, and editing, along with mise-en-scène, help constitute an ethical drama so that more theoretical and abstract concepts of time, space, movement, narrative, and identity can come into play in providing complex critical depth to film's ethical argument. In this particular scene the filming of the face resonates with the importance Levinas gives to the idea of the face and the face-to-face as the expression of the human.

The Joads are on the road, out of money, without enough gas to get anywhere, almost out of food, and desperate in every possible way. They get to a "transient camp," or Hooverville. The truck, with Tom Joad (Henry Fonda) at the wheel and his "Ma" (Jane Darwell) and sister Rosasharn (Doris Bowdon) on the front seat next to him, enters the camp and proceeds through it.

In one of the truly great sequences in American film a subjective camera view from inside their truck shows the faces, bodies, and situation of the people of the camp as they in turn observe the Joads driving slowly along. The front window of the truck becomes a window onto misery, a camera eye, as people appear before the Joads to stare back at them in a hopeless search for some sign of deliverance. This point-of-view shot establishes a vital dynamic between the subject and the other, an alienated other. The exchange in this scene between positions of the subject and the other becomes a visualization of Levinas's demand that the subject should achieve ethical subjectivity in the relationship through time and the other. As Critchley says, "Levinas insists that the subject discovers itself as an object, in the accusative case as he puts it, as interlocuted by the demand of the other" (*Infinitely Demanding*, 57).

Accordingly, the organization of shots in this scene emphasizes the eyes and reactions of the other, the people outside looking back at the Joads in this exchange of subjective and objective positions. The looks of these people outside the truck as they react to the Joads, the new arrivals, constitute a fascinating tension of perspectives. Ford structures this amazing sequence primarily by using the faces and the gestures of the people rather than the awful conditions of their existence. A middle-aged couple stares into the windshield of the truck but continues walking, a physical gesture that counters the intensity of their expression. Their physical movement also contrasts with and accentuates the solidity of the expressions of a cluster of people shown in depth of field, including children around a matronly figure on the road, all of them staring into the truck. As the woman and the children move along in front of the truck, two other women come into view behind them, one of them looking demented, and also stare into the Joads' vehicle. Then others look. The series of faces achieves a kind of momentary visual climax as another couple, a man and a woman, literally stops in front of the truck and looks at the Joads, anxiety on their faces. They look resentful about the newcomers who possibly could compete for work or housing. They also seem to yearn for something new to happen. The sequence places the emphasis on the rendering of hopelessness as written on the faces and told through the eyes of the people. Of course, the austere black-and-white photography, the documentary-style shooting, the powerful personages of Fonda and Darwell and the rest of the cast, and the brilliant timing and editing help account for the power of the scene.

While the camera shots from the interior of the truck create an extraordinary exposure of Depression-era abandonment, they also signal an ethical awakening. By the time the truck stops, an ethical transformation has occurred for the Joads. They have seen through the eyes of the other.

When the Joads first enter the camp, the situation centers primarily on them—their poverty, their desperation, their loss of hope. When the truck stops, more faces of people look starkly at the Joads while Pa and others on the truck look back at them in painful disbelief. The camera turns on the Joads in the cab of the truck, a famous medium close-up three-shot of Tom, Ma, and Rosasharn. The faces of Tom and Ma dramatize their reaction to what they have seen. They have seen the other faces that give a frightening welcome to this hellish place. The rhythm of these shots sets up a comment from Tom. When Tom remarks with brilliant understatement and powerful restraint that conditions in the camp "sure don't look none too prosperous," the world has been turned around so that it is no longer about them alone but about the other, which now includes the Joads as the other to the people in the camp who have observed these new transients arriving. In part, through the power of the camera's representation of the face, the Joads have undergone the kind of ethical transcendence that constitutes Levinas's argument. A Levinasian exchange of asymmetrical positions of responsibility has occurred, with priority placed on responsibility for the other.[29]

So in the transient camp, when Tom stops his truck, the Joads also have come to a special stop in a different kind of time, a Levinasian ethical time that breaks from the regular chronological order of misery. They have encountered through the faces and the eyes of the other and engaged through their own physical presence a diachronic form of Levinasian ethical transcendence, a domain that puts the priority on ethics before being. Even in their desperate condition, the Joads now can break through their own circle of need to sense their relationship of responsibility to others. The Joads, as they arrive and make a temporary stop at the camp, insinuate a Levinasian diachronic time of ethical transcendence into the scene.

In this scene from *The Grapes of Wrath* the drama of the faces of the people occurs to a considerable extent in the tension between medium close-ups and the organization of space and depth of field as the frame changes through layers of human misery. This construction emphasizes the relationship of the faces in the shots to other people and the environment. It suggests a kind of social aesthetic as envisioned by Ford and his cinematographer, Gregg

Toland, an aesthetic that emulates the growing significance of documentary photography, filming, and sensibility during the years of the Depression in the work of such people as Walker Evans, James Agee, Erskine Caldwell and Margaret Bourke-White, and Dorothea Lange.[30] Interestingly, the transient camp scene in *The Grapes of Wrath* constitutes an intersection of fiction and history that enables, in Ricoeur's phrase, "the actual refiguration of time" (*Time and Narrative*, 3:180).[31]

BEYOND LEVINAS: ETHICS, POLITICS, AND THE FEMININE

The Searchers, La dolce vita, and *The Grapes of Wrath* indicate the value of a Levinasian understanding of ethics, time, and transcendence for insight into film. This value obtains in spite of Levinas's religious and philosophical resistance to the potential idolatry of art, a subject I will discuss in a later chapter.[32] The controversial nature of his limited view of art and the image illustrates the need to go beyond Levinas to reconsider many of his arguments, not only about art but about other areas as well, such as politics and, especially, the feminine.[33] Derrida, in light of his great regard for Levinas, confirms the importance of rethinking Levinas's work.[34] Such engagement should challenge Levinasian ethics to maintain its role of providing an alternative way when compared to other movements in modern philosophy.

The important potential for philosophical, political, and ethical renewal that Critchley and others find in Levinas points to some current feminist thinking about the possibility for overcoming his sexism to strengthen the feminine.[35] These feminists put the notorious sexism of Levinas's work in the context of his radical critique of much of modern philosophy. They discover in their study of his writings interesting possibilities for their own work. In his rethinking of the Western philosophical emphasis on being and ontology, Levinas, for these scholars, helps to open territory for reconsidering ethics, the feminine, and alterity. These writers, therefore, discount Levinas's sexist thinking and language in favor of using his ideas for creating a better future for women and men. They engage Levinas in order to create new ethical and feminist paradigms. As Alison Ainley says,

> What makes Levinas's thinking initially appealing for feminist philosophers is the critique it provides of the structure of philosophical thinking. For Levinas, it seems that most or all philosophical thinking

is determinate, if it takes others as objects and fixes them under a conceptual category. The identity of the other is thus determined relationally and placed or theorized accordingly. Levinas objects to this primarily because it appears to him to be reductive, making otherness equivalent to "the same," and recuperating alterity under the scope of representational thinking, in a way that, although it may try to make subsequent assertions of ethical legitimacy, is actually denying the possibility of anything other than its own modes of representation and relation.[36]

Such thinkers emphasize Levinas's struggle throughout his work to distinguish between women as social beings and women and the feminine as the basis in his philosophy for difference and alterity. For Levinas "the feminine does not designate a being, but," as Chanter says, "is understood by Levinas as a tendency, a way, or a regime." Levinas does not intend, she claims, to "invoke" any "actual empirical women" but only to identify this "tendency" or "regime" of the feminine.[37]

Diane Perpich explains that in Levinas's *Existence and Existents* and *Time and the Other* "the feminine is identified with radical alterity." She says that Levinas "sought a relation to an alterity whose difference was not incidental, but essential."[38] Levinas emphasizes this "essential" difference of the feminine in his philosophy. Thus, in his preface to *Time and the Other* Levinas says, "Femininity... appeared to me as a difference contrasting strongly with other differences, not merely as a quality different from all others, but as the very quality of difference" (*Time and the Other*, 36).

Unfortunately, in making the feminine as a "regime" so crucial to his case for difference as to be the essential "quality of difference," he was not so much helping real, living women with their burden of supporting his ethical argument as conceiving another way through his philosophy of confirming the historic position of women as a lower order of humanity. Levinas's efforts to establish the feminine as radically other often only stereotype the feminine as a separate inferior ontology.

Chanter succinctly describes the dilemma feminist philosophers face in regard to feminist thought when they work on Levinasian ethics: "By allowing women to signify otherness, Levinas continues a long tradition of male-authored texts that figure the feminine as unknowable, mysterious, ineffable, unrepresentable, and intractable. Does he thereby repeat, however unwittingly or unwillingly, the same exclusionary gesture that denies women language and confines them to a gestural, corporeal, asocial psychosis? Or does his insistent privileging of alterity over sameness, even when it suffers a relapse at certain strategically predictable points, open up a space for the radical rewriting of the feminine?" (Chanter, introduction, 25). Accordingly, while Levinasian thought opens a new domain to the ethical imagination, feminists also find in his work outright disparagement regarding the feminine.

The problematic role of the feminine often highlights dilemmas in the Levinasian project. The subordinate status of the feminine in his philosophy engenders a feminine perspective on his work that can provide fresh insight into Levinasian issues. Thus, for Perpich the feminine accentuates the tension in Levinas between transcendence and immanence ("From the Caress to the Word," 48). As Perpich explains, the situation of the feminine makes the struggle against an irreversible return to immanence especially important. The feminine has a vested interest in countering the tendency to reduce transcendence to a condition of the encirclement of immanence for women.

Perpich's discussion of Levinas's notion of "the caress" in his early writings demonstrates the importance of a feminist perspective on his work in general and on the dilemma of transcendence and immanence in particular. She describes the caress "as an incessant recommencement of the movement toward the other." She says, "It is a seeking that is not satisfied by the presence of the other, but only renewed at a deeper level; it is a flight toward the other that does not involve return to the self." This maintaining of "distance" with the caress prevents the relapse into immanence and the self and therefore, she suggests, "seems to offer a perfect model of transcendence" (42).

Perpich proceeds to argue, however, that "the transcendence sought in the caress appears flawed" by perpetuating the secondary status for the feminine of either immanence or isolation. She notes that "the transcendent relation lapses into the immanence of knowledge and the sensuous" if the caress actually "'reaches'" and achieves "the presence" of the other. At the same time, if the caress "preserves the alterity of the other required by transcendence," then the feminine becomes "silent and withdrawn" in the condition of the isolated self (44). As Stella Sandford says, "Love is thus an event situated at the limit of transcendence and immanence" (*The Metaphysics of Love*, 50).

The caress, then, that should help concretize the connection of the feminine and transcendence in the relationship to the other, actually maintains the marginality of the feminine by either falling back into immanence or remaining in remote detachment. The feminine suggests how in Levinas transcendence can return to representation, being, and the same—precisely what Levinas wishes to overcome.

Ewa Ziarek confronts the dilemma in Levinas of immanence and the feminine by going directly to her idea of the source of the problem for Levinas in sexuality and the body. She proposes a revivification of the sexualized body for reconstructing the relation of the feminine to ethical transcendence. Ziarek develops the work of Luce Irigaray, among other thinkers, to answer Levinas's resistance to sexuality as a key to his resistance to the feminine.

Ziarek argues that "the radical potential of Levinas's work is undercut . . . at the moment it confronts sexuality." She maintains that Levinas "repeats the classical Kantian gesture of purification and dissociates those passions from any association with sex."[39] She asserts that "female sexuality in Levinas's work is relegated to animality, profanation, shame, indecency, and irresponsible infancy, and is thus associated with all the terms that evoke and justify the Kantian exclusion of 'pathological passions' from the domain of ethics" (59). Following Irigaray's interest in the fluctuation in Levinas between sublimation and an ethics without eros, Ziarek proposes an "ethics of sexuality" (59) as part of her program for an ethics of dissensus.

The influence of such feminist thinking could help Levinas in *Time and the Other* to develop his "notion of a transcendent alterity—one that opens time" (*Time and the Other*, 36). Demonstrating once again how his thought, especially regarding the feminine, can be stimulating, suggestive, and fertile while also proving vexing, Levinas claims that "a transcendent alterity" starts "with femininity." This assertion of the feminine still proves insufficient, however, to mitigate the impact of his view of the basic condition of women.

MESSIANIC TIME

With varying degrees of success and frustration, the films in the cinema of redemption engage a Levinasian ethical position of transcendence, ethical responsibility, and alterity. In Levinasian ethics such challenge involves a sacrifice of the self, almost at times to the point of martyrdom, in favor of the ethical priority of the other. As Levinas said in an interview with François

Poirié, "The I subordinated to other. In the ethical event, someone appears who is the subject par excellence" (Robbins, *Is It Righteous to Be?* 46). The films of redemption vary greatly in their responses to this ethical challenge.

Accordingly, for Levinas redemption involves what John Llewelyn calls "the temporality of recuperable time" and "regenerated time."[40] For Levinas such time becomes "messianic time": "Truth requires both an infinite time and a time it will be able to seal, a completed time. The completion of time is not death, but messianic time, where the perpetual is converted into eternal. Messianic triumph is the pure triumph; it is secured against the revenge of evil whose return the infinite time does not prohibit." Levinas then asks, "Is this eternity a new structure of time, or an extreme vigilance of the messianic consciousness?" and coyly confesses that "the problem exceeds the bounds of this book" (Levinas, *Totality and Infinity*, 284–85). Llewelyn nicely completes Levinas's thought in a way that expresses the relationship of Levinasian "messianism" to the concept of redemption. Llewelyn writes, "The Messiah of this messianism is not someone expected to come and bring about the end of history, but the human being acknowledging responsibility toward other human beings at this very moment. The Messiah is me, accused and categorized, summoned to appear as witness for the other" (Llewelyn, *The HypoCritical Imagination*, 129–130).

Llewelyn gains support from Levinas himself, who confirms Llewelyn's view by professing the universality of the messianic time of redemption through the human in his understanding of "a magnificent meditation of Jean Paul II" to mean that God "would be incarnated not solely in Christ but through Christ in all men." Levinas says, "This divine filiality of humanity is nothing new for Jews: the divine paternity experienced by Jewish piety, as it has been formulated since Isaiah, should be taken literally" (Robbins, *Is It Righteous to Be?* 109).

In Llewelyn's view, which follows Levinas's point on the pope's meditation on the potential spiritual salvation of all people, the meaning of the Messiah and messianic time becomes a kind of exalted moment of humanity. Humanity comes closest to divinity through the appreciation of the transcendent humanity of the face of the other in relation to the infinite. Messianic time becomes the time of redemption by breaking the bounds of selfhood to go beyond being to the time of the other.

The great promise of such messianism for universal redemption, however, also contains great challenges within crucial contradictions. For example, in

Levinas's words regarding the pope, the promise of redemption places special emphasis on "divine paternity." For Levinas the responsibility for redemption assumes a vital linkage between a Heavenly Father and humanity. In this regard Levinas consistently diminishes the feminine, dissipating the thrust of his project for universal ethical redemption.

Also, messianic time, the regenerated time of ethical responsibility, can inspire for good or ill national and cultural ideologies, most important for this study, the mythology and symbolism of American national regeneration. The idea of America historically has assumed a special relationship to the messianic time of redemption. The American mission figures heavily in the American version of the cinema of redemption. A messianic time of national responsibility for universal redemption for all humanity plays a less prominent role, however, in films in the cinema of redemption from other nations. In these other films the prominence of a national mission for redemption tends to recede before the shadow of the individual's confrontation with the crises of modern cultures of self-enclosed immanence. The struggle with the ambiguities of nihilism, disillusionment, and uncertainty imbue the journey toward redemption in these films.

THE CINEMA OF REDEMPTION

The cinema of redemption comes closest to a movement in its American version in classic films from the 1930s to the 1960s that I have described elsewhere as constituting a "Hollywood Renaissance,"[41] but American films before this period and up to our own time also fall within the pattern of redemption, from a work such as *The Jazz Singer* (1927) to *Gran Torino* (2008). Chapter 1 provides the literary, historical, and cultural context of the American version of the cinema of redemption. These films engage the American idea and experience in an aggressive dialogue comparable to the currents of thought that have been part of American history. The films participate in an American dissensus of difference, democracy, and redemption. Such dissensus as a foundation for democracy counters arguments for contemporary forms of radical dissensus as proposed by leading Levinasian scholars Critchley and Ziarek.

In chapter 2 I return to the enduring Frank Capra–James Stewart classics *Mr. Smith Goes to Washington* and *It's a Wonderful Life* as serious examples of an American cinema informed by Levinasian ethical thought, although other classics could perform the same function, such as John Ford's major films, Rossen's *Body and Soul* or Kazan's *On the Waterfront*, among many other films. Continuing the examination of the American version of the cinema of redemption, in chapter 3 I examine four major American performers in four important films that exemplify the diversity and durability of this pattern of film narrative. Henry Fonda in *The Grapes of Wrath*, Marilyn Monroe in *The Misfits*, Paul Newman in *The Hustler*, and Denzel Washington in *Glory* provide portraits of ethical challenge that become the faces of American redemption. This four-faces approach, so to speak, shows in one coherent chapter the importance of contrasts, changes, and continuities in the American version of the cinema of redemption. This focus on the face also compels explanation of the complex ethical and theoretical issue in Levinas's philosophy of the unrepresentable face as holy, especially as this problem manifests itself in film, an art form usually inseparable from the face.

As I have noted, other films within the multinational cinema of redemption diverge from the classic American narrative that often perpetuates a history of mission and the idea of the messianic time of ethical responsibility. Encountering crises of radical subjective immanence, these films become frustrated on the road to redemption, often confronting profound, and sometimes insurmountable, obstacles. Such a journey occurs in *The Unbearable Lightness of Being*, the film I examine in chapter 4. Directed by an American, Philip Kaufman, *The Unbearable Lightness of Being* immerses the search for redemption within modern European crises of ethics, sex, love, and politics. In this film version of the innovative novel by the Czech author Milan Kundera, Kaufman collaborates with an international group for the film's screenplay, music, and performances to create an ethical argument that challenges egoism, nihilism, repression, and the subjectivity of the same.

In chapter 5, the failure of Federico Fellini's *La dolce vita* to rethink the feminine in the ethical struggle for transcendence vitiates the ethical quest in the film. As a result of this failure the prolonged ethical struggle toward redemption ultimately collapses, providing an example of the complex variety of ethical encounters in this film narrative form.

I conclude this study with another Italian classic, Michelangelo Antonioni's *L'avventura*, a culminating work of both triumph and ambiguity that achieves an original film form of an ethics of redemption. In this film the feminine and Antonioni transform Levinasian ethical transcendence. The search in the film for redemption entails a search for a new cinema of redemption and a new sexual ethics.

In the cinema of redemption existence without ethical transcendence and time without spiritual regeneration often constitute the condition of the ethical challenge. The impulse toward redemption through transcendent time frequently encounters these conflicting forces of perception, belief, and experience. In the contest for transcendence in the cinema of redemption many forms of ingrained radical immanence counter the effort for redemption.

From a Levinasian perspective these forms of immanent subjectivity range over the spectrum of modernist sensibility from art to ethics and legal discourse. Eschewing ethical transcendence through the relationship with the other, the experience of immanence focuses on the ontology of the individual within complex social and cultural environments. In the absence of transcendence Levinas might characterize this mentality as "an act of knowing" that constitutes that "*immanence* of being, accessible to the subject in objectivity, that intelligibility of the objective in knowing" (*Outside the Subject*, 1). Such immanence encircles temporal experience. The ensuing sense of philosophical, ethical, and psychological enclosure provides the impetus for the journey of transcendence toward the other in life and in the cinema of redemption.

CHAPTER 1
AMERICAN TRANSCENDENCE
Levinas and a Short History of an American Idea in Film

LEVINAS AND AMERICAN FILM

Redemption and regeneration are old stories in America. The Puritans brought those concepts with them to the New World nearly four centuries ago, and in the mid-nineteenth century, Transcendentalists such as Emerson and Thoreau revivified regeneration itself, ingraining it, at least until our own era, in the American psyche. Hollywood, however, gave the story a new twist with the creation of a uniquely American version of the cinema of redemption.

From the 1930s until at least the early 1960s, some of America's most influential directors, actors, and producers developed a film form devoted to the idea of redemption. These films resonate with the history of American thought and the ethical project of Emmanuel Levinas. The coherent melding of these different ethical traditions and ways of thinking helps explain the diversity and continuity of the appeal of these films in the American version of the cinema of redemption.

The usual achievement of triumphal redemption distinguishes these classic American films from the broader international cinema of redemption that tends to encounter ambiguity regarding the struggle. In the classic American version of the cinema the hero undergoes a crisis of identity, culminating in a transforming or conversion experience. This event involves accepting a total commitment to an ethical order of belief and action, one that makes ethical relations with others more important than personal demands, success, and wealth. The American version of the cinema of redemption insinuates ethical issues into the film styles and genres that define popular American cinema—dramas, historical narratives, love stories, even westerns and comedies. Many of John Ford's classic films of this period exemplify this kind of film, including his version of John Steinbeck's *The Grapes of Wrath* (1940). James Stewart, however, especially in his iconic roles in Frank Capra films, and John Garfield could serve as poster children for such films. For example, even in such a minor movie as *They Made Me a Criminal* (1939), a heavy-handed film with Garfield, the Dead End Kids simply declare "regeneration" to be the purpose behind their removal from the crime-ridden streets of New York to Arizona.

While some form of institutional religion may be in the background of a particular film, such as Catholicism in *They Made Me a Criminal*, these films generally promulgate a nonsectarian religious sensibility. A representative list of such films includes *Mr. Smith Goes to Washington* (1939), *Sullivan's Travels* (1941), *Casablanca* (1942), *It's a Wonderful Life* (1946), *Body and Soul* (1947), *Force of Evil* (1948), *Breaking Point* (1950), *On the Waterfront* (1954), *The Searchers* (1956), *The Hustler* (1960), and *The Misfits* (1961). Martin Scorsese's *Taxi Driver* (1976) and *Raging Bull* (1980), among his other works, and Edward Zwick's *Glory* (1989) constitute more recent examples of the American cinema of redemption.

To a considerable extent these films of moral conflict and renewal reflect the response of American values to the multiple collective traumas of the Great Depression, the Second World War, and the cold war. In the face of such conflict these films generally reaffirm American ideals. They provide reassurance about the continued relevance of a historic system of ethics in a world of constant turmoil. For some, therefore, these films provide an unambiguous moralistic and emotional response to difficult issues in order to satisfy popular attitudes. As part of the broader multinational cinema of redemption, however, American films can also be viewed quite differently, as works deserving full discussion in several different cultural areas, including both European and American intellectual and ethical discourse.

In the sphere of ethical discussion the American version of the cinema of redemption and Levinasian ethical philosophy enlighten each other. The ethical conflict in these American films corresponds to Levinas's complex argument for ethical transcendence and dramatizes some of his most important ideas. Some key aspects of Levinasian philosophy include ethics as a "first philosophy" that precedes freedom and ontology, the total responsibility for the other as achieving priority over concern for the self, transcendence in the form of the relationship with the other, the face and face-to-face encounter as the sign of each individual's irreducible humanity, proximity and the importance of the neighbor, and religious sensibility in the midst of secular disorder and chaos. In the context of the work on time, narrative, and movement by Paul Ricoeur, David Wood, and Gilles Deleuze, the effort of Levinasian ethics to imagine an alternative temporal dimension for the revivification of ethical sensibility becomes increasingly interesting in its expression in the overall cinema of redemption, including, of course, the American version.

In the American cinema of redemption the surrender of the self for others and the sacrifice of personal gain for higher spiritual values generally affirm Levinasian ethical theory. Thus, the ethical position of the American cinema of redemption gains considerable credibility from its relationship to Levinas's philosophy of ethical transcendence. In the American cinema of redemption themes that compare to Levinas's arguments appear in the form of popular notions of moral behavior and ethical relationships.

EMERSON AND THE PURITANS

The original source for the ethical philosophy behind the American cinema of redemption, however, probably lies closer to home, on native grounds in America rather than in Levinas's native Lithuania or his adopted Paris. The roots for the ethical system that these American films articulate as popular culture expressions go back to the Puritans and the Transcendentalists. The moral argument that suffuses these films relates to Levinas's philosophy and achieves a native resonance from its connection to the ethical transcendentalism of figures such as Ralph Waldo Emerson. Emerson in turn reaches back to the origins of American intellectual history in the Puritans. In some ways the Puritans and Emerson presage not only Levinas's ethical priorities but also Levinas's way of seeing national and institutional purpose as fulfilling individual ethical calling.

Lawrence J. Buell generally dismisses a possible association of Emerson with Levinas: "Even though Emerson might have considered ethics more important than epistemology if forced to choose between them abstractly ... never would it have occurred to him to claim with Emmanuel Levinas that ethics was 'the first philosophy,' that relationality was more primordial than being itself." In his scholarly delineation of the array of interpretations of Emerson over the years, Buell focuses on comparisons of the New England Transcendentalist to a variety of thinkers, including Kant, William James, John Dewey, and, as Stanley Cavell suggests, "a Freudianized Wittgenstein and a Nietzschean Heidegger."[1]

While Cavell, as Buell says, "reads backwards to Emerson" from the Europeans, a more traditional direction to Emerson used to move forward from the Puritans. Buell writes:

> A half-century ago, New England Transcendentalism was still generally considered a "revival of religion" that happened to find its "new form of expression" in "literature" rather than in "formulations of doctrine"—to quote Perry Miller's concise definition in his influential *The Transcendentalists: An Anthology* (1950). For Miller, the chief force that animated Emerson's thought was the release of a radical "antinomian" spirituality inherent in Puritanism, apparent in figures like Jonathan Edwards, but held in check until Enlightenment rationalism and German "higher criticism" of scripture as myth eroded the dogmatic structures.[2]

Buell notes how resistance to imagining "Emerson as a religious thinker has lately intensified" so that in recent decades "Emerson studies have put much greater emphasis by comparison on Emersonian philosophy and social thought" (158–59).

A return, however, to moving on the intellectual roadway to Emerson from the Puritans may suggest how to find Levinas on that particular road, as well, by extending the intellectual journey some distance further. The Puritanism that Perry Miller, one of the most influential scholars of his time, believed eventually leads to Emerson rests on several crucial concepts that would not be alien to the extremism of Levinasian ethics, including the ultimate mystery of God, regeneration of the individual, election as a special responsibility, revelation as providing access to the spiritual meaning of life, and the immediacy of moral connections between people based on the face-to-face encounter. Miller writes, "The soul of Puritan theology is the hidden God, who is not fully revealed even in His own revelation."[3] In spite of such mystery, revelation was indispensable to seeking God. Miller asserts, "There was nothing essential to be learned outside revelation" (20). To the Puritans regeneration was the experience that made such anxiety worthwhile, and "there was of course only one interpretation" of it: "The moment of regeneration, in which God, out of His compassion, bestows grace upon man and in which man is enabled to reply with belief, was the single goal of the Augustinian piety. Without it individual life was a burden, with it living became richness and joy" (25). Referring to "a handbook that was widely used in New England," Miller proceeds to describe what regeneration meant to the Puritans: "It was the act of communion in which the infinite impinged upon the finite, when the misery of the fragmentary was replaced by the delight of wholeness. Regeneration was the receiving by man of 'the fulnesse of the infinitenesse of all perfections which are in the Lord,' who alone is 'able to fill up all the emptie chinks, void places, the unsatisfied gaspings & yawnings of the spirit of a man.' It was the resolution of the problem of sin, and of all other problems that torture humanity" (25–26). Miller adds that "regeneration was an inward ecstasy and not a ribbon of merit for distinguished services" (369). He notes, however, that not even the Puritans could monopolize regeneration for all humanity: "Other people have found other names for the experience: to lovers it is love, to mystics it is ecstasy, to poets inspiration. Even ordinary men have their ups and downs, know seasons when they are filled with something more than their usual vitality" (25).

This broadening of the concept of regeneration shows how Miller builds his intellectual roads and bridges from, for example, Jonathan Edwards, America's great eighteenth-century religious thinker, to Emerson. Miller confesses to building this mental structure "on the crudest of levels" by connecting "certain basic continuities" that "persist in a culture," namely a "history of ideas." He maintains that "on the crudest of levels, I am arguing that certain basic continuities persist in a culture—in this case taking New England as the test tube—which underlie the successive articulation of 'ideas.' Or, I might put it, the history of ideas."[4]

Many of these core beliefs of the Puritans strike close to home for Levinasian thought and relate to key concepts of his own reinscription of Hebrew theology and Talmudic learning into the terms of modern phenomenology and ethics. The method of intellectual history that for Miller overcomes the differences between Edwards's unique Calvinistic version of Puritanism and Emerson's Transcendentalism to link Edwards to Emerson also can extend to Levinas, establishing an intellectual connection for them all. Thus, Levinas's idea of the infinite in his overall philosophy in some ways repeats the concerns of the Puritans. Levinas argues in "Transcendence and Height" that "the idea of the infinite consists precisely and paradoxically in thinking more than what is thought while nevertheless conserving it in its excessive relation to thought. The idea of the infinite consists in grasping the ungraspable while nevertheless guaranteeing its status as ungraspable."[5] In this statement Levinas engages Husserlian phenomenology and Heideggerian ontology rather than Puritan theology. Nevertheless, like the Puritans, Levinas, with considerable help from Descartes, grapples with the spiritual significance of the infinite. In "Transcendence and Intelligibility" he writes, "According to Descartes, who identifies the idea of the perfect with the idea of God, the finite thought of man could never derive the Infinite from itself. It would be necessary for God himself to have put it in us. And Descartes's entire interest is concentrated on this problem of the existence of God. The incessant return of metaphysics!" He continues: "In the idea of the Infinite, which is also the idea of God, the affection of the finite by the infinite precisely produces itself" (*Emmanuel Levinas*, 157).

Also, Miller's language for describing the significance of the face-to-face relationship in Puritan thought invites comparison to Levinas's pressing insistence about the crucial centrality of the idea of the face to dramatize the spiritual relationship of one to another. Miller writes, "What is persistent, from the covenant theology (and from the heretics against the covenant) to Edwards and to Emerson is the Puritan's effort to confront, face to face, the image of a blinding divinity in the physical universe, and to look upon that universe without the intermediacy of ritual, of ceremony, of the Mass and the confessional" (Miller, "From Edwards to Emerson," 185).

With some similarity, Levinas notes in "Ethical Subjectivity" that "in the situation of the face to face, there is no third party that thematizes what occurs between the one and the other."[6] In the language that Miller and Levinas use, the face constitutes a revelation of the relationship to the infinite. Fully appreciating the impossibility of ever totally understanding this relationship signifies the beginning of the making of a form of regeneration.

EMERSON, PROPHECY, AND TRANSCENDENCE

The linkage of interests and the continuity of ideas that connect Levinas and the Puritans actually gain strength by going through Emerson, whose position on transcendence creates a bridge of shared beliefs between them. The ideas indicate Emerson's own relationship to the Puritans and Levinas in spite of important differences on many matters that Buell and others note. So even after recognizing the variety of Emersons to be found by Buell, Cavell, and others in the likes of Freud, Nietzsche, Heidegger, and Wittgenstein, Emerson as the open-ended, pragmatic American Transcendentalist still persists.

And Emerson the American Transcendentalist allows for yet another metamorphosis that ties him to Levinas.

Soul, spirituality, and transcendence are bedrock concepts of Emerson's major essays. In the power of his words Emerson's ethical radicalism compares to Levinas at his most eloquent. Emerson's essays constitute an ethical language that describes humanity's relationship to transcendence. In Emerson transcendence becomes a living project, and the infinite manifests itself in part through ethical responsibility between the individual and the community.

In such essays and in his public stance in America as a voice of conscience, Emerson achieves what Levinas calls prophecy. In "The Same and the Other" Levinas sees *"inspiration"* in *"prophecy,"* which becomes "the very spirituality of the spirit" (Levinas, *God, Death, and Time*, 142). Describing the "anachronism of the prophet" as more "paradoxical" than the powers of "prediction," he maintains in "Truth of Disclosure and Truth of Testimony" that "it is in prophecy that the Infinite eludes objectivation and dialogue" (Levinas, *Emmanuel Levinas*, 106). Similarly, in "God and Philosophy" he describes "prophesying" as "pure testimony" and claims, "It is in prophesying that the Infinite passes and awakens. As a transcendence, refusing objectification and dialogue, it signifies in an ethical way. It *signifies* in the sense in which one says *to mean an order*, it *orders*" (Levinas, *Emmanuel Levinas*, 146–47).

Surely, Levinas's conception of the prophet would characterize the Emerson of his most influential ethical essays. Thus, while Emerson's "American Scholar" (1837), "The Transcendentalist" (1843), and "The Poet" (1844), for example, are seemingly about very different topics and kinds of activity, Emerson's readers for nearly two centuries have seen the same figure in them, one curiously similar in many aspects to Levinas's prophet. Although he proclaims in "The Poet" that "all that we call sacred history attests that the birth of a poet is the principal event in chronology," he would say the same for any individual who aspires to moral transcendence.[7] Agreeing with Spencer that "the soul makes the body" and that the "universe is the externalization of the soul," he argues that "every thing in nature answers to a moral power" so that "every man is so far a poet" (Emerson, *Ralph Waldo Emerson*, 126, 127). The poet is not made by any special talent for poetry but by the ability to put "moral power" in action: "For it is not metres, but a metre-making argument that makes a poem" (ibid., 124). The poet overcomes the "intellect used as an organ" in order "to take its direction from its celestial life" (133). He avers, "Poets are thus liberating gods" (134).

Searching for the American Poet, as he had looked just a few years earlier for the American Scholar, Emerson repeats the theme of the earlier essay that true knowledge lives not in books but in a spiritual realm of moral values and action. In "The Poet" he says, "I think nothing is of any value in books excepting the transcendental and extraordinary" (135). Because the soul takes precedence over the intellect in Emersonian ethics, the American Scholar overcomes conventional time and achieves a kind of Bergsonian duration, what Levinas would call diachronicity, as another temporal order for ethical discourse. Emerson writes in "The American Scholar" that "the scholar is that man who must take up into himself all the ability of the time, all the contributions of the past, all the hopes of the future. He must be a university of knowledges" (Emerson, *Ralph Waldo Emerson*, 54).

Reminiscent of the spiritual fire of the Puritan Jeremiahs who excoriated New Englanders for their failure to maintain the ethical demands of earlier generations, Emerson declaims in "The Transcendentalist": "Where are the old idealists?"[8] In a litany of names of idealistic figures that could be updated to include Levinas, in spite of their many important differences, Emerson preaches a new way of thinking to achieve the kind of ethical transcendence that both men sought.[9]

Today, Levinas could join Emerson's historic line of dissidents and his extensive pantheon of moral prophets when he challenges the direction of what we think of as modernism and tries to replace such predilections with his own ethical priorities. He sounds prophetic in an Emersonian way, when he asserts in "Peace and Proximity" that "the conscience of the European is henceforth guilty because of the contradiction that rends it at the very hour of its modernity" (Levinas, *Emmanuel Levinas*, 163). Levinas maintains this prophetic voice throughout "God and Philosophy" and elsewhere when he promulgates his ethically transcendent alternative to modern conceptions of justice.

The American cinema of redemption gains moral clarity and intellectual significance when viewed through the perspectives of the Puritans, Emerson, and the contemporary ethical philosophy of Levinas. The prophetic demands of such different visionary thinkers lend credibility and legitimacy to what many today would consider the simplicity of the moral position of these films. The association with the Puritans and Emerson gives these films as social and cultural documents continuity with American history and thought. Similarly, the moral passion of Levinas also suggests the relevance of these films to the argument for ethics as a transcendent relationship to the other. Thus, when Levinas in "Transcendence and Height" describes his work as "an attempt to justify the transition to moral consciousness or the primacy of the moral" (*Emmanuel Levinas*, 25), it would seem unfair to deny the same justification, even if on another cultural level, to films that take seriously precisely that ethical demand.

Accordingly, the resonance of Levinasian ethics in the films of the American cinema of redemption does not occur in an intellectual vacuum. Other ethical forces that inform this cinema, such as the Puritans and Emerson, also have their own serious intellectual connections to Levinasian thought. Thus, various writings of the Puritans, Emerson, and Levinas connect in vital ways to help provide insight into the relationship of the American cinema of redemption to American culture and to contemporary philosophical movements.

AMERICAN NATIONAL REDEMPTION

Both Levinas and Emerson place the ethical self in vital cultural contexts. Since the Puritans, the idea of redemption has been connected to the meaning of America to the world. Individual redemption became inescapably involved with the national mission as a beacon to the world. Emerson, in his works and in his public role, personified the national prophet of this mission. He became the quintessential modern American Jeremiah, insisting on adherence to an American ethical ideal. As Sacvan Bercovitch argues, Emerson, in his major essays, takes the position of the "consummate figure of dissent, the representative/adversarial American Self."[10] The American cinema of redemption assumes the moral tradition of that ethical argument as a legacy.

Levinas also has much to say about the connection between individual regeneration and the mission of the state. *In the Time of the Nations* and *Beyond the Verse* not only elucidate the religious, ethical, and political significance of Israel to the Jews and the world. Their language and symbolism also compare to a historic self-understanding of American culture as a New Jerusalem, founded in Massachusetts and propelled through history to fulfill its symbolic destiny.

Thus, both Levinas and the historic symbolism of America hitch their arguments for a national calling to biblical metaphors of the New Jerusalem and the Promised Land. In *Beyond the Verse* Levinas delineates the origins of the idea of "the earthly Jerusalem" as "the unavoidable antechamber of the heavenly Jerusalem" that becomes "the city of refuge."[11] Attempting to follow the example of the biblical Hebrews, the Puritans lived out their awareness of the contrast between the New Jerusalem they wanted to build in the wilderness of America and the challenge of the historic realities that made up their daily lives. In the knowledge of that conflict between the ideal and the real they managed to set forth a mission for themselves and their posterity that compares to Levinas's understanding of Israel as "a State which will have to incarnate the prophetic moral code and the idea of its peace" (Levinas, *Beyond the Verse*, 194). Levinas's position on the importance of the state of Israel to the potential for individual redemption has been criticized in the light of the history between Israel and the Palestinian and Arab populations. Slavoj Žižek reads this history as disproving "Levinas's hope that the State of Israel will be a unique state directly grounded in the messianic promise of Justice."[12] Levinas never reconciled such difficulties for himself and others.

Nevertheless, in spite of great controversies in the histories of both Israel and America, individual redemption for Levinas and for American ideology remains bound to national renewal. For both, the idea of a regenerated being, a redeemed self, also involves a national vision in which a new idea of human beings compels a new understanding of the earthly city. As Levinas says, "the Messianic City is not beyond politics" (Levinas, *Beyond the Verse*, 183).

THE CINEMA OF REDEMPTION: BOGART AND GARFIELD

The American cinema of redemption consistently enacts prophetic consciousness for the relationship of the individual self to others. Regardless of variations in narrative structure, plot development, or relationships, these films profess with almost a didactic regularity a transformation or conversion from egoistic self-obsession to transcendence based on others. In effect, they become lessons in Levinasian ethics and metaphysics. For example, *Casablanca*'s apparently self-absorbed Rick Blaine (Humphrey Bogart) is eventually unveiled as a one-man American arsenal for the survival of others. Although some scholars such as Tina Chanter proffer a radically different reading of *Casablanca*,[13] it could be argued that Humphrey Bogart's Rick gives a farewell speech to Ilsa (Ingrid Bergman) that epitomizes how a language of ethical responsibility imbues American ideology: "Last night we said a great many things. You said I was to do the thinking for both of us. Well, I've done a lot of it since then, and it all adds up to one thing. You're getting on that plane with Victor, where you belong." Overriding her protests and insisting that Ilsa must leave with her husband, Rick's tone and attitude capture in a couple of sentences the mixture of ethical language and political rhetoric of a generation and an era: "Ilsa, I'm no good at being noble, but it doesn't take much to see that the problems of three little people don't amount to a hill of beans in this crazy world. Someday you'll understand that." Of course, Ilsa must understand only too well that Rick's redemption and ethical commitment to others come at her expense. She must realize that Rick barely has managed to disguise his turn of the ethical tables on her, as he adopts the ethical position she initially used to influence him.

In *Body and Soul*, another film of moral struggle, John Garfield plays Charlie Davis, a New York street kid who becomes a boxing champion, acquiring money, fame, and visible success at a great ethical cost to himself and others. Choosing to betray himself and the principles of those who love and have faith in him, Davis takes money to throw his last fight and lose his championship. Nearly too late, Charlie realizes that rather than keep his word to let him leave the ring in relatively decent physical condition, Roberts (Lloyd Goff), the crooked boss, has told Charlie's mediocre opponent to surprise Charlie with a brutal beating that will help make the fixed fight look somewhat more legitimate.

Charlie is pummeled into a groggy psychic state in which time changes for him. His inner consciousness struggles against the structured time of the boxing match—the ten-count knockouts and three-minute rounds. Charlie experiences a mental state at this moment that involves a view from his own different inner experience of time; he must find his own time. Like James Stewart in *Mr. Smith Goes to Washington*, he must break the hold the clock has over him to realize the power of an order of time other than the synchronic sameness that often expresses ethical conformity.

Until now he has thought only of himself. As a sign of such self-centeredness, he has measured time in terms of his own potential end. He learns suddenly in the face of his existential crisis to think of death in terms of a time greater than himself. In a deadly battle consistent with the crisis of

Levinasian ethics, Charlie Davis, the champion prizefighter, by virtue of his own experience, comes to appreciate the meaning behind the "invitation" from Levinas "to think death on the basis of time, and no longer time on the basis of death" (Levinas, *God, Death, and Time*, 104). A revelation occurs to Charlie that demands a search for more meaning to life than mere survival. Charlie recognizes another conception of time in the struggle to achieve a form of redemption.

In *Body and Soul* Charlie must decide not just to retain or lose his championship but to gain or lose his soul, to rethink his last chance to change, in the Levinasian sense, his ethical relationship to others. In the film's concluding fight scene Charlie decides to fight to win but only after his opponent's manager has pounded on the floor of the ring to signal a change in the tempo of the fight that will unleash the sudden surprise attack on him. Throughout the match the minute-by-minute time of the fight clock beats a numbing awareness of the tyranny of time. Such actions suggest an existential dread of imminent doom marked by regulated, abstract time. The fight gives Charlie a brutal lesson about time. As Levinas asserts, "We have an opening of the time of suddenness, which is the *beating of the Other in the Same*" (Levinas, *God, Death, and Time*, 139). The disjunctive experience of time conveys the paradox for Charlie of his inescapable separation from the other, as well as his responsibility to the other. Levinas recalls that the Hebrew for *blow*, as in beat and in the striking of the clock, derives from the same verb as *agitate*, suggesting agitation for a new relationship to time. He proposes an understanding of time that involves more than simply being beaten moment by moment but instead recognizes an immemorial time that supersedes ordinary time and engenders a new relationship with the infinite.

Accordingly, *Body and Soul* dramatizes the Levinasian theory of the relationship to death as part of the ethical responsibility to the time of the other and the priority of the other's life. The temporal dimensions of the violent drama of the prizefight intensify these ethical paradoxes—difficulties about time, ethics, and transcendence that are familiar subjects in the writings of the Puritans and Emerson.

After leaving the ring, victorious but bloodied and horribly bruised in his physical embodiment of moral martyrdom, Charlie faces Roberts, the boss who wanted him to throw the fight. Roberts asks Charlie how he thinks he can get away with beating the mob by winning the fight. Charlie declares, "What are you going to do, kill me?" and repeats the boss's own ominous words from earlier in the film, "Everyone dies!" He then tells his jubilant, morally vindicated girlfriend, Peg (Lilli Palmer), "I never felt better in my life."

Battered and financially ruined after losing his own bet against himself by winning rather than throwing the fight, Charlie's words constitute a testimony of revelation and redemption, a statement of Levinasian "awakening" to moral and ethical priorities greater than himself. Just as Charlie awakens in the ring to his responsibilities to others, the film suggests the need for an awakening about time and money. Indeed, the films of the American version of the cinema of redemption generally enact calls for a Levinasian awakening regarding ethics and the demand to prioritize responsibility for the other. As Levinas says in "God and Philosophy," "Awakening is like a demand that no obedience is equal to, no obedience puts to sleep; it is a 'more' in the 'less.' Or, to use an obsolete language, it is the spirituality of the soul, ceaselessly aroused from its state of soul, in which *wakefulness* itself already closes over upon itself or falls to sleep, resting within the boundaries it has as a state" (Levinas, *Emmanuel Levinas*, 132–33).

At a crucial tipping point *Body and Soul* graphically dramatizes the darkness that existentially and ethically confronts Charlie before his awakening. Peg tells him that he must leave Roberts, even if it means surrendering his dreams for money and success. Since Roberts owns and controls him, Charlie has nothing under his management. That means she also has nothing, so she forces him to choose between her or Roberts. In a sense Charlie has to decide between two different managers and two ethical systems. He complains that such a choice "is not fair" when he has come so close to all he has wanted. Interestingly, even as the moral messenger, Peg has her own issues involving the relationship of the body and soul. She first appears in the movie in a bathing suit for the amusement of neighborhood men at a political function. Charlie finds her intriguing because her work as an artist complicates his first impression of her as a beauty queen at the political gathering. Peg ultimately seems to give up her artistic ambitions for a career in fashion and merchandising. In a sense she therefore also has to deal with the same kinds of compromises and choices that confront Charlie. Contemplating his dilemma, he sits by himself on the steps of a stoop in total isolation and deepening darkness, his face a portrait of desperate, lonely abandonment. It is one of the most moving images of the entire film. The rest of the film becomes the story of his emergence from the darkness with the revelation of the priority of ethical responsibility that is greater than demanding fairness and equality for the self.

The films in the American cinema of redemption vehemently profess such Levinasian "wakefulness" to the importance of the moral and ethical dimension of human affairs. They place a priority on ethical relations and on adherence to human values. Without participating in the complex philosophical analysis of Levinasian ethics, the American cinema of redemption adopts his notion of the "obsolete language" of the "spirituality of the soul" into its own cinematic language to revivify hope for the soul.

A COMPLEX MORAL VISION

A sign of the genius of the American cinema of redemption involves its complex double, or even multiple, vision. In these films temporal structure and a multilayered mise-en-scène integrate individual, national, and metaphysical narratives. The story of individual redemption transpires in a context of social and cultural forces that are themselves part of a greater metaphysical mise-en-scène of ethical relationships. The camera in the cinema of redemption gives full exposure to the crises of the modern condition but does so in a way that incorporates a transforming American vision. Thus, Frank Capra, with all of his corny sentimentality, does not pretend that his heroic "fool with faith," Jefferson Smith (James Stewart) in *Mr. Smith Goes to Washington*, will end corruption in the country with his single, miraculous victory in the Senate. Similarly, in another of Capra's cinematic time experiments, George Bailey (James Stewart again) in *It's a Wonderful Life* undergoes a rebirth amid his family and friends on Christmas Eve in Bedford Falls, but this still fails to mark a new age of the triumph of economic and political reform. Also, Ethan Edwards (John Wayne) in John Ford's *The Searchers* fulfills his search in Texas for redemption but remains basically the homeless outsider, and Terry Malloy (Marlon Brando) in *On the Waterfront* carries a burden of redemption for his fellow longshoremen, who themselves remain driven, sullen sheep within a failed system. In a sense Garfield speaks for all of them in never truly escaping the problems of the world. They all may find a transcendent moment of a new vision that enables them to achieve a redeeming entry into the heavenly city, but they take the earthly city with them. The mise-en-scène of ethical transcendence does not displace the mise-en-scène of poverty, despair, inequality, and injustice.

In these films transcendence places the earthly city in a new light. The mise-en-scène of ethical transcendence compounds, sometimes in biblical proportions, the weight of moral responsibility and ethical expectation for those living under the conditions of the earthly city. These films raise the moral and ethical demands in the battle for putting ethics before self. Such challenge helps motivate the drama of what Levinas terms, as we have seen, the "ethical adventure of the relationship to the other person."[14]

The high ethical demands in the American cinema of redemption also convey in the cinematic form of narrative and characterization, among other elements of the cinetext (cinematography, mise-en-scène, editing), some of the difficulties associated with Levinasian ethical extremism. An exultant feeling of moral triumph sometimes occurs in these films in a way that recalls the putative sense of moral superiority of the American Puritans and the famous tendentious reformism of many of the Transcendentalists. Thus, Ricoeur's argument about the "hyperbole" of Levinas's radical ethics could also apply in many instances to the American cinema of redemption.[15] In these films extremism often manifests itself in a moral martyrdom that touches many of the male protagonists, often played by Stewart and Garfield but by Brando and Wayne as well.

The moral narcissism of such masochism also can mobilize a seemingly opposing but in fact complementary reaction in the form of complacent self-satisfaction. Such self-centeredness becomes dangerous as a kind of ethical adventure that differs markedly from Levinas's version of that adventure, erupting into the adventurism of a super-heroic John Wayne figure. This character type often possesses a ferocious moral certitude to match his trigger-readiness to act. In *The Searchers* Ethan Edwards exemplifies this attitude and character type in his chauvinistic and racist treatment of women and Native Americans throughout his long search on the frontier for his niece, Debbie (Natalie Woods), who was captured by Indians.

Indeed, Ethan has been seen as representative of the sexism and racism evident in many of the films and much of the culture of the American cinema of redemption. Such redemption, as previously discussed, often means redemption for white men. Embattled during these decades with fascist and communist regimes and forces, the United States propounded the American creed of freedom, fairness, equality, and opportunity throughout the world while engaging in its own ethical and political battles at home to realize precisely those ideals for women and minorities. Interestingly, *The Searchers* has been interpreted by several critics as part of this domestic battle through the dramatic education of Wayne's character in overcoming his innate racism as a manifestation of his own self-hatred.[16] Thus, his adventurism becomes an example of the ethical adventure.

Such complexities constitute the substance and structure of the ethical adventure. Levinas, the Puritans, and the Transcendentalists inform that enduring journey. The American cinema of redemption strives to enlighten it.

ETHICS, DEMOCRACY, AND A CASE FOR THE FUTURE

To Simon Critchley the nurturance of genuine democratic cultures requires the transformation of contemporary politics. This change, in turn, depends on establishing a new ethical foundation for politics. For him, "facing" political problems must resonate with the Levinasian ethical commitment to the face as an ultimate, absolute revelation of responsibility for the other. Only such a combination of ethics and politics can begin the effective creation of democratic movements and environments: "It is this meta-political moment that propels one into facing and facing down a wrong or confronting a situation of injustice, not through sovereign legal norms backed up with the threat of violence, but through an ethical responsiveness to the sheer precariousness of the other's face, of their injurability and our own. An ethical politics flows from our constitutive powerlessness in the face of the other."[17]

For Critchley the mutual dependence of ethics and politics necessitates going beyond Levinasian ethics: "There is no pure ethical experience and no simple deduction from ethics as the relation to the other to politics as a relation to all others, as Levinas sometimes appears to believe" (Critchley, *Infinitely Demanding*, 120). In the relationship between ethics and politics each has what the other needs. In the exchange of qualities and powers one provides body and substance, and the other offers sight and insight. Critchley proposes that "if ethics without politics is empty, then politics without ethics is blind. The world that we have in sight overwhelms us with the difficult plurality of its demands" (120). Critchley thus politicizes John Llewelyn's powerful idea of a "spiritual optics," claiming, "My view is that we need ethics in order to see what to do in a political situation" (120).[18]

For Critchley the politics that can help effect Levinasian ethics involves an anarchic politics of democracy and dissensus. Reflecting the Levinasian focus on the other, he says, "It is an anarchism of the other being who places me under a heteronomous demand rather than an anarchism of the autonomous self" (Critchley, *Infinitely Demanding*, 126). He believes that "politics consists in the manifestation of a dissensus that disturbs the order by which government wishes to depoliticize society" (129). Emphasizing that "democratization consists in the manifestation of dissensus," he proposes that such dissensus dramatically refuses to countenance the manufacturing of an artificial consensus (130). Ethics, for Critchley, should not be sacrificed in the name of consensus, not even to make the political system work or to accommodate the desires of the majority. Critchley believes that a fusion of dissensus and Levinasian ethics will help generate the kind of motivation to make a new politics for a real democracy work: "On my view, ethics is the experience of an infinite demand at the heart of my subjectivity, a demand that undoes me and requires me to do more, not in the name of some sovereign authority, but in the namelessness of a powerless exposure, a vulnerability, a responsive responsibility, a humorous self-division" (132).

Significantly, when Critchley calls on Levinas for help to articulate a philosophy for a democratic future based on ethics, the thread of ideas that binds his system together intertwines in interesting ways with classic American ideology. Critchley himself notes something of this interesting relationship between these seemingly very different worlds, namely, on the one hand, ideas by contemporary advocates of radical democracy and anarchy and, on the other hand, the American experience. He says an idea of the "anarchist recovery of direct democracy" could be "as American as apple pie (or the death penalty)." He asserts, "One can find the idea of democracy as a way of life as far back as Thomas Paine's radical distinction of society from government in *Common Sense*, or again in John Dewey's 'Creative Democracy,' written on his eightieth birthday at the dark moment of 1939" (Critchley, *Infinitely Demanding*, 126).

Critchley obviously has some sympathy for this radical American impulse toward democracy as a viable "notion of anarchist democratic self-organization" (127). For Critchley, however, any such connection between American ideology and Levinas would also have to engage the deep concern that Critchley shares with Derrida and others about the dangers to democracy from any national hegemony. He also resists associating American ideology too closely with his own espousal of both anarchic dissensus and a Derridean "democracy to come."[19] Accordingly, Critchley castigates Richard

Rorty for his political view in *Achieving Our Country* of "American national pride." For Critchley, Rorty's politics is "only a cigarette paper away from a rather unpalatable chauvinism of American exceptionalism."[20]

Ewa Ziarek also considers Levinasian thought as a potential source for bringing ethics and politics together in a new social philosophy for radical change. Noting the relatively recent recognition of "the importance of Levinas's ethics for democracy," Ziarek shares Critchley's interest in dissensus as a key term for the new ethics.[21] Ziarek, however, proposes dissensus as part of a theory of a "feminist ethics of dissensus": "Feminist ethics of dissensus raises an important question concerning the relevance of Levinas's ethics for contemporary democratic politics." Using Levinas in conjunction with other radical thinkers, such as Patricia Williams, she sees feminist ethical dissensus as forming a common front for battling "the history of racism, anti-Semitism, and exploitation." She reads Levinas, among other thinkers, to propose a "reformulation" and a "redefinition of human rights in the context of the theories of radical democracy." Seeing a clear complicity of liberalism, property rights, and racism in perpetuating contemporary social injustice, Ziarek hopes that Levinas's ethical passion can provide impetus "for the ethical redefinition of rights based on the notion of responsibility" (Ziarek, *An Ethics of Dissensus*, 62, 63, 68). Such responsibility must resist reduction to the ideological temptations and myths of liberalism concerning rights, property, and freedom.

Ziarek, of course, appreciates that for Levinasian thought to fulfill its potential for helping to shape a new radical feminist ethics of dissensus, it becomes necessary to go beyond "Levinas's definition of political discourse" as delineated in some of the basic works of his "philosophical system." In such works as *Totality and Infinity* and *Otherwise Than Being*, Levinas maintains too strict a separation, she says, between the infinity of ethics and the totality of politics or between the disruption and diachronicity of the ethically ineffable saying versus the "systematicity" and "synchrony" of the said (Ziarek, *An Ethics of Dissensus*, 66, 65).

The force of dissensus, however, in democratic theory also occurs in a context somewhat removed from the postmodernism that Ziarek espouses and somewhat closer to the American "exceptionalism" that Critchley disdains. Sacvan Bercovitch's use of dissensus can provide another bridge for Levinasian thought to both American democratic ideology and its expression in the American cinema of redemption. Although Critchley and Ziarek probably would challenge such a connection, dissensus—as articulated in the American ideology, the American Creed, and the American Way—extends the relationship between radical thought and American democracy beyond the limits Critchley perceives while also advancing some of the causes for democracy and equality that Ziarek advocates.

Bercovitch sees a paradigmatic relationship between consensus and dissensus as the foundation for American ideology, literary history, and culture. Bercovitch's theory of dissensus and American culture makes dissensus the energy behind the historic reenacting of a "ritual of consensus" built on generations of dissent.[22] In contrast to Critchley's anarchic anticonsensus argument, dissensus in American thought, as Bercovitch sees it, historically constitutes the core of American democracy by providing the basis for an "ideology of consensus." Dissensus, then, creates a new kind of consensus out of the very opposite of *consent, dissent.* America for Bercovitch becomes a culture of dissent and consensus, and the power of dissent keeps the culture together. Dissent in America becomes the vehicle for inclusion and for upward mobility. The ethics at the core of the impulse for dissent fuels the ideological process.

Of course, any similarity between Critchley's conception of dissensus and the American experience as Bercovitch analyzes it separates over the inherently conservative nature of American dissent as a force for eventual cohesion and conformity. Bercovitch notes that for many "the American ideology . . . undertakes above all, as a condition of its nurture, to absorb the spirit of protest for social ends" and achieves "this most effectively through its rhetoric of dissent." Making dissensus part of the ontology of America, of its very fabric and being, constitutes a form for controlling dissent and change. Noting that this American ideology was "adopted from the start precisely for its ability to transmute radicalism of all kinds, from religious protest to revolutionary war, into varieties of ideological consensus," he says that "this approach implies a fundamental challenge both to the old consensus and to large parts of the current dissensus."[23]

Moreover, for Bercovitch dissensus becomes a crucial element in enabling the ideology of consensus to define and confine the contours of American identity and discourse. Consensus and dissensus help cast all issues in terms of the American ideology and what it means to be American. Bercovitch speaks of the articulation of the American idea through its representation in classic American literature: "The point here is not that these classic writers had no quarrel with America, but that they seem to have had nothing *but* that to quarrel about. Having adopted the culture's *controlling* metaphor—'America' as synonym for human possibility—and having made this tenet of consensus the ground of radical dissent, they defined radicalism as an affirmation of cultural values" (*The Rites of Assent*, 367).

In these terms of the process of mutual dependence between consensus and dissensus, American dissensus may seem irrelevant to Critchley's anarchic impulse for a renewed democracy or inadequate for Ziarek's passion for reinventing human rights for women, minorities, and the poor. The history of American dissensus, as delineated by Bercovitch, certainly could appear dated before the great challenges for democracy posed by Critchley and Ziarek, among many other contemporary thinkers. For example, Ziarek, thinking about Patricia Williams, refers to the need to address and assuage the suffering of "the historically disempowered—slaves, the homeless, mental patients" (Ziarek, *An Ethics of Dissensus*, 68).

In the context of the discussion of ethics, dissensus, and democracy, however, it could be of benefit to consider that "the historically disempowered" also have a history that could help inspire change for the future. It could be claimed that in the past America was defined in part by its response to the disempowered when the word *disempowered* described almost everyone in Europe, just as today it could be applied to the many millions of people around the globe living in poverty and under oppression.

Thus, a Frenchman before deconstruction and postmodernism, Hector St. John de Crèvecœur, famously wrote in 1782 in *Letters from an American Farmer*: "In this great American asylum, the poor of Europe have by some means met together." He then proceeds to list the sufferings inflicted on Europeans by conditions in their home countries. He also indicates how the disempowered of that time achieved empowerment and renewal in America: "Everything has tended to regenerate them: new laws, a new mode of living, a new social system; here they are become men: in Europe they were as so many useless plants, wanting vegetative mould, and refreshing showers; they withered, and were mowed down by want, hunger, and war; but now, by the power of transplantation, like all other plants they have taken root and flourished!"[24]

Crèvecœur sets forth indelible imagery of America as a sanctuary for the world. Equally important, he helps initiate the idea of the American asylum as a new kind of environment for the cultivation of a universal nation comprising all the peoples of the world. Although he originally conceived of this new identity as primarily northern European and certainly white, the symbolism became the engine for the perpetual transformation of American identity and culture.

Thinking of this promise of America, Crèvecœur, in some of the most famous words associated with America, asks, "What, then, is the American, this new man?" He immediately answers his own question, forecasting America as the home for a new mongrel people: "He is neither an European nor the descendant of an European; hence that strange mixture of blood, which you will find in no other country." He then adds, "Here individuals of all nations are melted into a new race of men, whose labours and posterity will one day cause great changes in the world." America gives new meaning to life for ordinary people: "The American is a new man, who acts upon new principles; he must therefore entertain new ideas and form new opinions" (Crèvecœur, *Letters from an American Farmer*, 63–64).

Crèvecœur's political and ethical imagination also encompasses the political dynamic of his own cultural symbolism. Regeneration as an indispensable element of his cultural ideology and mythology engenders the craving for dissensus. Dissensus fuels the mechanism for constant change and renewal. This purpose manifests itself in American democratic political theory, in part, as Jefferson's argument for so-called continuing majorities. Jefferson wrote in 1824, "The Creator has made the earth for the living, not the dead. Rights and powers can only belong to persons, not to things, not to mere matter unendowed with will." He then adds, "A generation may bind itself as long as its majority continues in life; when that has disappeared, another majority is in place, holds all the rights and powers their predecessors once held, and may change their laws and institutions to suit themselves. Nothing then is unchangeable but the inherent and unalienable rights of man."[25] Jefferson's theory of change based on "unalienable" human rights gains more dramatic expression in his argument to James Madison in 1787: "I hold it that a little rebellion now and then is a good thing, and as necessary in the political world as storms in the physical."[26]

As part of his theory of democracy and dissensus, Jefferson's argument for revolution resonates in Levinas's own language for dissent and revolution in his writings of 1972 in "Ideology and Idealism." Not quite matching Jefferson's genius for succinct immediacy but approximating his passionate conviction, Levinas argues that "rebellion against an unjust society expresses the spirit of our age. That spirit is expressed by rebellion against an unjust society." Thus, he makes reference to "disorder or permanent revolution, a breaking of frameworks, an obliteration of ranks, liberating man, like death, entirely, from everything and from the whole."[27] Ziarek calls this argument "the most stunning reversal of his own initial presuppositions" that "affirms rebellion against the unjust society" while still maintaining responsibility toward the other (Ziarek, *An Ethics of Dissensus*, 73). Seán Hand places this argument in the context of Levinas's thought regarding religion, politics, philosophy, the Holocaust, and the Talmud.[28] Levinas's comments also reflect, no doubt, the many political and cultural crises in Paris and throughout the world during these years.

Similarly, in the light of his case for achieving human rights, Levinas also attests to the importance of fighting for such rights of the other. In the name of a modern conception of rights and freedom, especially against the "exploitation by capital" and for "the right to social advancement," Levinas proclaims "the right to fight for the full rights of man, and the right to ensure the necessary political conditions for that struggle."[29]

The rhetoric and history of American dissensus and consensus, as discussed by Bercovitch, incorporate the struggle for rights into the culture's very language. Such rhetoric propels dissensus forward as part of America's mission to the world. The rhetoric thrived as a counterforce to totalitarian ideologies and nations in the last century but also makes the argument against America's own aggressive imperialistic adventures throughout our history. In brief, the American model of democracy as an ideology of consensus based on regeneration and dissensus goes back to John Winthrop's vision in "A Model of Christian Charity" of an American New Jerusalem as a "city upon a hill," to Jefferson's notion of America as "an empire for liberty," to Emerson's argument in "The Fortune of the Republic" that "this country, the last found, is the great charity of God to the human race," to Lincoln's insistence in his Second Message to Congress that America remains "the last best hope of earth."[30]

The idea of America's mission of redemption and dissensus informs the American version of the cinema of redemption and helps to link the meaning of the ideology of such films to both the American past and the contemporary continental ethical philosophy of Levinas. The proclivity for change in the American ideology of dissensus can provide the political counterpart to realize the ethical demand of Levinasian philosophy for placing a priority on responsibility for the other, including maintaining, protecting, and advancing the human rights of the other.

Just as a linkage of ideas of ethical transcendence extends from the Puritans through Emerson to Levinas, so also a history of dissensus and regeneration operates from early sources of American identity in the Puritans and Emerson to the latent radicalism of Levinas. The historic importance of the American ideology of democratic dissensus justifies comparing American dissensus to the history and practice of other more recent theories of radical democratic dissensus.

Accordingly, the ideology of dissensus and consensus and the American cinema of redemption can be part of a new discourse for reconstituting a new idea of dissensus, one that engages the radical innovations of thinkers such as Critchley and Ziarek, especially in their call for a reaffirmation of human rights for the oppressed. American dissensus can participate in its own transformation in its engagement with these other theories that place democracy in a modern context for a new century.

Critchley's call for the creation by "contemporary anarchists" of "a new language of civil disobedience" should resonate with a theory of dissensus that the works of Thoreau and Emerson embody (Critchley, *Infinitely Demanding*, 123). Critchley suggests a promise for the future with this new language. At the same time, he and other dissensus advocates such as Ziarek also may find a potential in American dissensus for energizing their ambitions for a new fusion of ethics and politics in domestic politics and international relationships. Together a potential may exist for creating a new language of dissensus into a fresh force for ethics—literally a force for good in a world still wracked with the evils and crimes that made the last century such a disaster. The need for such a revolution in the realm of ethics and politics helped inspire the move for a new fusion of politics and ethics in the first place.

The radical Levinasian demand for absolute ethical responsibility for the other compels discussion and action. To many, the mixture this demand requires of ethics and politics becomes particularly explosive when it encourages serious intervention for the other in personal relations, as well as in national and international politics. For example, Jackson Lears makes a powerful argument that challenges the value and meaning of the ideology and myth of regeneration in "the making of modern America."[31] Yet at some point the responsibility for the other requires an ethical politics. Indeed, Levinas's own vision of the significance of the idea of Israel in *Beyond the*

Verse and elsewhere compares to America's self-conceived messianic mission in history of responsibility. As Derrida and others have noted, Levinas never quite managed to reconcile these conflicting ethical issues of absolute responsibility to the other in his philosophy or his inchoate politics. Certainly aware of the totalistic danger involved in the potential incarnation of universal power in a particular entity or individual, Levinas also knew the ethical and political danger in fleeing from individual and national ethical responsibility for the other.

In a cinematic context of such issues of ethics and politics, Sarah Cooper's theory of the creation in film of a "space of responsibility" proves useful. This space involves the intersection between what can be perceived phenomenologically and what the "excess" of perception and image suggests of the infinite and transcendent.[32] The "difference" between these two forces of the phenomenological image and the excess of its infinite temporal and ethical potential constitutes a space for ethical debate.

Such a debate can facilitate the search for a new ethical subjectivity in relation to changing political contexts. No doubt this search requires new political and ethical thinking. Conceivably, the work of aesthetics can carry a considerable share of the ethical burden. To a certain extent, the significance of the cinema of redemption, including the American version, derives from its participation in the search for a new mutually sustaining relationship between ethics and politics.

CHAPTER 2
FRANK CAPRA AND JAMES STEWART
Time, Transcendence, and the Other

At the beginning of *Totality and Infinity* (1961) Levinas prophetically wonders if the idea of morality still obtains in the contemporary world: "Everyone will readily agree that it is of the highest importance to know whether we are not duped by morality."[1] Levinas, of course, committed several decades of his life to articulating an original philosophy that answers his own question by affirming that morality and ethics not only remain relevant but inescapable in the human experience. The publication of *Totality and Infinity* signified his growing influence on the philosophical world of his time. From being a student of both Edmund Husserl and Martin Heidegger to becoming an important primary source of Jean-Paul Sartre's introduction to phenomenology, Levinas steadily matured into a significant counterforce in European thought whose prolific writing required recognition. In his discourse with more famous Continental thinkers, including Jacques Derrida, Levinas challenged dominant intellectual trends to propagate his interpretation of the relationship of ethics to modernism. He insisted on prioritizing ethics over ontology, pluralism over totality, transcendence over empirical investigation and conceptualization. Whereas Sartre promoted a philosophy of freedom based on the idea that existence precedes essence, Levinas, as Richard J. Bernstein says, proclaimed responsibility to the other takes precedence over oneself. After Levinas died, during the early hours of December 25, 1995, Derrida's funeral oration, entitled "Adieu," on December 28 confirmed that Levinas's ethical argument had become a significant part of modern philosophical debate.[2]

It could be argued that the great American director Frank Capra spent much of his career answering Levinas's question about the relevance of morality. Like Levinas, Capra insists that not only are we not duped by morality but that the real duping occurs when we try to cheat morality and hope to escape the consequences of such avoidance. Moreover, in giving priority to this ethical theme in *Mr. Smith Goes to Washington* (1939) and *It's a Wonderful Life* (1946), Capra underscores the centrality of this idea in many of the movies from this period in the American cinema of redemption. While all of these films articulate by definition an ideology of redemption, Capra's films become especially interesting for their varied use of time in making the argument for ethical transcendence.

The salience of moral and ethical issues in Capra's greatest films helps sustain his place in the pantheon of America's classic directors. For many, Capra remains the quintessential American director. America at the time of his death, on September 3, 1991, was a dramatically different place from the country of his classic films from the 1930s to the early 1950s. The differences between the America of small-town values, railroads, radio, and classic cars and the America of the computer, instant media, and sexual liberation perhaps were as significant in their own way as the differences between his origins—Capra was born in Sicily, on May 18, 1897—and what he had become as a Hollywood icon. Along with *Mr. Smith Goes to Washington* and *It's a Wonderful Life*, his most successful films, such as *It Happened One Night* (1934), *Mr. Deeds Goes to Town* (1936), *You Can't Take It with You* (1938), exude qualities of simplicity, honesty, and sentimentality that many people termed "Capracorn" but many others still consider the truer, ideal America. While Capra's style runs counter to many current trends in popular and critical thinking, years of scholarly criticism by Robert Sklar, Ray Carney, Robert Ray, Charles Maland, Joseph McBride, John Raeburn, among others, demonstrate the complexity of Capra's best work.[3]

Indeed, Capra's most important films incorporate within their artistic structure a complex examination of American culture. At the time of the emerging hegemony of America in the world, Capra's cinematic dramatization of a changing sensibility became part of a developing national dialogue.[4]

Arguably, two of his most important films during this period of American transformation helped to form the vocabulary for broader cultural and political debate. These films, *Mr. Smith Goes to Washington* and *It's a Wonderful Life*, became part of American national consciousness, not as mere celebrations of American uniqueness but as complex cinematic articulations of deep ambiguities in American culture.[5] Rethinking these two films in light of Levinas's thought on ethics and time can provide new insights into the significance of these films to our own era.

MR. SMITH GOES TO WASHINGTON

In many ways *Mr. Smith Goes to Washington* serves as a case study for how the relationship of time to a variety of matters, such as movement, space, and narrative, becomes part of an ethical drama, ultimately leading to an experience of alterity and transcendence in the manner that Levinas discusses in his ethics.

In terms of Gilles Deleuze's theory of time and movement in film, a typical sequence in *Mr. Smith Goes to Washington* literally exemplifies not simply moving dynamic frames but the action and interaction of closed sets and ensembles that invariably point to an open process with metaphysical implications. Even as an indirect image of time, with time subordinate to the intervals, breaks, and false continuity of the movement-image, the Capra sequence remains open to endless possibility yet connected and integral to the whole of the film. Montage, as the composition of movement-images, in Capra emphasizes change. Absent a solid center or solid anchorage in the image, the fluidity of the film movement compares to the ephemerality of human relations. Even given the limitations of the movement-image, the Capra montage points to what for Deleuze would be the possibility of infinitude.[6]

Viewing the dynamics of classic montage through a Deleuzian prism brings into sharp relief the temporal aspects of the Capra montage in a way that also highlights the ethical implications of the film's frame. For example, one famous scene, when Jefferson Smith (James Stewart) arrives at the Washington, D.C., train terminal, exhibits great internal and external movement with the activities of aggressive young women who welcome him with flirtatious teasing and of political operatives who disparage him. The dynamic composition, spatial relations, and depth of field of the scene all emphasize movement and positioning that dramatize Smith's physical displacement while also demonstrating the ethical implications of his situation as he stands as the object of public ridicule, in some ways connected to the black porters who also occupy positions of inferiority.

The movement in and out of the spatial dynamics of the scene also suggests, however, a temporal displacement. Smith has arrived at the Washington train station, and in a sense, as a fresh, young senator, his time has come. In fact, however, he really functions in his own temporal dimension. Although he has arrived physically, he still lives in his mind and in his relations to others in a different world—the world of the classic American West. Thus, when Smith looks at the Capitol dome, itself framed by the door of the train station, he envisions a personal connection to what could be deemed for him a spiritual domain.

Capra's framed image in the train station demonstrates the relevance to time and ethics in film of Paul Ricoeur's paradigm of time and narrative and Wood's time-frame. Ricoeur's space of experience and horizon of expectation and Wood's horizon of being readily apply to the dynamics of time and change in the film frame. The view of the Capitol dome injects a vital temporal dimension into the scene, indicating an extension of distance and time and a special historic temporality. The Capitol dome presents a horizon of Smith's expectation of his movements for his day of sightseeing. The vision of the Capitol dome also projects a national horizon of political meaning based at least in part on history, thereby dramatizing Ricoeur's notion of multiple temporalities in narrative or the intersections of cosmological and phenomenological time into "human time."

Moreover, for Ricoeur, the terms for describing spatial organization and relationships, itineraries and traversals, accentuate the temporal aspect to movement and physical connection within the spatial frame. *Itinerary* especially suggests temporality in the linkage of parts of a scene or space. Itineraries and traversals wonderfully describe the time of the action within the framed scene at the train station as the political hacks realize their new senator has disappeared on them. With Washington, D.C., the nation's capital, as the background and politics as the subject matter of the film, *Mr. Smith Goes to Washington* also dramatizes the importance to film of Ricoeur's idea of the interweaving of fiction and history in narrative, including the documentary aspect of the city itself and of the political processes that occupy its attention.

In addition, the visual images of Jefferson Smith in this scene of his arrival in Washington provide a powerful example of the crucial difference for Ricoeur between identity as the same and identity as selfhood. The film brilliantly shows Smith's steady transformation from simply being an archetypal cultural image of American innocence and a study of the sameness of Hollywood's idea of American male identity in the late 1930s to the emergence of his mature singularity as a morally sensitive ethical hero.[7]

For nearly seventy years people throughout the world regularly summon James Stewart to the screen as Jefferson Smith for what has become something of a ritual of viewing *Mr. Smith Goes to Washington* to witness the triumph of good over evil. The movie insinuates itself into the structure of our most pervasive myths of national self-identity. For many, it clearly provides reassurance that in the face of overwhelming odds the youth and integrity of an American David will defeat the evil of the Goliath of great power in the service of greed. Over the years narrative development, characterization, dialogue, cinematography, editing, and performance have all been analyzed to explain how the film works so successfully to make Smith's transformation from an innocent bumpkin to a cultural and political hero convincing.[8] Melding elements of a love story, romantic comedy, urban melodrama, and national epic, the film also enacts a basic religious metaphor of a journey through evil to gain redemption. In many ways the political, religious, and cultural rhetoric of the film dramatizes the basic ethical metaphysics that Levinas advocates. The film espouses an ethical ideology with religious connotations that resonate with American values of fairness, honesty, justice, and morality.

Moreover, Capra's direction in *Mr. Smith Goes to Washington* dramatizes relationships between time and ethics that Levinas, Ricoeur, Wood, and Deleuze elucidate. An important example of this connection between Capra and philosophy occurs during the early stages of the film in one of the most famous montage sequences in classic Hollywood film. As in the entire film, Capra's montage editor, Slavko Vorkapich, deserves considerable credit for his creative expertise. In the scene Smith has just arrived at the Washington train station from the hinterland, most likely Montana since the film was based on an original Lewis R. Foster short story called "The Gentleman from Montana." After seeing the Capitol dome framed through the doors of the station, he eludes the greeting party at the station to go on his own tour of the city.

The montage sequence operates on several different time levels and compresses different time frames—different temporalities that Ricoeur probably would appreciate. First, it compresses into a matter of minutes the hours that Smith's tour would take. While he visits the various sites throughout the city, others anxiously wonder and wait to learn where he has gone. The montage of sites on his tour intercuts with Jean Arthur as Clarissa Saunders and Thomas Mitchell as Diz Moore, idling their time in the senator's office awaiting news of Smith's whereabouts. Ostensibly, the new senator's secretary and administrative assistant, Saunders personifies a Washington insider. Personally involved with Moore, the venerable poet and dean of the Washington press corps, Saunders will become romantically involved with Smith to work as the instrument for the film's multiple meanings. By both loving and advising him, she will serve as the brains behind his actions that move the film to its melodramatic conclusion. Meanwhile, the dialogue and dramatic action between Saunders and Mitchell during their wait in the senator's office add depth to Smith's character as a figure whose roots in the West and in old frontier values of honesty, integrity, honor, and service make him an anachronism in modern Washington.

Along with the montage editing that presents the day's events for Smith, Saunders, and Moore, the film also achieves a cinematic milestone in the way it contrives another montage of national history to insert into the original story of the day. Powerful nondiegetic music of a nationalistic nature provides a provocative background and emotional cues for the overlapping images of historic sites that illustrate the nation's history from the time of the founding fathers to the Civil War. Thus, in *Mr. Smith Goes to Washington* Capra presents an imaginative rendering of American history that illustrates the kind of complex temporalities Ricoeur describes.

The sequence ends at the Lincoln Memorial, where Smith observes and listens to a young boy read the end of the Gettysburg Address to an elderly man with a distinct profile. A cut shows a humble black man enter the monument with his hat in his hand. When the boy states the word *freedom* from Lincoln's address, the film cuts immediately to the black man, thereby allowing the boy to speak for this idea of emancipation for the grown man of color. Nevertheless, in spite of the cautious stance on racial inclusion, this moment at the Lincoln Memorial intends to make the monument into a national cathedral of democracy. Lincoln looms over the scene like a national deity. Smith's face shines in key light that turns him into a supplicant who embodies a deep devotion to a secular religion of democracy, freedom, and equality.

In terms of tone, timing, and cultural and political significance, this moment at the Lincoln Memorial provides a strong conclusion to the montage. It summarizes the significance of the historic images that precede it and injects all the energy of the montage with an attitude of solemnity regarding the ultimate importance of the serious themes of the movie that underlie its comedic overtones. Also, the scene foreshadows a crucial later scene of ultimate significance at the Lincoln Memorial on which the film will turn.

From beginning to end, the montage of Smith's initial tour of Washington dramatizes how classic montage operates as a movement-image that subordinates time to movement in film construction. The relationship of Capra's montage technique to his development of diachronicity and transcendence can be explained to a considerable degree by D. N. Rodowick's study of Deleuze's complex theory of the movement-image and the time-image.[9] As Deleuze and Rodowick describe it, montage tends to show time indirectly as it relates to movement. Montage links different movements and intervals in a way that produces time indirectly. Rodowick says that "because time is reduced to intervals defined by movement and the linkage of movements through montage," the movement-image produces an "indirect image of time" (Rodowick, *Gilles Deleuze's Time Machine*, 11).

No matter the source, structure, or nature of the montage, Rodowick proposes that "the idea of montage is in every case founded on managing the number of rational segmentations of movement per unit of time" (*Gilles Deleuze's Time Machine*, 12). This explanation obtains for the montage in Capra's films, as well as the intellectual montage of Sergei Eisenstein or the analytical montage of Dziga Vertov. Rodowick describes this aspect of montage as an "organic movement-image" of "relatively determined and predictable relations" within a "deterministic universe" (15). Since for Rodowick time in the movement-image "serves here as the *measure* of space and movement," time becomes subordinate to movement and "can only be 'seen' through the intermediaries of space and movement" (9–10).

Accordingly, for Rodowick, even with the fluidity of constant mobile framing and editing of montage, such movement-images constrict imagination by imposing spatial boundaries on time. In contrast to the organicism of the movement-image, the time-image becomes "probabilistic" as opposed to determined (*Gilles Deleuze's Time Machine*, 15). In the time-image, filmic elements form "incommensurable" relations of inexorable divisions that make absolute certainty impossible (15). Instead of the regulated time of the movement-image, the time-image suggests a different time order of unpredictability. Rodowick writes, "The chronological time of the movement-image fragments into an image of uncertain becoming" (15). He explains how even thinking and knowing vary between movement-images and time-images: "Where the movement-image ideally conceives the relation between image and thought in the forms of identity and totality—an ever-expanding ontology—the time-image imagines the same relation as nonidentity: thought as a deterritorialized and nomadic becoming, a creative act" (17). With all of its fluidity between shots, images, and frames and its diversity of time frames, the Capra montage of Smith's tour of Washington typifies the linkages of movement-images in montage in general as described by Deleuze and Rodowick.

One aspect of the montage, however, operates differently from the usual movement-image. Like Smith's election itself, this element suggests a different temporal order. In the sequence of shots of historic landmarks and sites, founding documents, and statues of the founding fathers, the famously enlarged signature of John Hancock for the signing of the Declaration of Independence takes shape. For some, perhaps, the physical action of writing the signature at this point in the montage can be dismissed as a mere visual conceit in keeping with the grandly patriotic and celebratory rhetoric of the whole sequence. Nevertheless, what Ricoeur would call the "reenactment" of the signing, even without the dramatic context of the historic moment itself, suggests a different kind of temporal regime, one closer to the idea of the time-image or thought image that so impresses Rodowick and Deleuze. The action of the signing derives from an order of time different from the linear continuity of the movement-image. The moment of signing suggests a break from the synchronic order of coherent events to indicate Levinasian diachronicity.

Moreover, considered in the context of the American "religion of democracy" that the Lincoln Memorial represents in this film, this signature-signing moment can be compared to other renditions of insinuations of Levinasian transcendence or diachronic time into traditional temporal order. Thus, in his extended tribute to Levinas, Derrida recalls in a footnote a Talmudic story that emphasizes the impact of transcendent time in the ordinary temporal regime. Derrida quotes, "'According to a Talmudic parable, all Jews, past, present, and future, were there at the foot of Sinai; in a certain sense, all were present at Auschwitz.'"[10] Similarly, the enactment of the Hancock signing, seemingly out of nowhere, can be seen as a sign of transcendence, a form of summons or call to the movie viewer of a temporal world with a meaning and significance that exceed historical time. In this light the signature writing constitutes a form of Deleuzian time-image, what for Levinas would signify the diachronic time of transcendence beyond ordinary linear time, synchronicity, or chronological order.

Throughout his writings Levinas expatiates with great passion on the issue of the relationship between time and ethical transcendence and explains in detail the contrast between ordinary synchronic time and the diachronic time of transcendence that Jefferson Smith ultimately achieves in *Mr. Smith Goes to Washington*. Thus, in "Inside Heidegger: Bergson," which is part of Levinas's lecture courses that have been published as *God, Death, and Time*, Levinas distinguishes between "linear time," or the ordinary time of daily life, and "a more profound, or originary, time behind linear time."[11] Following Bergson, Levinas says, "the idea that there are various levels of time is affirmed here" in a manner that follows "the entire Western tradition" that "approaches time through measurement" (*God, Death, and Time*, 55). He continues: "For Bergson, linear time is a spatialization of time in view of acting upon matter, which is the work of intelligence. Originary time he calls *duration*; this is a becoming in which each instant is heavy with all of the past and pregnant with the whole future. Duration is experienced by a descent into self. Each instant is there; nothing is definitive since each instant remakes the past" (55).

For Levinas this "diachronic" as opposed to "synchronic" time breaks the bounds of spatialized time to gain access to the infinite. "Time is not," he says, "the limitation of being but its relationship with infinity" (19). Of course, diachronicity and transcendence must function along with the more traditional temporal organization of narrative form in *Mr. Smith Goes to Washington*. Time in the form of Levinasian diachronicity and transcendence persists as a crucial part of the film's significance in conjunction with the predominance of montage and the movement-image.

One scene in the film constitutes an extended form of time-image. This scene finds Smith in severe depression after his demoralizing humiliation at the hands of Paine, Taylor, and their cronies. He returns to the Lincoln Memorial as a gesture of defeat before his guilt-ridden flight from Washington. What earlier had been filmed as a temple for celebrating the promise of American democracy and the fulfillment of Lincoln as the Redeemer President is cast now in somber darkness and functions as a tomb of lost idealistic hopes. Smith sits alone in the shadows of the monument and weeps, totally abandoned. Observing him as she emerges from the shadows, Saunders appears to save him and salvage his spirit. Barely acknowledging the extreme unlikelihood of her being at the monument at the precise time as Smith, she simply indicates that she figured she could find him returning to what once had been a source of his highest idealistic dreams.

The emotion of the scene successfully blurs the fact of its utterly incredible, unrealistic nature. Other than her simple comment, the scene offers no explanation for how Saunders could possibly have found Smith at that particular moment. The film does not even pretend to explain the contingent nature of this meeting. In fact, the mystery of the scene actually serves its deeper purpose to suggest that it occurs in a different temporal dimension, one that for Levinas would involve a transcendent ethical connection. Indeed, her words of encouragement in this scene sustain a Levinasian theme of a realm of meaning beyond being. In an earlier scene with Diz, Saunders wistfully gained an insight into the true Smith by seeing him as a classic idealist and dreamer. She says, "I wonder, Diz, if this Don Quixote hasn't got the jump on all of us." She asks "if it isn't a curse to go through life wised up like you and me."

In the second Lincoln Memorial scene, however, her language acquires its own religious resonance after Smith expresses his deep disillusionment to her about the reality of the lies behind the ideals "carved in stone" on all the monuments. Similarly, without quite realizing it, he makes a confession of the misplaced direction and nature of his faith that would confirm Levinas's concern about idolatry. Speaking of Senator Paine, he complains to Saunders that he has been betrayed by "a man I worshipped." She responds to his inadvertent admission of worshipping false gods, with her own new faith in his profound beliefs. Picking up on the biblical notion of "fools for Christ's sake" (1 Corinthians 4:10), she recalls the power of belief of all the men Smith had believed in and dubs them "fools with faith" who had the courage to act on their hopes. So Smith in her eyes has grown from simply being a naive idealist to a potential religious figure, a "fool with faith."

The emphasis in this scene on language also recalls the importance in Levinasian ethical theory of the difference between the "saying" and the "said." Saunders has found Smith at the Lincoln Memorial shortly after he was reduced to silence by the lies of the corrupt politicians arrayed against him. Then, he stared tearfully in disbelief over their callous disregard for the truth. Having failed to find the will or the words to defend himself, Smith simply raced out of the Senate chamber during the hearing of his case. Like Melville's Billy Budd, he proves too innocent to articulate his own cause. For Levinas, saying suggests a domain of spirituality that depends on its reduction to representation in the said. As Tina Chanter observes, "There is an essential and irreducible ambiguity that marks the passage from the saying to the said, and the reduction of what shows itself in the said to the signification of the saying." Chanter emphasizes the paradox of Levinas's paradigm: "The restlessness, the lack of fixity, the resistance of the saying to its assembly in the said, its inexhaustible divergence from the said, defies thematization."[12] It becomes Saunders's mission to help Smith find the language to defend himself. Fittingly, this assumption of a new purpose to her life occurs at the Lincoln Memorial, a national monument to the recuperative power of language to regenerate.

After she has inspired Smith to act, Saunders and Smith leave the memorial together, fired up by mutual enthusiasm and motivated by his suggestion to get a drink. As they leave, a strange thing occurs. A security guard wearing a police cap stands with his back to the film audience at the corner of the frame and casts a distorted shadow across the floor that connects to the couple. Perhaps this shadow involves a rather gratuitous act of artistic design merely to tighten the sense of connection of the couple with the setting. Given the importance of transcendence to the scene, however, the shadow of a stranger—a protective security guard—raises the notion of the soul, a bodiless spirit. The scene also suggests a third man, as Rob White says in a different context, whose meaning can be found in part from Luke 24:13–15: "And behold, two of them went that same day to a village called Emmaus, which was from Jerusalem about three score furlongs. And they talked together of all these things which had happened. And it came to pass, that, while they communed together and reasoned, Jesus himself drew near, and went with them." T. S. Eliot develops this theme in *The Waste Land*:

> *Who is the third who walks always beside you?*
> *When I count, there are only you and I together*
> *But when I look ahead up the white road*
> *There is always another one walking beside you*
> *Gliding wrapt in a brown mantle, hooded*
> *I do not know whether a man or a woman*
> *—But who is that on the other side of you?*[13]

Throughout Levinas's writings, including his *Basic Philosophical Writings*, the third man achieves transcendent importance as the sign of religious witness of the total responsibility for the other, the force that ruptures the narcissistic bond of the individual or the couple to form a relationship of spiritual significance.[14]

Stella Sanford explains how for Levinas the third person becomes a guarantee of transcendence over immanence of even greater importance in a sense than the other. She says the third person "who looked at me through the eyes of the Other becomes that which *ensures* the very otherness of the Other." This notion of the third person or "the third way" suggests structure for an ethics of "beyond being" and for resisting the "reduction of the other to the same." She says, "illeity," which is what Levinas terms the third person, "refers not to the actual third person but to that which signifies in the third person from 'beyond': transcendence."[15]

Although not always diachronic or a time-image with the inspirational power of transcendence on Mt. Sinai, time retains its importance as a general theme as *Mr. Smith Goes to Washington* progresses. A political mechanism based on time, the filibuster, actually controls the concluding portion of the film. After saying a prayer for Smith, Saunders from the gallery above helps guide his attempt to filibuster control of the Senate floor. Because Smith has to talk without interruption for as long as he can, his enemy becomes the enormous clock on the Senate wall.

As Smith approaches the end of his filibuster, Capra has a famous working radio broadcaster of the time, H. V. Kaltenborn, broadcast the minute-by-minute effort by the young senator, noting how he has spoken for an amazing twenty-three hours and sixteen minutes. Several low-angle shots of Smith position him visually at the intersection of crossing lines of the Senate walls and galleries that suggest a form of crucifixion. Close-ups of Stewart's face, a face that epitomizes human suffering, suggest Levinas's conception of the face as the ultimate sign of the human. The close-ups emphasize Smith's martyrdom while also providing a contrast with the dehumanized face of the clock that he battles. While many critics have detailed the masochism, martyrdom, and male hysteria ingrained in Stewart's portrayal, the prominence of time and spirituality in the film also suggests a portrayal of ethical transcendence.[16]

In one of the film's most powerful visual and rhetorical expressions of the relationship of time to ethics, Smith pleads in the Senate chamber with Senator Joseph Paine (Claude Rains), the senior senator from his home state who has been a surrogate father to him. Smith thought that like his own father, Paine, who knew Smith's father, was committed to fighting for the great "lost causes" of ethical and political importance. Instead, Paine has betrayed Smith by showing greater loyalty to corrupt bosses who support his political ambitions.

Nearing the end of almost twenty-four hours of filibustering, Smith is filmed and framed by Capra from below with the large Senate clock over his shoulders, signifying a crucifixion by ordinary temporality. In this frame a diagonal line of moral elevation moves from a low-angle shot of the back of Senator Paine, at the bottom left of the frame, to Smith who looks at and beseeches Paine from the center of the frame while the clock hangs over Smith's shoulders. The visual diagonal of attention through the center of the frame extends to the top of the frame that reveals, as several of my students have noted, a celestial light of heavenly inspiration that glimmers from a kind of skylight on the ceiling of the Senate chamber. The frame thereby literally becomes a Levinasian ethical horizon and Ricoeur's horizon of expectation.

Smith must somehow reverse the burden and overcome the tyranny of the deadly, chronological time of the clock and answer the call for ethical transcendence. As Levinas says, "To let time signify according to its diachrony, disengaged from the simultaneity through which knowledge would grasp it, is to think time under the figure of the ethical, under the figure of the responsibility for the other in the gratuitous generosity of love renouncing

FIGURE 2.1. James Stewart carries time on his back in his appeal to Claude Rains in *Mr. Smith Goes to Washington* (1939).

reciprocity."[17] Smith must place time precisely "under the figure of the ethical, under the figure of the responsibility for the other," to educate and reform other senators and the public. To compel such an ethical understanding of responsibility, Smith repeats in an exhausted whisper to Senator Paine the command to "love thy neighbor." Interestingly, Ricoeur sees in the "secret of the commandment 'Love thy neighbor as thyself'" a fundamental equivalence in ethics between "the esteem of the *other as a oneself* and the esteem of *oneself as an other*," putting him at odds with Levinas over the asymmetry of greater ethical responsibility to the other (Ricoeur, *Oneself as Another*, 194, 194n32).

For Smith the ethical achievement of seeing himself in terms of his responsibility to the other rather than to the moral narcissism of his naive devotion to abstract ideals constitutes a form of resurrection. Standing alone against the mass in his commitment to a different temporality of transcendent ethics, Smith experiences regeneration in the midst of terrible despair and defeat. As John Llewelyn writes, "So the future of temporality is not the ecstatic projection of possibility. Nor is it merely the future as measured by clocks, the future of a time rendered timeless by being construed according to the analogy of physical space whose limitations are exposed by both Heidegger and Bergson.... The future is the good infinite. Not the bad infinite of replicative repetition, but the good infinite of resurrection."[18] Llewelyn concludes by pointing to Levinas, who writes in *Totality and Infinity*, "Resurrection constitutes the principal event of time. There is therefore no continuity in being.... In continuation the instant meets its death, and resuscitates; death and resurrection constitute time" (284).

In so well enacting the conflict between contrasting forms of time in the filibuster scene, Stewart's performance achieves what Rodowick describes as one of Kant's great successes. Using a term I have emphasized for Levinas on time, Rodowick writes that "Kant discovers a way of defining the subject through his 'unhinging' of time from movement" (Rodowick, *Gilles Deleuze's Time Machine*, 128). Stewart performs a Kantian action in the film by also "unhinging" time as he battles oppressively ordered time with his own transcendent time. Stewart accomplishes this in part by enacting what Rodowick terms "the cinema of the body": "The cinema of the body is not a picturing of the literal body. Rather, its goal is to give expression to forces of becoming that are immanent in bodies, as well as the body's receptivity to external forces through which it can transform itself" (*Gilles Deleuze's Time*

Machine, 154). Stewart's acting turns his body into the point of intersection for the ethical, political, spiritual, and cultural forces in contention in the film. His body expresses the power of these forces as he leans toward Senator Paine, with the burden of his many hours of talking, fighting, and filibustering weighing down upon him.

A well-known statement from a classic rabbinic source conveys Smith's message of love and responsibility, while also accentuating the bond of time to ethics and moral transcendence. The saying comes from Rabbi Hillel, as it is written in the "Sayings of the Fathers" or "Pirkei Avoth" in the *Traditional Jewish Prayer Book*: "If I am not for myself, who will be for me? But if I am for myself alone, what am I? And if not now, when?"[19] Rabbi Hillel's suggestion of a possible asymmetry of greater responsibility for the other would uphold the Levinasian relationship of transcendent time in the relationship to the other. Transcendent time never disappears or wavers but insists on immediacy, the inescapable now for ethical belief, action, and commitment.

Smith's battle with the clock in his filibuster encapsulates the paradox of the struggle with time, being, and death. In his fight he uses time to engage his opponents, but he also must recognize time's message of his own impending defeat. Levinas thinks Heidegger makes this dilemma of time, being, and death the crucial concern for understanding the meaning of life. In contrast, Levinas determines to go beyond this dilemma, to a realm of transcendent moral responsibility. In *God, Death, and Time* Levinas muses on Heidegger:

> For Heidegger, death signifies *my* death in the sense of my *annihilation*. For him, the inquiry into the relationship between death and time is motivated by the effort to assure oneself that, in the analytic of *Dasein* in which being is in question, being-there is grasped and described in its authenticity or its integrity. Because death marks from the start the end of being-there, it is through death itself that being-there—or man, who, in the form of a being, is the event of that being-there—is the totality of what it is, or is properly there. (50–51)

For Smith, the time of the filibuster, the ominous, looming, relentless stare of the Senate clock, the facial expressions of ambiguous support of the deific president of the Senate (Harry Carey) force him to confront destruction. The situation compels him to move beyond his own ambitions to consider ideas that exceed the politics of ordinary history to a realm of greater ethical demand.

Smith thus moves existentially, ethically, and emotionally toward a position that Levinas elucidates in his ethical metaphysics. As opposed to understanding life in terms of being and the anxiety imposed by time in the face of death, Levinas reads Kant's "transcendental ideal" to proffer another possibility of rethinking life and death. Rather than focusing on death as the end that structures thinking about life, Levinas interprets the transcendental ideal as understanding experience as going beyond death to possibility. For Levinas it becomes "necessary to appeal to the *whole* of reality, to the whole that is a transcendental ideal that is never given" (*God, Death, and Time*, 60). In this understanding, death becomes a "problem" rather than an absolute end: "So the death included in the finitude of being becomes a *problem*. Time reveals itself to be a relative concept" (60). Accordingly, Levinas argues for a sphere of meaning of "hope" that goes beyond being and the certainty of death: "Kant certainly does not think that we must think of an extension of time beyond limited time; he does not want a 'prolongation of life.' But there is a *hope*, a world accessible to a hope; there is a motivation proper to a hope that signifies. In an existence determined by death, in this epic of being, there are things that do not enter into the epic, significations that cannot be reduced to being" (61).

Exhausted on the Senate floor, Stewart portrays his character as finally drained of his egoism and self-centeredness, incapable of acting on his promise to keep fighting. Instead, he must appeal to the realm of hope that Levinas describes. Capra and Stewart ostensibly grasp intuitively and convey artistically what Levinas spent decades proposing through his philosophy and ethical metaphysics. Facing the failure of all his efforts, Smith finally finds what he has been searching for throughout the film, a transcendent realm of belief that goes beyond the existence he sees and experiences every day. He undergoes a kind of religious epiphany and conversion to a realm beyond even the political ideals that originally motivated him. Indeed, with amazing perspicacity, Capra and Stewart anticipate the recent project by Simon Critchley, as previously discussed, for a politics based on the ethics of "infinitely demanding" responsibility.[20]

The conclusion of *Mr. Smith Goes to Washington* thereby fulfills the promise of the film's beginning, an intimation of diachronic intervention, a sense of a man "chosen" to redeem the people and the corrupt society and political culture festering around them. *Mr. Smith Goes to Washington* begins with a call that dissimulates a transcendent event as an ordinary random act. The call will prove to be a charge for action from another temporal order. Ignorant of the deeper purpose of their errand, ordinary, corrupt politicians pick Smith to fill a Senate seat vacated by a senator's death. To his great surprise, Smith discovers he also has been chosen to be tested for his ability to meet responsibilities of an ethical nature greater than the demands of dishonest politicians.

Thus, a vital spiritual challenge complicates this story of good and evil in the nation's capital. Smith's selection becomes an act of "election" that differs from the usual political meaning of the word. Because of his moral character and his sense of responsibility toward others, Smith finds himself chosen for a mission of personal and cultural redemption. This aspect of the story dramatizes Levinas's conceptualization of election. In "Transcendence and Height" Levinas describes election as "the promotion to a privileged place on which all that is not-I depends":

> This election signifies the most radical possible engagement, namely, total altruism. The responsibility that empties the I of its imperialism and egoism, albeit the egoism of salvation, does not transform it into a moment of the universal order. Responsibility confirms the I in its ipseity, in its central place within being, as a supporter of the universe. Such an engagement is happy; it is the austere and noncomplacent happiness that lies in the nobility of an election that does not know its own happiness, tempted as it is "by the slumber of the earth" ("and yet Lord, I am not happy..."). (Levinas, *Emmanuel Levinas*, 18)

For much of this film Jefferson Smith must learn to accept the kind of responsibility that accompanies election as Levinas describes it. Although from the beginning Smith feels the overwhelming weight of the expectations placed on him as a newly appointed senator, the self-denial of responsibility still must be learned and tested. Smith's election represents a "summons" that is extended to any person who gives priority and proximity to the neighbor as opposed to the individual self. This places Smith in the paradox of being absolutely unique while also dramatizing the potential of every man to assume ultimate moral responsibility. In "God and Philosophy" Levinas says, "Before the neighbor I am summoned, and do not just appear; from the first I am answering to an assignation." He argues that "here no one can be substituted for me.... It obliges me as someone unreplaceable and unique, someone chosen" (*Emmanuel Levinas*, 143). Thus, Smith's plea to Paine to "love thy neighbor" marks his fulfillment of the summons to his election to a moral responsibility for which there can be no substitution.

Time, transcendence, diachronicity, and ethical discussion place the focus of *Mr. Smith Goes to Washington* on ideas as opposed to religious doctrine. Ultimately, the Christian imagery of crucifixion becomes less important than the psychology of transformation and the importance of accepting absolute responsibility for people in terms of the sanctity of the face.

As in Capra's time, many today may greet with skepticism and even mockery the insistence of *Mr. Smith Goes to Washington* that "fools with faith" can create a renewable time for changing the lives of others for the better. Then as now such belief could seem ludicrous. Capra's espousal in the film of this view helps connect him to the interpretation of Levinas that the existential scholar John Wild proposes. Wild links Levinas to William James.[21] Levinas's opposition to totalistic truth, as well as the importance of affectivity and sensibility to his project of transcendence, links him not only to James but also to Jonathan Edwards's commitment, as Perry Miller says, to "the human heart" as much as to "the human mind."[22] Such comparisons associate Levinas with pluralism, pragmatism, democracy, and humanitarianism. These concepts, in combination with the Levinasian argument for ethical responsibility beyond being, constitute a body of belief that probably could help Senator Smith with his next speech or even a possible campaign.

IT'S A WONDERFUL LIFE

Another Capra classic, *It's a Wonderful Life* casts James Stewart once again as the small-town naif-with-a-heart-of-gold in the character of George Bailey, who experiences an epiphany and undergoes a conversion comparable to Jefferson Smith's. Bailey's transformation also occurs through the narrative's manipulation of time. In fact, the film, as often noted, can be considered a story about an extended time experiment. It revisits Bailey's past, reconstructs his history, dramatizes his crisis of faith, demonstrates the power to foresee and determine his future, and, in the last part of the film, contrives an alternative temporality to challenge his way of being in the world. As in *Mr. Smith Goes to Washington*, time in *It's a Wonderful Life* ultimately involves a transcendent ethical dimension. In the beginning of the film, God, represented as a twinkling heavenly light, responds to prayers to save George in his troubled state of mind and situation. Questions of redemption in a different temporal context immediately pertain.

It's a Wonderful Life also dramatizes the relationship of time to film art in terms of film direction. In the film Joseph (Joseph Granby), the twinkling star, who speaks as and for the Deity, functions as a heavenly film director. He visually focuses on George Bailey and describes him to Clarence Oddbody (Henry Travers), an angel second class who has not been able to earn his wings and will try to do so by saving George. Significant for a film about time and ethics, Clarence is called a clock maker with a last name of Oddbody, which symbolizes the incommensurability of the tension between the body and the soul. Also, as Robert Sklar notes, in Capra's film "the other filmmaker is the Deity" who makes the "film within the film" of George's trials. Sklar sees this dual collaboration between Capra and God as "clearly an act of faith, perhaps an effort to reinforce religious belief in the face of postwar secularism, by depicting God as committed to human welfare and capable of using His powers to fulfill that commitment."[23]

As a dual authorship between Capra and God, the film becomes a cinematic commentary on the implications of the potential linkages of time, space, and transcendence. By "linking his godlike capabilities—to be omniscient, to move freely across space and time—with the Deity Himself," Capra tells us "that while the subject of God's film is George Bailey, the subject of *his* film is not only George Bailey's destiny but also God's hand in that destiny—in a larger sense, God's overseeing of the world" (Sklar, "God and Man in Bedford Falls," 212–13). Considering God to be the all-powerful director of all things, Capra articulates George's particular story, therefore, as part of the greater story about the meaning and purpose of life.

While Capra dramatizes a story based on the power of temporal manipulation, his own film art in It's a Wonderful Life generally deals conservatively with time. The film primarily works with time as indirect and subordinate to movement. Beginning with his documentary-style use of the heavenly voice-over, Capra's direction in It's a Wonderful Life constitutes a prime exhibition of classic Hollywood organization of narrative and time as an extension of movement. Accordingly, Capra compresses the story of George's youth in the beginning of the film. He carefully selects moments of consequence to depict the relationship between George and Mary (Donna Reed); and toward the end he summarizes the Second World War in a brief montage sequence.

In one of the most famous scenes in *It's a Wonderful Life*, however, Capra subordinates movement to time. Time stops and movement ceases in God's interior film. In this scene George extends his arms to demonstrate the size of a suitcase he wants to buy. The frame freezes while God in a voice-over talks about George to Clarence, thereby suggesting a kind of special temporal dimension for God and film directors. As a self-conscious lesson on how a film works, the scene brings attention to itself as a filmic element in a way that differs from the invisible editing of most Hollywood filmmaking. The scene especially accentuates the temporal aspect of film as an artistic medium. Nevertheless, throughout most of *It's a Wonderful Life*, time generally remains subordinate to movement. The indirect representation of time as a function of movement limits the film's artistic potential. The dominance of movement and the absence of what Levinas terms diachronicity tend to limit the potential for the creative use of time for suggesting renewal.

This containment of time contributes to the paradoxes concerning God and time in *It's a Wonderful Life*. The intervention of God from the very beginning of the story implies a view of time as an inescapable ordering of events that must adhere to a predetermined design. This predetermined world under God's absolute control, however, still must enable freedom and choice. George also must have the freedom to undergo the challenge to mature by acquiring the moral character to assume responsibility for himself and others. Replaying the classic dilemmas of determinism, free will, and contingency, the film dramatizes the conflict between the individual's moral responsibility and freedom before the all-powerful and all-knowing Deity. It acts out Rabbi Akiva's famous statement in the "Pirkei Avoth" that "All is foreseen, yet free-will is given to man."[24]

As in *Mr. Smith Goes to Washington*, the meeting of time and transcendence in *It's a Wonderful Life* reaches a climactic stage when the hero confronts his own destruction. Whereas Jefferson Smith experiences an existential crisis as he faces final defeat in the Senate, George Bailey intensifies his own existential and metaphysical stakes by considering suicide.

The culminating event occurs when George Bailey's Uncle Billy (Thomas Mitchell) absent-mindedly misplaces Bailey loan company funds. Potter (Lionel Barrymore), the villainous banker, finds the money and seizes the opportunity to take it and hide it to discredit George, who has battled

Potter's greedy schemes for gaining total economic control of Bedford Falls. George assumes the responsibility for the situation, although he is innocent of any wrongdoing. This leads to the justifiably famous Christmas Eve scene at the Bailey household when George goes home in the belief that he and his family face complete ruin. While George cannot hold back tears of impotent despair as he hugs one of his children, his wife, Mary (Donna Reed), stops decorating the tree to begin confronting the crisis. The close-ups and eyeline matches as Mary observes George reaffirm Donna Reed's poise and sensitivity in this role as she develops Mary's character. The scene ends with George's explosive outburst of frustration and guilt. Overlapping images show George headed in the wrong direction to Potter to beg for help while Mary, after telling the children to pray, gets on the phone to begin correcting the situation.

In Potter's office the gloating banker tells George that facing scandal, bankruptcy, and possible legal indictment, George is "worth more dead than alive." George then goes to Martini's Bar, where he appeals to God but gets hit in the face by the enraged husband of a teacher he insulted. George then decides to end his life. He goes to a snow-covered bridge, planning to leap into the icy waters. At this point the narrative shifts its focus from being God's inner-film narrative account about George to being the story of Clarence's actions to save George. As Sklar writes, "Here ends God's screenplay of George Bailey's story. Clarence Oddbody now knows all there is to know. It is time for divine intercession. The spectator at God's film-within-a-film will himself enter the frame. And God's role as Frank Capra's collaborator shifts from codirector to leading performer" ("God and Man in Bedford Falls," 217).

Although God lets Clarence take control of the film, the story remains consistent with the amazing assumptions of *It's a Wonderful Life*. Clarence operates as God's agent so that he can invoke divine powers. Thus, by leaping into the water before George, in the knowledge that George would sacrifice his plan for suicide to save another's life, Clarence actually saves George, an inconceivable notion to George but one that he will grudgingly come to appreciate. Also, both the scene of the rescue at the bridge and the subsequent scene in the tollbooth beautifully evoke the look, atmosphere, and feeling of icy, snowy upstate New York in winter, a factor that lends physical authenticity to the emotion of the mise-en-scène.

Often overlooked in comparison to so many other famous scenes in *It's a Wonderful Life*, the tollbooth sequence again exhibits Stewart's extraordinary ability to hold a scene together as an actor and personality. The scene operates on several different levels, and Stewart integrates them all through the skill of his speech and body expression, as well as his charm. On one level the scene is thoroughly fantastic, as a depiction of an angel striving to save a good man in trouble. On another level it develops the great psychological crisis of George Bailey into a deepening existential and ethical dilemma. In addition, it directs the education of George toward reconsidering the meaning of his life in particular and life in general to gain recognition of his infinite responsibility to others. In this way *It's a Wonderful Life* fulfills its promise to deal with time and transcendence.

Stewart plays the tollbooth scene marvelously, with a perfect mixture of irony, skepticism, and cynicism. These qualities give a special cutting edge to the despair and desperation that underscore Bailey's situation. Dealing with the bizarre and incomprehensible nature of the situation in the only way that at first makes sense, Stewart as George regards Clarence at best as an oddball or at worst a madman, a sick person who only adds to his own misfortune, his miserable night, and his current state of confusion, which he attributes to "what Martini put in those drinks." When Clarence informs George that he is George's "guardian angel," George responds sarcastically, "I wouldn't be a bit surprised"; and when Clarence further explains, "I know everything about you," George says, "Well, you look about like the kind of an angel I'd get. Sort of a fallen angel, aren't you? What happened to your wings?" Clarence tries to explain that he has not yet earned his wings. George mocks, "I don't know whether I like it very much being seen around with an angel without any wings." George's annoyance with the craziness of the man surfaces after he sardonically tells Clarence that he could use eight thousand dollars to replace the lost money and that that would be the "one way you can help me." Clarence states matter-of-factly, "Oh, no, no. We don't use money in Heaven." George responds bitterly, "Comes in pretty handy down here, bub." Throughout the scene a line that has been strung up in the tollbooth for George's and Clarence's wet clothes divides the frame diagonally, balancing Clarence in the upper part with George in the lower, a division that replicates their relationship to heaven and earth.

When George finally says, "I suppose it would have been better if I'd never been born at all," Clarence gets the idea of miraculously taking back George's life. The snow stops, and an ominous wind suddenly blows the door open. Significantly, the first signs of change for George affect his body. His lip stops bleeding from the blow he received in Martini's Bar, and although he has been deaf since childhood, he now can hear. Clarence has fixed things so that George has a body but never did exist. He embodies Clarence's symbolic name of Oddbody.

The idea of nonexistence works brilliantly. George never happened. This puts George in the amazing position of being there and not there, visible and invisible, present but not himself. In the subsequent noirish nightmare scenes George revisits his life, and no one, not even Mary or his mother (Beulah Bondi), knows him. George gets to see the consequences of his absence. Potter controls the town, now called Pottersville. A friend since childhood, the flirtatious and sexual Violet Bick (Gloria Grahame) has grown up to become a dissolute vixen and alcoholic, while the town itself has become an open city of bars, blatant sexuality, and vulgar entertainment. George learns that because he was not there, he never got to save his brother from drowning in the ice. He also was not available to prevent Uncle Billy from being institutionalized for his apparent insanity. Among many other calamities that result from George's absence from the world, Mary endures life as a spinster librarian and is condemned to wear glasses, obviously unable on her own to see clearly.

While this concatenation of horrors ostensibly epitomizes "Capracorn" exaggeration and sentimentality, negating George's birth serves as a brilliant device for elaborating on pervasive issues of time, transcendence, and existence. Never having been born, George goes through the scene in another kind of time than the people he once knew. He has succeeded in reaching a nonsynchronous temporal dimension. Capra convincingly dramatizes George's entrapment in this other temporal order. In different ways the situation for both Jefferson Smith and George Bailey follows what Rodowick terms "the incommensurability of thought and determination in relation to identity or being" (Rodowick, *Gilles Deleuze's Time Machine*, 133). Both men function in another order of time and a different kind of place than the people around them. As Rodowick says, "the quality of incommensurability demonstrates that we cannot think otherwise than in the streams of time or in the form of nonidentity" (133).

Similarly, George's experience follows what Ewa Ziarek calls "the paradoxical structure of embodiment": "Enabling and preceding the movement of loss and recovery characteristic of the identification of consciousness with itself, the paradoxical structure of embodiment exhibits a disjunction between two opposite yet inseparable moments: between an irremissible attachment to oneself and the radical exposure to the outside. If one can still use the term 'identity' for such a knot in which exposure to exteriority constitutes what is most intimately one's own, it is an identity of nonessence, evocative of Lacan's term of 'extimacy' or Derrida's 'transcendence within immanence.'" This "non-coincidence with form" that entails for Ziarek "the materiality of embodiment" creates a "disjunction" for George.[25] The disjunction occurs between, on the one hand, George's bodily exteriority or negotiation with the physical environment and, on the other hand, his sense of being that ultimately will enable him to find himself through others and achieve a form of transcendent alterity and redemption.

What Rodowick terms "nonidentity" in "streams of time" and Ziarek considers "an identity of nonessence" seems to characterize Bailey's situation when Clarence takes his life away but still allows him to function. George now operates in a situation that is neither life nor death. Nor is it quite a kind of existential death in life that exudes Heideggerian anxiety. Without an identity but denied the opportunity of death, George seems beyond being in his nightmare scene as he frantically, rather hysterically, races through Pottersville trying to find himself.

By the film's conclusion George will have undergone a rethinking of life and death that differs from his previous conceptions. The film will suggest what he gained from the experience of being beyond death and life in the temporal dimension of his Pottersville nightmare. He learns what Levinas suggests as an alternative view of death that perpetuates the commitment to transcendence and ethical metaphysics. Levinas writes, "Death is not, then, the ending of a duration made up of days and nights but an ever open *possibility*. This ever open possibility is the most proper possibility, exclusive in regard to an other, isolating, and extreme or unsurpassable as a possibility" (*God, Death, and Time*, 47).

As in much of *It's a Wonderful Life*, George's eventual appeal to get his life and his wife back operates on multiple levels of meaning. Again on the bridge where he first encountered Clarence, George cries out to the angel, "Clarence! Clarence! Help me. Clarence! Get me back. Get me back. I don't care what happens to me. Only get me back to my wife and kids. Help me, Clarence, please. Please! I want to live again!" George's desperate cry constitutes a simple recognition of his fundamental need for life and family. This allows the story to have the requisite Hollywood happy ending that fulfills the divine gesture at the beginning to help George and make things turn out all right. In this view of the film George accepts his life in the world and understands his failures as simply part of his destiny within a grander scheme of being.[26]

George's serious engagement with time, death, and being also opens the metaphysical implications of *It's a Wonderful Life*. The film powerfully suggests that George learns more than mere acquiescence to failure, mediocrity, and the acceptance of life with only the small, ordinary pleasures and triumphs that most people know. Arguably, George returns to his old life with a new vision gained from his experience with nonidentity, nonbeing. For the entire film, from beginning to end, George does his duty and sacrifices for others. He does so for the members of his family and for the entire community. Capra and Stewart clearly present George Bailey as a flawed but good man. He becomes the embodiment of the ordinary American, democratic hero who represents a generation that survived the Great Depression, won the war in Europe and the Pacific, and stood ready to fight the cold war. As a sign of the genius of *It's a Wonderful Life*, it takes this good and honest man and imposes on him the demand to do better. It takes him to another ethical level, one that goes beyond mere duty and obedience of conventional moral codes.

As opposed to proposing that doing one's duty, obeying the rules, and acceding to the expectations of others constitute an adequate ethical position in life, the film indicates at its end the need to transform George's nightmare episode of temporal separation and incommensurability into an alternative vision of life and human relations. The film suggests adherence to a transcendent dimension of a greater ethical demand. The lesson of this journey through evil and loss insists that we look at people not just as eminently touchable but profoundly holy—in other words, in Levinas's terms of the face. George's story of redemption and rebirth that he enacts with his plunge into the river, involves achieving what Levinas calls in *God, Death, and Time* "the transcendence of the one who is *for* the other" (158). In other words George learns to see himself in terms of the eyes and place of the other. As Levinas says, "My basic posture is the for-the-other" (*God, Death, and Time*, 158).

Rather than understanding George's story by merely studying his past and the context of his life, the greater ethical question in the film indicates a profound appreciation for a different temporal order. It suggests a greater origin of George's life than the simple history of his birth, beginnings, and days in Bedford Falls.

Thus, Levinas could be thinking of the opening moments of *It's a Wonderful Life* when he writes, in *God, Death, and Time*, "Raising itself toward the sky, the gaze thus encounters the untouchable: the sacred" (163). The twinkling stars and heavenly voices in the beginning of the film invite an interpretation that intimates a mise-en-scène of infinite dimensions. The infinity of the heavens contrasts with the material values of daily existence in Bedford Falls. The film takes seriously the idea of the importance of this realm of ethics beyond being. So does Levinas:

> In an age in which movement toward the heights is limited by the line of the summits, the heavenly bodies—stars fixed in their positions or traveling along closed trajectories—are intangible. The sky calls for a gaze other than that of a vision that is already an aiming and proceeds from need and to the pursuit of things. It calls for eyes purified of covetousness, a gaze other than that of the hunter with all his ruse, awaiting the capture. Thus the eyes turned toward the sky separate themselves in some fashion from the body in which they are implanted. (*God, Death, and Time*, 163)

In a manner that dramatizes Levinas's idea of "the eyes" separated from the body, George's separation from his body, his incommensurability, instructs him in a new way of seeing that changes his thinking about his old life as George Bailey. Instead of seeing himself as trapped in a predetermined world, the life he regains involves what Levinas calls being a "hostage" to a time and responsibility with "no beginning." He explains: "The subject as hostage is a referral to a past that was never present, to an immemorial past, that of its preoriginal affection by another" (*God, Death, and Time*, 162). This view of time and an immemorial past indicates a dramatic difference for Levinas with Ricoeur, who concentrates on the temporal aporias of the inescapable ecstasies of the past, present, and future. For Ricoeur the dilemma of multiple temporal realms cannot be avoided through Levinas's kind of emphatic ethical assertion of total and inescapable moral responsibility.

George, however, experiences a rebirth outside of the usual understanding of time. His joy in this rebirth involves a new perspective that minimizes his trials in comparison to life's benefits. This rebirth also involves an appreciation for his place not just in his family's and his community's time but also in a transcendent, diachronic time that revolutionizes how everything looks and means.

Thus, George comes to appreciate his life in terms of what Luce Irigaray calls the "passion" of "wonder." Reading Descartes, Irigaray writes, "Wonder is the motivating force behind mobility in all its dimensions." Thinking of wonder as the "advent or the event of the other" and "the beginning of a new story," she writes: "Wonder would be the passion of the encounter between the most material and the most metaphysical, of their possible conception and fecundation one by the other."[27]

In the nightmare segment George's loss of identity in a temporal regime beyond existence and death enables him to discover such "wonder" in his life that Irigaray describes through his new understanding of his relationship to a transcendent time. He goes from the kind of "unhinged time" of Levinas's imprisonment by the Nazis to the transcendent time of redemption that Levinas worked to promote for himself and others. Ironically, if George felt tied to responsibility in his old life, the new life proffers infinite responsibility to others that stems from spiritual origins that defy total understanding.

George's regeneration in this transcendent realm maintains the development of savior figures as heroes in many of Capra's most important films, including, of course, Jefferson Smith in *Mr. Smith Goes to Washington*. As Sklar points out, "In George Bailey the identification of the hero as suffering savior is all but complete. God's miracle for George occurs on Christmas Eve: the people whose money saves George sing in praise of the new-born King to accompany George's rebirth into life—one might almost say resurrection" ("God and Man in Bedford Falls," 219).

Sklar questions whether the form of "consolation" George receives would really be adequate for him and whether it would suffice for Capra himself, who was facing his own crisis during this period of his life as a result of his efforts to achieve artistic and financial independence from Hollywood studio domination. Whatever Capra himself truly believed, the thrust of his films testifies to a deep need for the kind of understanding of experience that his films dramatize and Levinas articulates. As in *Mr. Smith Goes to Washington*, in *It's a Wonderful Life* religious imagery works as a metaphor for a way of seeing and thinking and living that goes beyond religious dogma and sectarian pursuits and practice. The film argues for an ethical metaphysics that speaks directly to the skepticism of Capra's time and our own. The growing importance of Levinas's work to contemporary thought perhaps suggests why Capracorn remains so relevant long after many thought Capra and his work had outlived their appeal.

It's a Wonderful Life suggests not just that life can be wonderful but that it involves a quality of wonder and awe. It indicates an origination in a temporal dimension that cannot be measured or spatialized. The return of George Bailey to his own life and family insists on the idea of life as a gift from an ultimately unknowable and mysterious source. Mostly, it argues not that friends and popularity constitute the greatest joys in life but that an absolute commitment to others makes life meaningful and, as William James might say, worthwhile. It makes sacrifice more important than self. Responsibility proves to be more fulfilling than personal reward. These simple concepts perhaps constitute Capra's response to Levinas's question, stated at the opening of this chapter, about the possibility of our being duped by morality. To answer Levinas, Capra suggests there is no real life without morality.

CHAPTER 3
THE CHANGING FACE OF AMERICAN REDEMPTION
Henry Fonda, Marilyn Monroe, Paul Newman, and Denzel Washington

THE FACE AND THE CINEMATIC IMAGE

Faces, it would seem, should dramatically help to establish the relationship between ethical philosophy and film. Given the importance of the face to cinema and to Levinas, the medium and the philosopher appear made for each other. For many, the cinema proffers a unique means for studying the face. To the Swedish auteur director Ingmar Bergman, cinema is about the face. As Bergman says, "Our work begins with the human face.... The possibility of drawing near to the human face is the primary originality and the distinctive quality of the cinema."[1] Throughout his writings Emmanuel Levinas refers to the face and the face to face to epitomize the ultimate moral responsibility of each individual for the other. Thus, the Levinasian face and film seem ready to inform each other.

However, the relationship between the film image of the face and the Levinasian face in fact entails a crisis of representation, a crisis that must be confronted for any Levinasian theory of film. As a philosopher with profound religious belief, Levinas's problem with the artistic image, especially the image of the human face, stems from the Second Commandment prohibition against idolatry. For Levinas, the commandment prohibits a way of thinking that reduces thought to the thing it thinks. In "Reality and Its Shadow," for example, he proposes that simply by "becoming an image," any "represented object" constitutes "a disincarnation of reality." The "picturesque" invariably becomes "to some extent a caricature."[2]

Thus, describing Levinas's position on visual images of the face, Libby Saxton notes that "the suspicion of images of beings at the heart of Judaism may also be interpreted" for Levinas "as a denunciation of a certain reductive or acquisitive mode of thought." Saxton emphasizes Levinas's disavowal of such reductive thought and reflexive representation in order to proffer the transcendent. "The face," she says, "cannot be captured in representation, which would reduce it to immobility, reappropriate its alterity and silence its address."[3]

Sarah Cooper summarizes the significance of the paradox of the Levinasian argument about the face, indicating how for Levinas the physical, visible face differs philosophically from the face "that transcends its own sensible expression." She notes the difficulty for many to appreciate the complexity of the apparent simplicity of the Levinasian notion of the face: "Much misunderstood, the face has had certain commentators unable to move beyond the phenomenological counterpart, thinking solely in terms of the actual faces of others we may see and recall in our day-to-day dealings with people." Cooper maintains that the Levinasian "face cannot be seen, since vision is not a relation of transcendence."[4]

To Cooper the confusion between the visible phenomenological face and the transcendent *visage* indicates the closeness of their relationship of mutual dependence. She says that "the confusion between the two is useful" and maintains that such confusion "prevents us from ever severing the link between a phenomenal point of contact with human others and the ethical dimension that cuts through this to extend beyond the spatial and temporal co-ordinates of such encounters" (Cooper, *Selfless Cinema?* 17).

The Levinasian face as *visage*, therefore, exceeds in meaning any conventional representation of the physical face. This contrast between the visible, physical face that casts the face into a representation, as opposed to the Levinasian face as a *visage* that evokes the transcendent, the ethical, and the holy, encapsulates the complexities involved in learning how to read the face in a Levinasian understanding of film. The contrast also indicates a great potential for ethical debate.

The tension between face and *visage* becomes a powerful force for delineating ethical engagement in film. Speaking of the "documentary subject" in a way that can apply to film in general, Cooper finds that such tension between face and *visage* has "carved out within the space of the films themselves" a unique place for the intersection of conflicting forces of representation and transcendence. The crossing of these forces creates an energy that informs the ethical debate. In the contrast between representation and transcendence, between visual image and Levinasian concept, Cooper says, "It is the difference between an excess of the image that we cannot know, and what we actually perceive, that becomes a space of responsibility which persistently resists any attempt to reduce those we see either to their image, or to an image of ourselves" (*Selfless Cinema?* 23).

Cooper's idea of a "space of responsibility" that emerges from the conflict between perception and infinite ethical demand presents a valuable conceptual instrument for ethical analysis. Instead of acceding to the impossibility of ever adequately representing a conclusive ethical position, Cooper's space of responsibility provides a realm for pursuing debate rather than ending it: "The Levinasian ethical encounter, as we have seen in our discussion of the face, is not rooted in, or restricted to, an experience of the senses. It traverses them nonetheless to exceed full comprehension. This excess is signalled through a limit to what can be perceived, but also through a connection to another time that cannot be contained within the present" (*Selfless Cinema?* 24). Cooper, thereby, manages artfully to transform Levinas's certainty of the impossibility of achieving adequate ethical representation of the face through art into an argument for forcing an encounter between the perception of the senses and the impulse for a time of infinite ethical demand.

Judith Butler, as Saxton suggests, makes a somewhat comparable case for dealing with this dilemma of the face by exploiting rather than repressing the break between the face as representation and the face as beyond representation in its relationship to the infinite. Maintaining that "the human is not *represented* by the face," Butler says, "the human is indirectly affirmed in that very disjunction that makes representation impossible, and this disjunction is conveyed in the impossible representation. For representation to convey the human, then, representation must not only fail, but it must *show* its failure. There is something unrepresentable that we nevertheless seek to represent, and that paradox must be retained in the representation we give."[5] For Saxton, "Butler's argument rehabilitates representation as revelatory of the face precisely to the extent that it fails to represent it and—crucially—acknowledges this failure" (Saxton, "Fragile Faces," 11).

Clearly, for these writers the obvious simplicity, immediacy, and directness of the face mask profound paradox. The face for Levinas marks the holiness of every human being while also signifying the ultimately unknowable source of that holiness. The face occurs in the instant of its appearance, but its most important time touches infinity in its own invisibility. Thus, in Levinasian ethics the importance of the ontology of the face derives from its suggestion of infinite ethical demand.

The problem of the face, however, especially for the analysis of film, has been pondered by others, including Gilles Deleuze. In his discussion of Bergman and the close-up, Deleuze studies this mystery of the meaning of the face and the difficulties the face presents for film: "The facial close-up is both the face and its effacement. Bergman has pushed the nihilism of the face the furthest, that is its relationship in fear to the void or the absence, the fear of the face confronted with its nothingness" (Deleuze, *Cinema 1*, 100).

Throughout its history, cinema has had to respond to the difficulty of filming the face as a mirror of immediate experience. To this problem the cinema of redemption adds the impossibility of adequately representing the face in light of its relationship to infinity. The response of the cinema of redemption has been to use all the artistic means available to film the face without paradoxically reducing it to a cliché or a false image. Thus, the film-face dilemma involves a kind of double impossibility of adequately portraying the face by using the entire art of cinema—performance, setting, mise-en-scène, cinematography, editing—without actually reducing it by depicting it. Saxton claims that ultimately this can be achieved and that, ironically, Claude Lanzmann does it by subverting his own antirepresentational ethical stance, which compares to Levinas's position, with his images in *Shoah* (1985). She argues that Lanzmann shows in his historic documentary of the Holocaust that "the cinematic image has a vital ethical role" in representing violence, death, and all aspects of the human condition (Saxton, "Fragile Faces," 12).

The face in the cinema of redemption invariably tests the power of the cinematic image to operate in the space between face and *visage*—Cooper's space of responsibility—to suggest the transcendent, ethical relation to the other. Since by definition the cinema of redemption struggles (with varying degrees of success) with the challenge to articulate the ethical relationship to the infinite, the dilemma of the unrepresentability of the face constitutes an important specific problem for these films of ethical conflict. The face in this cinema highlights the ethical challenge to visually articulate Levinas's argument for ethical responsibility for the other.

The discussions by Cooper, Butler, and Saxton indicate that there is no easy formula for overcoming Levinas's epistemological and transcendental reservations regarding art and the image. These writers, however, do suggest that rather than attempting to impose a final solution to such dilemmas, in what would be a rather un-Levinasian gesture, it would be more effective for meaningful ethical discourse to exploit the tensions of the dilemma to articulate the issues. Certainly, a scientific way to measure redemption as seen on a face on a movie screen would not be feasible. In terms of Levinasian ethical discussion, however, it should be possible to study how, as previously suggested, key elements of film—acting, editing, narrative, characterization, mise-en-scène—project that same face at the signifying center of Cooper's space of responsibility. The face becomes a visual field or stage for the intersection of the fallible, physical representative image and the suggestive source of infinite, ethical responsibility.

Throughout the history of international cinema the American faces that have been instantly recognizable have often been faces from the American version of the cinema of redemption. Such faces during the classic period of the cinema of redemption conveyed the struggle for regeneration. They include many figures I have already discussed—Henry Fonda, James Stewart, John Wayne, John Garfield, Humphrey Bogart—and many others, such as Marlon Brando, Marilyn Monroe, Montgomery Clift, Canada Lee, Katharine Hepburn, Spencer Tracy, Robert De Niro, Dorothy Dandridge, Jane Fonda, Audrey Hepburn, Cary Grant, Charlton Heston, among so many others from classic American cinema.

As *stars* who manifest all the implications of that word, the actors in the American cinema of redemption and their images become power sources in a space between the creative energy of cinema and the meanings associated with the symbolism of American redemption. The significance of these faces derives from more than just physical appearance and personality. The faces become part of film narrative as synecdochical expressions of the tensions that make the greater narratives of America. Faces and culture interact to exceed portraiture and image and to suggest ultimate relationships of transcendence and ethical responsibility.

The American cinema of redemption presents a variation of Cooper's space of responsibility. The fluid dimensions of this space incorporate the physical images of a multiplicity of different faces that intersect with the excess of meaning of American transcendence. These faces in the American cinema of redemption become the faces of the mystery and multiplicity of the ever distant and elusive American experience.

Four faces that can be studied for how they relate to contexts of the American experience in specific roles and films include Henry Fonda in John Ford's *The Grapes of Wrath* (1940); Marilyn Monroe in John Huston's

The Misfits (1961); Paul Newman in Robert Rossen's *The Hustler* (1961); and Denzel Washington in Edward Zwick's *Glory* (1989). These actors suggest variation and transition, as well as durability and continuity, in the American cinema of redemption.

THE CLOSE-UP AND THE AURA OF THE IMAGE

The intense close-up of the face as a force for the retrieval of the soul has been a key idea for directors since the early days of cinema. Such notable filmmakers as Jean-Luc Godard, Ingmar Bergman, Jean Renoir, John Ford, and Woody Allen have been identified with such uses of the facial close-up.

On one of the occasions when Levinas refers directly to cinema, he discusses the close-up and its connection to modern art without even referring to the spiritual potential of this technique or its possible relationship to the face. In *Existence and Existents* Levinas resists the almost instinctive association of the close-up with spirituality and inner being; rather, the close-up is consistent with the fragmentation of painting: "The limitation at work in a painting, due to the material necessity of making something limited, constitutes a positive condition for the aesthetic, in the abstract and abrupt lines of its limits." He goes on to develop the comparison between such art and the close-up: "Effects of the same kind are obtained in cinema with close-ups. Their interest does not only lie in that they can show details; they stop the action in which a particular is bound up with a whole, and let it exist apart. They let it manifest its particular and absurd nature which the camera discovers in a normally unexpected perspective—in a shoulder line to which the close-up gives hallucinatory dimensions, laying bare what the visible universe and the play of its normal proportions tone down and conceal."[6]

Unlike Levinas, directors such as Godard, Bergman, and Allen emphatically propose the idea of the close-up's intrinsic connection to the soul. Godard, as has been noted often, famously suggests in *Le petit soldat* (1960), "To photograph a face is to photograph the soul behind it. Photography is truth. And the cinema is the truth, twenty-four times a second."[7] Similarly, Allen, in a review of Bergman's autobiography, *The Magic Lantern*, deems Bergman a pioneer in his use of the close-up to gain access to the interior life of his characters: "Bergman evolved a style to deal with the human interior, and he alone among directors has explored the soul's battlefield to the fullest. . . .

One saw great performers in extreme close-ups that lingered beyond where the textbooks say is good movie form. Faces were everything for him. Close-ups. More close-ups. Extreme close-ups. He created dreams and fantasies and so deftly mingled them with reality that gradually a sense of the human interior emerged. He used huge silences with tremendous effectiveness."[8]

Jean Renoir, as David Mamet recalls, "made movies for the close-ups."[9] Béla Balázs summarizes the intrigue of the close-up for many as the discovery of "the soul of things in the close-up." He says that "good close-ups radiate a tender human attitude in the contemplation of hidden things."[10]

Brief as it is, Levinas's discussion of the close-up avoids the Godard-Bergman-Allen paths of interiorization that go toward layered approaches to the depths of the soul. Levinas and these directors have different worldviews, which in turn lead to different ways of thinking about film. For Levinas the search for the soul compels movement toward exteriority as opposed to interiority. Finding the soul for Levinas involves the intersubjective search for the other as opposed to the struggle for the self. The effectiveness of the close-up for both approaches—interiority or intersubjectivity—relies on what can be deemed the aura of the photographic image, especially regarding performers. On aura, Gilberto Perez describes the semiotic blending in the photographic image of icon as likeness and index as connection to an idea, while Theodor Adorno calls aura "the atmosphere of the artwork."[11] For Perez, blending icon and index gives the photographic image in cinema a unique quality that can be compared to Walter Benjamin's classic notion of aura. Benjamin, of course, uses aura to describe the unique quality of original art as opposed to mechanically produced art, which he believes lacks such uniqueness. Perez, however, disputes the argument that photography lacks aura. "In photography," he writes, "there is no original image, only copies, and thus, according to Benjamin, no aura. Yet a photographic image has its own kind of aura—the aura of a remnant, of a relic—stemming from the uniqueness, the original particularity, not of the picture but of the referent whose emanation it captures" (Perez, *The Material Ghost*, 33).

The theory of the aura of the cinematic image adds to our understanding of the impact of faces in film. The concept of aura in the cinematic and photographic image provides insight into how such images become meaningful, including, of course, images of performers. Iconic and indexical aspects of the image of a performer—likeness and connection—combine with the other elements of the cinematic image to help account for the power actors acquire. The aura of the photographic image cultivates the qualities of appearance and personality, as well as the acting, talent, and individual genius that go into film performance. Thus, the glamorization that occurs with images of stars constitutes an aspect of aura. Also, documentary shots, portraits, and even negative images gain interest from the visual and social contexts that help create the aura of the photographic image.[12]

The aura of photographic images of actors in film informs the cinematic use of Levinas's idea of the face. This aura helps to suggest the ethical transcendence of characters as played by actors who diversify the faces of redemption in the American cinema of redemption, actors such as Fonda, Monroe, Newman, and Washington.

LEVINAS AND THE FACE

The concept of the face, as noted throughout this study, constitutes the key to Levinas's ethical philosophy. As John Llewelyn says, "If the face is the source from which all meaning appears, as Levinas says that it is, then the face is the source of the meaning of being."[13] Levinas says that "the face is meaning of the beyond." He writes, "The meaning of the face is not a species whose indication or symbolism would be the genus. The face is alone in translating transcendence."[14] In its connection to ethical transcendence, the face not only defies simple explanation; it proposes a genuine impossibility of total definition. Levinas maintains that "it is impossible to contain the meaning of the human face in any concept" (Levinas, *Outside the Subject*, 39). Thus, clearly Levinas persists in speaking of the face as more than its visual representation of the individual. It comes to mean the entire ethical relationship that makes people human. According to Llewelyn, Levinas "tells us that a distinction must be made between the visibility of the phenomenal face at which I look and the invisibility of ethical face that looks at me."[15]

Thus, Levinas talks about the face "as a breaking of the plastic forms of the phenomenality of appearance" (Levinas, *Outside the Subject*, 44). "It is," he says, "that radical separation, and the entire ethical order of sociality, that appears to me to be *signified* in the nakedness of the face illuminating the human visage, but also in the expressivity of the other person's whole sensible being, even in the hand one shakes" (102). In this view the hand or human body could serve for the face in the ethical relationship to the other.

What makes the face rather than the hand or the toe or the nose so crucial concerns the face's exposed vulnerability that becomes an absolute Levinasian ethical demand for responsibility. Levinas asks whether we have not "already been exposed—beyond the presence of the other, plainly visible in the light—to the defenseless nakedness of the face, the lot or misery of the human?" He continues to question whether we "have not already been exposed to the misery of nakedness, but also to the loneliness of the face and hence to the categorical imperative of assuming responsibility for that misery?" (*Outside the Subject*, 158). As Llewelyn says, "One reason for describing absolute responsibility as face-to-face is that the face and the eyes are vulnerable parts of the body" (Llewelyn, *The HypoCritical Imagination*, 128).

The recognition of absolute moral responsibility for the other proves more important than the self-satisfaction that may come from an emotional response to the other. In his reconsideration of the importance of Levinas's ethics to modern politics, Simon Critchley emphasizes the "asymmetry" of Levinas's idea of responsibility, meaning the lack of equivalence in the relationship of responsibility. Responsibility to the other means the denial of the need for reciprocation. The concept of the face encapsulates all of the asymmetry entailed in such extreme ethical responsibility. Critchley writes, "From Emmanuel Levinas, I will try to show how this moment of asymmetry that arises in the experience of the infinite demand of the other's face defines the ethical subject in terms of a split between itself and an exorbitant demand that it can never meet, the demand to be infinitely responsible. So, my normative claim, if you will, is that at the basis of any ethics should be a conception of ethical experience based on the exorbitant demand of infinite responsibility."[16] For Levinas the face constitutes exactly such a demand for infinite responsibility.

In essence, then, the face puts a face on the enormous idea of absolute ethical responsibility. As Critchley proposes, "The ethical relation begins when I experience being placed in question by the face of the other, an experience that happens both when I respond generously to what Levinas, recalling the Hebrew Bible, calls 'the widow, the orphan, the stranger,' but also when I pass them by on the street, silently wishing they were somehow invisible and wincing internally at my callousness" (Critchley, *Infinitely Demanding*, 56).

As Critchley notes, Levinas contrives a fascinating term to express this relationship of the face and the other; it is a "curvature of intersubjective space," by which Levinas wishes to emphasize the priority of the other. Levinas distinguishes this "'curvature' of the intersubjective space" from mere "'points of view'" in relationships: "This 'curvature of space' expresses the relation between human beings.... Man as Other comes to us from the outside, a separated—or holy—face. His exteriority, that is, his appeal to me, is his truth." Levinas suggests this face constitutes a kind of "surplus of truth over being" or mere existence so that "the metaphor of the 'curvature of intersubjective space' signifies the divine intention of all truth." The face, for Levinas, ultimately signifies the sanctity and holiness involved in all human life. Maintaining that "the face to face is a final and irreducible relation," Levinas says, "this 'curvature of space' is, perhaps, the very presence of God."[17]

HENRY FONDA: TOM JOAD'S REDEMPTION

The Levinasian argument concerning the face presents not only an ethical challenge but an artistic one as well. The artistic triumph of John Ford's *The Grapes of Wrath* concerns the drama of the ethical triumph of the Joads in recognizing the face of the other as opposed to merely dwelling on their own pain. The exchange of looks between the faces of the Joads in the transient Hooverville camp and the people around them creates, in Sarah Cooper's phrase, a space of responsibility between visual recognition and unspeakable moral crisis. In their look from their crippled truck, the Joads recognize the horror of the difference between what they see before them, the image, and a moral responsibility that will be impossible to fulfill. Moreover, their recognition of this difference as seen on the faces of others constitutes a special moment of humanity in the film. They appreciate the face of precisely those others who most concern Levinas—the poor, the homeless, the orphaned, the widowed.

In *The Grapes of Wrath* the special, lasting significance of the image of Henry Fonda's face during his "I'll Be Everywhere" speech also comes from its evocation of that inexpressible gap between the image's representation of visual reality and the impossibility of fully articulating the holiness of the face. The visual drama on Fonda's face of that difference between the physical face and transcendence also conveys the depth of the ethical transformation that Tom Joad undergoes. Fonda's face becomes more even than the significant achievement of a beautifully composed portrayal of the common man in crisis as a martyred victim of economic disaster. It conveys an attack

FIGURE 3.1. Henry Fonda in *The Grapes of Wrath* (1940)

on the human spirit under inhuman conditions; it evokes the desire for the recognition of the infinite in the human. The ethical suggestiveness of the face reinforces the speech that Fonda repeats from the novel. The Levinasian "saying" of the ineffable face strengthens the "said" of his words. Thus, Ma says she doesn't quite understand, and Tom admits that neither does he fully grasp the complete meaning of his own words. The honesty of the family's helplessness before all they have witnessed emphasizes from a Levinasian perspective the nature of the Levinasian ethical commitment that goes beyond total understanding.

In the scene, sitting with Ma Joad and preparing to leave the family, a transformed Tom acquires a social consciousness and commits himself to following the ethical lead of the activism of the Reverend Jim Casy (John Carradine), the prophetic Christ-like figure whose initials obviously signify the application of religious symbolism to the crises of the times. Shot beautifully by Gregg Toland and John Ford, shadows and light on Tom's face and on the scene suggest ethical extremes and accentuate the depth of Tom's sincere commitment. Fonda speaks with dignified clarity so that his soft, well-modulated speech gives Steinbeck's words a humble eloquence. Fonda makes convincing the romantic political idealism of Tom's rhetoric about being everywhere a man is needed for the helpless. The visual and verbal language of the scene, its tone and attitude, all come together for Fonda in this scene.

Thus, the range of elements in film art of mise-en-scène, cinematography, editing, and narrative all work brilliantly to suggest their ultimate failure to portray the impossible. But the same elements succeed magnificently in suggesting the gap between the visual image and ultimate, absolute ethical responsibility for the other. A heavily lined scar by Tom's left eye stands out on his gaunt, unshaven face. He received the scar when he was clubbed across the head by a vigilante "deputy" in retaliation for killing a "deputy" who had unjustifiably clubbed and killed Casy for his union organizing and preaching. The deputy describes the mark as a "trademark" that will lead to his capture. The wound brands him like Cain as a murderer but also testifies to the fact that his mission for the downtrodden has been inscribed on his body as a permanent sign of unwavering commitment. Assuming Casy's mantle of leadership, Tom also now carries a heavier burden of guilt for murder. For Levinas, even the thought of murder ultimately makes it incumbent on all people to assume absolute responsibility for the other. In Tom's speech in the scene with Ma, the intensity of Fonda's deep, piercing eyes, the powerful purposefulness of his stare, and the mixture of sensitive fragility and aggressive intent in his look and bearing make for a performance that puts an unforgettable face on Tom's words of ethical and political embattlement. He breathes new life into a message of a new politics of ethical responsibility for the other.

Fascinatingly, throughout the scene Fonda projects an ethical vision that goes beyond his audience just as it goes past Ma and even exceeds Tom's own total comprehension. He speaks to the idea of the other. So Fonda suggests Tom's immersion into another kind of temporal realm of serious ethical commitment as he prepares to leave the family with a kiss on the forehead of his sleeping father and his memorable good-bye speech to Ma.

At one point a train whistle intrudes into the scene between Tom and Ma, creating a sense of departure and distance, an auditory horizon and a sensory disjuncture over what can be seen and heard in the darkness of the night. The sadness of the train's call conveys the unknown, a reality beyond ordinary time, and suggests the path of ethical demand that Tom now takes. Carrying Casy's burden and walking in his steps and speaking in his place, Tom answers the call in the darkness and night to a new life that anticipates but surpasses death with a greater commitment of ethical purpose. Ma even says that with Tom's disappearance into the night, he could eventually die without anyone in the family ever knowing about it. By taking on this new ethical mission, Tom already in a sense has gone to another world.

The gap between Fonda's physical face and the face of the fictional Tom compares to the space between the face and the Levinasian *visage*. Fonda as Tom vivifies that tension into an ethical experience. Fonda shows that through a complex construction of the elements of film, the innocence, nudity, and vulnerability of the face can be made to suggest the Levinasian face of infinite ethical engagement. In *The Grapes of Wrath*, shot, image, and narrative—in conjunction with the documentary delineation of conditions and the development of all the characters—converge in the aura of Fonda's face. Like Stewart, Bogart, Garfield, Brando, and others, Fonda, in his portrayal of Tom, becomes the face of redemption. As Tom Joad, the face of Henry Fonda insists on an answer for the meaning of life and human relations that remains at once simple enough for a child to understand and yet so incomprehensible as to challenge ordinary knowing.

MARILYN MONROE: THE LOST REDEEMER

In an increasingly pornographic society and culture, Marilyn Monroe takes the Levinasian ethical philosophy to extreme alternatives between the face of redemption and the reduction of the self to erogenous body parts. Seeking redemption herself in *The Misfits*, she becomes the face of redemption, certainly for the men in the movie but also for her men outside of the movie, including her husband at the time, Arthur Miller, who wrote the screenplay, and Norman Mailer, who writes about her as an extension of his own imagination. Initially, however, it was not the amazingly soulful, graceful nudity of her face, with its beauty, vulnerability, innocence, joy, sensitivity, neediness, and fear that made her famous. It was, instead, a calendar that made her the American Nude. It also made her the world's most famous sex symbol. Arguably, Monroe's image helped initiate a culture that has made pornography fashionably respectable for some today. Noting that Marilyn Monroe came "to the attention of the film industry" when she posed for "a pornographic photograph," Susan Griffin insists that Monroe became "a pornographic symbol in pornographic culture."[18]

In Marilyn Monroe, however, Norman Mailer saw more than the "virgin and the whore, Justine and Juliette" dichotomy that inflames Griffin or "the transcendent body and the seamy, sensual body" that S. Paige Baty sees.[19] For Mailer, Monroe becomes no less than a sexualized myth of America. He, therefore, tries to go beyond the usual easy dichotomies of the whore-goddess syndrome when he writes about Monroe. He strives to develop the contradictions that actually persist in his own understanding of her. Mailer begins his provocative biography of Monroe with what must be among the most quoted words written about her:

> So we think of Marilyn who was every man's love affair with America, Marilyn Monroe who was blonde and beautiful and had a sweet little rinky-dink of a voice and all the cleanliness of all the clean American backyards. She was our angel, the sweet angel of sex, and the sugar of sex came up from her like a resonance of sound in the clearest grain of a violin. Across five continents the men who knew the most about love would covet her, and the classical pimples of the adolescent working his first gas pump would also pump for her, since Marilyn was deliverance, a very Stradivarius of sex, so gorgeous, forgiving, humorous, compliant and tender that even the most mediocre musician would relax his lack of art in the dissolving magic of her violin. (Mailer, *Marilyn*, 15)

Mailer goes on to tie this general public vision and cultural apprehension of Monroe to her specific relationship to her husband, Arthur Miller, and *The Misfits*. He notes that with *The Misfits* Miller, who had won the Pulitzer Prize for his play *Death of a Salesman* (1949), promised to give her a screenplay and film "that would bestow upon her public identity a soul" (Mailer, *Marilyn*, 203). Mailer writes, "Her existence as a sex queen will be reincarnated in a woman. It is not that her sex will disappear so much as that the sex queen will become an angel of sex." Mailer sees Miller working like Gatsby in his quest to reinvent his love according to the transcendent conception of her in his own mind. Mailer writes of Miller's "early and enraptured idea of her" that would enable them both to "wipe away" the past so that Marilyn could assume a kind of national destiny: "It was as if she wanted to become the angel of an American life; as if, beneath every remaining timidity and infirmity, she felt that she had deserved it. Perhaps she did. Are there ten women's lives so Napoleonic as her own? So she had to hope (with the part of herself not without hope) that the final version of *The Misfits* would be her temple" (ibid., 203–4).

To make a film into a "temple" for the sanctification of "an angel of sex," as Mailer here proposes Miller and Monroe hoped to do, would require the writing of a script that would be the literary and cinematic equivalent of an architectural design for such a cathedral. To be successful would mean seeing that design for a script evolve into a film that would be comparable to an edifice of great aesthetic and spiritual value with the primary purpose of representing the deification of one human being. Thus, "the picture," as Mailer says, "must become nothing less than her canonization," and to this end "Miller has committed everything" (186).

Such high ambitions naturally invite disappointment. Many agree that Miller's relentless revisions never adequately resolved the screenplay's conflicting conceptions of Monroe's character, Roslyn Taber, a former dancer and a divorcee whose sad past and fragile temperament do not defeat her idealism, sensitivity, and innocence. In Nevada for her divorce from Raymond Taber (Kevin McCarthy), she befriends Isabelle Steers (Thelma Ritter) and meets three men who will change her life (and who will find their own lives dramatically transformed in turn) — Gay Langland (Clark Gable), Perce Howland (Montgomery Clift), and Guido (Eli Wallach). Together they form a band of misfits, the men being modern cowboys who no longer can work cattle and the range. Instead, they drive wild mustangs from the mountains onto the desert and rope them from a truck to sell for dog food, a brutal business that horrifies Roslyn when she ventures out with them. Of course, the clash between Roslyn's beauty and sexuality, which determines how the world perceives her and how she often sees herself, and her inner nature of sensitive sympathy and love, adds to the idea of her as the embodiment of a misfit unable even to fit comfortably into her own skin. Like the men, she remains an outsider to conventional middle-class lifestyles.

Accordingly, in spite of all Miller's efforts and intellectual pretensions, the screenplay for *The Misfits* never completely comes together, in part because of his inability to create Roslyn with all of her ambiguities as a truly coherent character. As Barbara Leaming says in her study of Monroe, "In fact, the playwright had devoted the better part of three years to a mediocre screenplay." She adds, "In the end, Roslyn's emotions during the hunt are not as moving as they ought to be, because they seem disconnected from the story."[20] Similarly, Mailer suggests that "it is also possible, however, that Marilyn does not begin to assess how unplayable will be her part by the end" (Mailer, *Marilyn*, 204). Throughout the film Miller's script has her veer radically between being a wondrous, loving figure of grace and an insecure, displaced loser.

The turmoil at the center of the making of *The Misfits* has been well documented by many who have written about Monroe, Miller, and the film. The story behind the film includes the unnerving relationship between Monroe and Miller as their marriage disintegrated, the tensions of national politics during the McCarthy era of blacklists and investigations by the House Un-American Activities Committee, the clash of personalities and interests involved in the production itself. This background to the film's story not only has become a legend in film history and filmmaking; it also becomes part of the film itself and contributes to our understanding of it.

As much as *The Misfits* tells the story of the characters in Miller's screenplay, it also documents the activities of the actors themselves, inevitably connecting the lives, psyches, and biographies of the real people onscreen to the fictional characters in the film. As the story of the characters unfolds, so also the actors themselves play out their fate. Such documentation of actors inexorably occurs in any film with performers. Every film or documentary becomes a record of the people in it. This becomes most noticeable for stars or leading figures. Thus, James Naremore notes that "people in a film can be regarded in at least three different senses: as actors playing theatrical personages, as public figures playing theatrical versions of themselves, and as documentary evidence."[21]

In *The Misfits*, especially, fictional characters and real lives work off each other. The real interacts with the fictional, providing an extra dimension of meaning to the film. The prominence of Monroe during this horribly tumultuous stage of her life, the drama of her relationship with Miller, the political background of the film, and the legendary status of other stars such as Gable and Clift all make *The Misfits* as much of a documentary about them and the film itself as it is also a major film directed by one of America's great directors, John Huston, with a screenplay by the country's leading playwright at the time. Distraught and disturbed like Roslyn in the film, Monroe's own instability became part of the film's history, as did Gable's aggressive masculinity as an older man trying to match the sexuality, beauty, and glamour of the younger love goddess. So it becomes part of the experience of the film that Gable performed his own stunts, including being dragged on the rough desert ground by a wild mustang, a brave act that probably contributed to the occurrence of the massive heart attack that killed him just eight days before the film finally was finished on November 24, 1960. Similarly, it helps us to appreciate the historic, cultural, and cinematic significance of the film to know that apparently drugged and incapacitated through much of the filming, Monroe would never finish another film and would die from a drug overdose on August 5, 1962. Accordingly, the public images of Monroe, Gable, and even Clift in this film support their roles.

The successes *The Misfits* achieved along with its failures derive in part from its focus on Monroe's promise as a force for redemption and from her role as the face of the film's ethical argument. In this sense Monroe fulfills the vision Mailer and Miller had of her as a redemptive power for those who could see it and believe it, a power energized for them by their idealization of her as a highly sexual angel of love and as a symbol of national and cultural renewal.

In *The Misfits* the images of Monroe herself, more than the script or a speech or a particular part of the film's developing story line, dramatize her redemptive role. In these images Monroe triumphs over psychoanalytical readings of her face as the sign of the whore-Madonna syndrome. Instead, the images invoke a radical ethical appeal for infinite responsibility from the men in the film who seek to find their redemption in her. Glamorized and sexualized, her face becomes the focus of that ethical demand.

Monroe as Roslyn preaches a lot in the movie. Expressing values of compassion, love, and caring that reflect the proclivities of Miller and his New York circle of liberal friends, she becomes a secular version of the film's church lady (Estelle Winwood) in the Reno bars, hustling drunks for contributions. She quite vociferously pronounces about human relationships. She notes how people have lost touch with their own emotions, with themselves, and with each other. People are around physically but not there as emotionally or spiritually accessible, including her ex-husband. "We're all dying, aren't we? All the husbands and all the wives," she says, and "not teaching each other what we really know." She cringes over the pain people inflict not only on each other but on animals as well, at one point berating Gay for trying to kill the rabbit that eats lettuce from their desert garden. Her morally judgmental statements often sound stringent. She notes how Guido's thoughtless lack of preparation in regard to complications with his wife's pregnancy led to her death. His wife died, she says, because Guido didn't have a spare tire for his vehicle to get her to the hospital. When they dance together and Guido remarks about her gracefulness, the word has a religious connotation about her attitude toward life and people, but she responds harshly to the remark. She tells Guido that his reluctance to teach his wife how "to be graceful," to dance well, suggests that "to a certain extent maybe you were strangers." Such heavy pronouncements sometimes make her a cruel moral consciousness and voice for the film as she draws attention to the way people harm each other.

Monroe's real authority as Roslyn comes, however, from the power of Monroe's image that in turn gives credence to her speech. Monroe's face, not her spoken words, indicates the authenticity of her character's sensitivity that makes her so attuned to the pain of others. Sarah Childress has pointed out one moment in particular that dramatizes Monroe's own vulnerability as a key to Roslyn's moral sensitivity. The moment works as an example of the kind of interiorization that close-ups in film make possible and that so many directors regard so highly. In the scene Roslyn shows Guido how much she has done to brighten and domesticate Guido's desert home that he has allowed her to share with Gay as she and Gay develop their own love affair. An open closet door in the bedroom reveals several publicity-style photos of

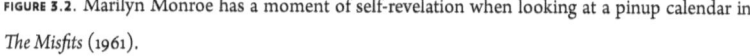

FIGURE 3.2. Marilyn Monroe has a moment of self-revelation when looking at a pinup calendar in *The Misfits* (1961).

Roslyn. She says excitedly, "Oh don't look at those. They're nothing. Gay just had 'em up for a joke." The photos that embarrass Roslyn, however, clearly reflect back on Monroe's own photos that in reality helped to establish her career. Roslyn tries to close the door but Guido persists in opening it to look at the photos. Pushing the door closed one more time, she tries to distract him again, as she moves out of the room lightly saying, "Come on! Let's have lots of drinks. Come on."

As Childress notes, however, an amazing close-up of Monroe dramatizes the depth of her actual distress during this moment of exposure. Her face indicates genuine uncertainty about her place in the scene and suggests a similar uncertainty about the meaning of her existence in her real life. In this shot Monroe the actor and Roslyn the character truly share and compound the despair the camera reveals. In this self-reflexive moment Monroe's own weaknesses strengthen her portrayal of Roslyn, a lost character, who becomes a kind of alter ego for Monroe's yearnings for love and approval. In a film of carefully prepared shots and sequences this close-up of Monroe turning inward on herself comes as a surprise, probably even an accident, just as her eyes blink in a way that signifies a kind of revelatory self-recognition of the joining of character and actor.

Another seemingly incidental shot of Monroe that occurs after the calendar scene also takes on surprising significance. This shot assumes great potential importance because of what it says about Roslyn's sense of concern for others as opposed to primarily demonstrating her own insecurity. In this shot Monroe, rather than turning inside herself, goes outward toward the other with a silent, beautiful, indeed graceful gesture of sympathy and understanding. In the scene Gay, Roslyn, Guido, and Isabelle encounter Perce Howland. They are driving to a rodeo and find Perce by a roadside public telephone trying to call his mother. Again, the scene reflects reality in that Perce's efforts to call his mother recall Monroe's own difficult childhood and her abandonment by her mother who apparently endangered her life. Marilyn's abandonment resonates with Roslyn's earlier story of her mother's absence.

As Perce speaks to his mother, he closes the door of the phone booth, but he still can be heard by the others in the car. Monroe's face, as part of her reserved performance, speaks wonders. Her still face suggests subsurface suffering as she hears Perce's painful conversation with his mother. Since this is a grown man, a lone cowboy, living and surviving by himself, the scene has a special pathos. Monroe's quiet, reserved reaction to Perce makes it touching and real. She looks off in the distance at first, but then her eyes barely blink, as in the earlier calendar shot, as they shift toward Perce without noticeable facial movement. Absent the melodramatic theatrics and strained speech of much of her performance in this film, in this scene she enacts all of Roslyn's spoken anguish for the pain of others who need love. Monroe projects onto herself here the intensity of the ethical demands Roslyn requires from others. In this scene Monroe's face becomes a vision of excess beyond representation and image. It suggests an ethics of a relationship to the other greater than perception. In this space of excess Monroe refuses to be reduced to a visual cliché or the image of others' desires. Ethical transcendence exceeds totalization and closure.

All of the male characters in the film seek redemption in the eyes of Roslyn in a way that replicates Mailer's and Miller's views of Monroe—or at least their understanding of her most meaningful place in American culture. They each seek redemption in the sense of renewal of their identities. In this quest each of the actors gives a performance of a lifetime, Gable most of all. Gable, as Gay Langland, expresses veneration for Roslyn because of her beauty, suggesting the redemptive power of her face. Watching her sleep and wake up in his car after they all had been drinking too much, Gay feels compelled by the exquisite beauty of Roslyn's face to say, "You're a real beautiful woman. It's almost kind of an honor sitting next to you. You just shine in my eyes. That's my true feelings Roslyn." He marvels at her ability to bring sunshine into others' lives. Old enough to be her father and aware of his failures at parenting, Gay seeks another chance with her. Each of the men strives for regeneration through her by acting out this new story in their lives in terms of their individual past experiences. Thus, Gay remains ironical, sarcastic, and wisecracking throughout but finally succumbs to her demands to change.

Also, Perce fulfills his role as her friendly ally, a man without the others' sexual desire for her while Guido persists in a violent masculinity of jealous resentment that he never manages to disguise in spite of toasting, appreciating, and probably understanding Roslyn better than either of the other men. Commenting on how she finally made his house into a home, coming closer than he ever could to realizing his dream for it, Guido says, "You just walk in, a stranger out of nowhere, and for the first time it all lights up. And I'm sure you know why, too. Because you have the gift for life, Roslyn. The rest of us, we're just looking for a place to hide and watch it all go by."

As many, including Mailer, have noted, the outstanding performances in the film by the trio of male actors presented an intimidating challenge to Monroe. Ultimately, however, their work sustains her efforts. As actors, they convincingly suggest men who succumb not only to Roslyn's beauty but to her moral and ethical influence as well. Their performances give credibility to the authenticity of Roslyn's constant demands for a better way of living for each other.

The ethical and emotional climax of the story occurs with Roslyn's reaction to the hunt for the wild mustangs. She realizes that the horses, which in earlier times were captured and sold to become pets and riding ponies for children, now will be slaughtered for dog food. Distressed at the situation, she lets Gay, out of concern for her safety and comfort, set up a bed for her off of the desert ground on the flatbed of the truck. In a beautiful straight shot of her lying on the bed of the truck, Gay stands above and behind her, touching her, and appeals to her to be reasonable about the necessity for him of the hunt. He says he regrets how things have changed, but hunting the animals enables him to avoid regular jobs with "wages," so it becomes his way of maintaining his freedom and independence. This conversation for once simply and starkly presents ethical conflict: his freedom for the lives of the horses. Her own sense of conscience persists: "But you know what you're doing isn't right, don't you? You know that." He defensively responds that if he

FIGURE 3.3. Marilyn Monroe in *The Misfits* (1961)

didn't do the hunting, others would, at the cost of his own freedom. "But I don't care about the others," she says.

The horses obviously have become a metaphor for slaughter in general. The film at this point really constitutes a Levinasian statement of a fundamental ethical dilemma—the potential in all people to kill to keep their own "place in the sun." In an earlier scene Guido, finally the most destructive of the men, ironically sees, articulates, and marvels over Roslyn's personification of a kind of Levinasian ethical position. He relishes what he himself cannot have or be. Interestingly, his statement also summarizes a key argument in Levinas in the contrast between knowledge and ethics. Guido, a pilot and war veteran, has been impressing Roslyn and Perce with his knowledge of the stars. After being told how smart he is and how much he knows, he says to Roslyn, "Knowing things don't matter much. You got something a lot more important.... You care! Whatever happens to anybody, happens to you. You're really hooked into the whole thing, Roslyn. It's a blessing." She says people just consider her "nervous." Guido responds: "If it weren't for the nervous people in the world, we'd all still be eating each other." Thus, the Levinasian argument about ethics as the first philosophy that compels the inescapable responsibility for the other has been made by the most selfish and self-centered member of the group who least adheres to it.

In these scenes that set up the mustang hunt Monroe's performance has been relatively restrained and muted as the men prepare for the hunt. She already has established Roslyn's moral presence throughout the earlier scenes in the movie. The calm of the readiness for the hunt, however, works as a prelude to contrast with the emotional climax of her horror over the hunt, her battle with Gay to stop it, and Gay's own proud refusal until the end to relinquish his control of the situation by giving up his way of life. With all the violence in this part of the film, Roslyn looms as the face and figure of ethical exigency.

What Roslyn has called her nervousness carries as much emotional intensity and energy as the violence of the hunt, in part because her reaction propels the ethical burden of the film. Crying over a horse's pain as it is roped and wrestled to the ground, fighting with Gay to free all the animals, and then inadvertently insulting him, Roslyn's moral outrage finds its strongest expression in her confrontation with Guido in the cab of the truck as he offers to free the animals if she will be with him. Her facial expression in close-up signifies genuine moral conviction, and her voice echoes with real anger. As in previous scenes, a moment of Actors Studio inner thought registers in her voice and look. But then this internal movement projects outward in precise force back toward Guido. She says, "You a sensitive fellow. So sad for his wife. Crying to me about the bombs you dropped and the people you killed." Her voice becomes a growl as she leans into him. She continues, "You have to get something to be human. You never felt anything for anybody in your life. All you know is the sad words. You could blow up the world, and all you'd feel is sorry for yourself." Being human, feeling, and acting for others summarizes her purpose in the film. She embodies an ethics of responsibility.

Then, listening to Gay discuss with Guido the value by the pound of an old mare he has fought to the ground, the mixture of horror and outrage on her face carries a message about violence and human values that is intended to go beyond this moment on the desert to serve as a comment about the murderous history of the century. Roslyn runs off and from a distance calls the men "Murderers" and demands they kill themselves out of their love of death. Picking up on the nervousness of her character, Guido calls her "Crazy," and then speaking of women in general, he says, "They're all crazy!!"

Monroe's successful portrayal of Roslyn's nervousness as a sign of moral outrage helps secure her role as the face of redemption, although it operates in this case as a declaration of values more than an excess of representation and image. She persists as the face of redemption by turning trauma into an ethical energy for renewal. In her, ethical demand and neurosis come together. Monroe, thereby, enacts a vital theory of ethical thought that Simon Critchley considers an important aspect of Levinas's later work. As Critchley says, "Trauma was not a theoretical issue for Levinas, but a way of dealing with the memory of horror." Critchley, of course, recognizes that for Levinas the horror concerns the Holocaust. But for Roslyn in this performance by Monroe in *The Misfits*, the horror also involves the pain of everyday experience, including the pain from the challenge of insisting on both love and the ethical regard for the other. As Critchley says:

> Levinas makes the extreme claim that my relation to the other is not some benign benevolence, compassionate care or respect for the other's autonomy, but is the obsessive experience of a responsibility that persecutes me with its sheer weight. I am the other's hostage, taken by them and prepared to substitute myself for any suffering and humiliation

that they may undergo. I am responsible for the persecution I undergo even for my persecutor; a claim that, given the experience of Levinas's family and people during the Second World War, is nothing less than extraordinary. (*Infinitely Demanding*, 60–61)

Critchley's comment that "the Levinasian ethical subject is a traumatic neurotic" characterizes Monroe's performance in *The Misfits*. She performs some mental and psychological acrobatics by dramatizing the Levinasian idea, as described by Critchley, that "the inside of my inside is somehow outside, the core of my subjectivity is exposed to otherness." This means, he says, that "the ethical demand is a traumatic demand" (*Infinitely Demanding*, 61). Monroe turns her beauty into a convincing ethical argument for another way of living. She succeeds as the face of redemption because she follows a script greater than Miller's. Miller scripts the words of ethical demand, but Monroe provides an emotional music and theatrics to give those words a special power. She vividly enacts the Levinasian saying of the spirit of ethics over the completed, articulated said.

The trauma of Monroe's ethical demand as Roslyn ultimately becomes both compelling and problematic. Roslyn's cry for a world of loving care without killing not only echoes Levinas's argument; it also constitutes what could be deemed an example of unrealistic extremism that insists on the impossible. To demand a world without any violence, as Roslyn does in this film, can invite the very thing she dreads: suffering and death for the most vulnerable among us. But it also could open the way for redemption. As Gay says after his final victory over a wild mustang before freeing it, "Ah, just gotta find another way to be alive, that's all."

In the last scene in the cab of the truck, Gay and Roslyn again become a couple. Both faces show all the pain and tension and loss of their experience together. But the faces also express what has been learned. Gay says in his most paternal way, "God bless you, girl." She takes the comment as a true blessing as Gay looks down in humility. Her face radiates love. They follow this statement with words and symbols consistent with the blessing. She imagines "a child who could be brave from the beginning," and he contemplates a star in the heavens above the highway that will "take us right home." Redemption and a new life, it seems, wait for them at the end of their journey.

Considering the nearness of the end for both of these amazing actors, this last scene conveys deep sadness. In the final take, a straight shot of them through the windshield of the truck, their faces convey profound meaning and differences. Gay, the old cowboy, finally seems at ease and rested, apparently imagining a happy ending of a new beginning for him in his last years with Roslyn. Of the three men, Gay obviously comes closest to finding redemption through Roslyn.

Roslyn's face suggests something else, at least for a moment. Still the face of redemption for others, the idea of such redemption for herself, or even the possibility of happy endings, cannot come easily to her. Here, perhaps, Marilyn and Roslyn come closer together again, just as their very names resonate with each other. It becomes difficult to imagine either woman finding redemption in a relationship with another needy man. Thus, Roslyn's expression, body, and presence project an awareness of a deeper sadness about life than Gable's character, Gay, wants to or can recognize. Her sensitivity to the world's wrongs promises a future of more shock, trauma, and pain. Ethical acuteness for Roslyn means divided subjectivity, even if such moral intelligence also creates the opportunity for her to influence others, as Roslyn has done for the men, the other misfits in the film.

Unfortunately, for Roslyn, ethical subjectivity leaves her rather naked and defenseless, armed primarily with moral outrage. Echoing the film's real-life world of persecution in the style of McCarthyism and liberal impotence in the manner of Miller, *The Misfits* does not arm Roslyn with an ideology strong enough to fulfill her ethical demands, especially the feminist politics and sexual ethics she seriously needs.

For Roslyn redemption ultimately entails continuing the struggle for ethical engagement, being involved ethically and caringly with others. Roslyn, just before acquiescing to Gay's assurances and snuggling contentedly into his old shoulder, evidences another of her introspective moments of self-doubt and then looks, with more uncertainty, for the star he sees in the sky. Her face again tells us that for her, redemption will have no finality. With all of her innocence, vulnerability, and insecurity, Roslyn seems to realize her sense of time differs from Gay's, just as her perception of the stars contrasts with Guido's astronomy. Motivated by the trauma of her view of others, she inevitably feels their pain. While Gay has called for God to bless her, she ironically might say with Levinas, "'Thanks to God' I am another for the others."[22]

PAUL NEWMAN: ACTING FOR THE OTHER

Paul Newman's face bears witness to his character's redemption in *The Hustler*. Newman, under Robert Rossen's direction, acts out a great transformation that his face and his physical gestures convey. *The Hustler* begins with Newman as "Fast" Eddie Felson, a pool-playing con man and the epitome of cocky arrogance. As the film progresses, he experiences defeat by Minnesota Fats (Jackie Gleason) and then a crippling beating by thugs who break his thumbs so that he can't hustle pool. Worst of all, partly because of his own selfish thoughtlessness, Sarah Packard (Piper Laurie), the one person who truly loves him, commits suicide. Through all this Newman reveals in his facial expressions and gestures a steady maturation that indicates a transforming degree of ethical growth. He goes from Fast Eddie's total self-absorption to a passionate commitment to the other. In the end he stands ready to risk everything for a greater cause, redemption for himself and for Sarah by fighting to commemorate her life and what defined it.

The Hustler could be viewed as Rossen's remake of his classic boxing film, *Body and Soul* (1947). Both films dramatize stories of heroic redemption. *The Hustler* takes the story from the boxing ring and New York's Lower East Side to pool halls and the West Side of Manhattan. One contrast, however, between the movies stands out. Newman's character begins without any principles at all, only ambitions and needs. At the same time, the films are similar in presenting the hero's education in becoming a human being. As in classic stories of conversion and redemption, the greatest enemy often resides within the protagonist himself.

In *The Hustler* Eddie's inner enemy of arrogant aggression and blind ambition becomes externalized in the figure of a gambler named Bert Gordon, played brilliantly by George C. Scott. Rossen shoots Scott as a death mask of danger, a visual representation of evil with a high forehead, thin face, and stark profile that make him a devilish incarnation, the embodiment of threat. Yet even with his masterful performance of controlled explosiveness, Scott ironically justifies a statement by Levinas in regard to the Holocaust that "'Evil has no face.'"[23] Scott becomes a powerful caricature of evil, the kind of representation that for Levinas reduces ethics to images. It falls to Newman to bring greater nuance and complexity to his performance to suggest the ambiguities of redemption.

The climactic scene becomes a battle of close-ups of faces with a dynamic camera that organizes the space of a seedy pool hall to transform it into a mise-en-scène of conflict between forces of good and evil. In the sequence of events that sets up the concluding scene, Sarah's suicide follows her final humiliation by Bert after a long chain of humiliations. Weak, insecure, needy, she has sex with Bert as a complete surrender of her dignity and her ability to stand up to him in her own defense.

In a human jungle where only killers survive, Bert has hated Sarah for her relationship with Eddie and for her weakness. Even more important, he hates her for her beliefs and the way she thinks. Sarah functions in the film as Rossen's voice of conscience, a spokeswoman for the kind of liberal, humanistic politics that characterized Rossen's views after his own flirtations with communism and his personally disastrous acquiescence to the House Un-American Activities Committee.[24] Sarah's liberal humanism makes her Bert's natural enemy and target. Bert preys on and abuses her with the zeal of a true predator. A perennial student, Sarah's appreciation for literature, art, and the life of the mind signify weakness to Bert, especially combined with her limp and her alcoholism. Her views and lifestyle as a kind of Greenwich Village bohemian and misfit undermine Bert's avaricious values of power and materialism and threaten his dominance. Coveting Eddie's talents as a means of his own personal gain, Bert, as Eddie's manager, senses danger from the influence of Sarah's values on Eddie. Her ideas, ideals, and dreams are anathema to Bert, making her the composite of everything he abhors.

In the final scene Eddie returns to the Ames Billiards Parlor in New York City, for a rematch with Minnesota Fats. Everyone in the room understands that the real contest involves Eddie and Bert over the death of Sarah. Eddie's face conveys a new strength and purpose while Bert resembles a devil under siege in his fortress. Both faces register the activities on the field of battle, a pool table. Minnesota Fats becomes a kind of mediator between them. Close-ups of his face also register the volatile balance of the ethical and moral battle between Eddie and Bert.

As a setting for action, the world of the billiards parlor becomes a strangely enclosed, separated environment. A suffocating sense of congestive compression in black and white suffuses the pool hall. It resembles a tomb with a different temporal order. Although the clock on the wall insinuates an outside world of regular time that affects the pool hall, the world inside operates as well on a time of duration that depends on a continuous game without end. The clock tells the story of pool hall battles in minutes, just as the bell signals the rounds for Charlie Davis in his boxing matches in *Body and Soul*. Both Eddie Felson and Charlie Davis must fight in one temporal dimension while engaging in a greater battle of ethics and human relationships in another. Different temporalities exacerbate ethical and psychological disjuncture.

Remembering Ricoeur on how time operates in the contrast between a "horizon of expectations" and a "space of experience," and Wood on time and the horizon of being, we can see that in the pool hall the nature of the horizon becomes complex.[25] The temporal horizon becomes internalized within the hall as the ethical battle transforms the temporal dimension into a beyond of infinite demand. A dramatic sense of temporal disconnection occurs with the transformation of physical space into a mise-en-scène of ethical action. Eddie, Minnesota Fats, and Bert will be performing in an unfamiliar ethical arena. This allows for a change from closed space to a scene of ethical engagement.[26]

The scene begins with establishing shots of the pool hall. Minnesota Fats intently reads a newspaper while Bert flicks dice in a cup so that the popping and rattling sound announces his domineering presence and establishes an audial rhythm for the moment, a kind of rhythmic tattoo that asserts his power over the pool hall. In a classic theatrical set-up of oppositional forces, Eddie enters the billiards parlor, and a clear line of antagonism between the two men on opposite sides of the room cuts across the screen. Time seems to have stopped.

Minnesota Fats looks up, sensing a change in the pool hall. Similarly, Bert, usually cool, gets rigid, his shoulders pulled back as though preparing to receive an assault. As Eddie proceeds to shoot pool with a confident precision that conveys his invincibility, a sneer of fear and hatred stays frozen on Bert's face. Close-ups and cuts between Fats and Bert also show recognition of a coming moment of judgment. At the end of the match, when Fats concedes defeat, Eddie and Bert finally confront each other, Bert demanding payment and a return on his investment in the winning hustler. The close-up of Fast Eddie as he gives his speech in memory of Sarah reveals the change in his character in that he has gained precisely what Bert once accused him of lacking, "character." He achieves what Cindy Lucia says of another Newman character in Sidney Lumet's *The Verdict* (1982), "a nobility of spirit" and "the hope of redemption."[27] Instead of his initial cocky arrogance, he now demonstrates a deeply felt compassion and grief. Eddie says, "I loved her Bert. I traded her in on a pool game." As he speaks, a close-up of Minnesota Fats requires no verbal articulation. Just as he knew that Eddie was unbeatable and the pool game was over, his face indicates his awareness of the ethical stakes involved in the duel of wills taking place between Eddie and Bert. His expression becomes a visual echo of Eddie's words and look.

While Bert's face acknowledges defeat, even to the point of compelling him to justify his actions, the faces of both Eddie and Minnesota Fats suggest the impossible gap between Eddie's awareness of his betrayal of Sarah and the ultimate impossibility of rectifying it. The handsome face of Paul Newman signals the tragic impossibility of reconciling what Eddie now knows he learned from Sarah with the results of his inattentiveness during her life.

Rossen concludes the powerful engagement between Eddie and Bert with an effective long take of the two men confronting each other. They stand opposite each other in a straight line. When Eddie breaks that line to move briefly into the background of the frame before returning to his original position, the physical movement accentuates the point that a battle of ethical priorities, as well as a contest of individual egos, occurs between the men. When the tension finally breaks, Eddie wins his freedom from Bert by refusing to give the gambler his take. Only that gesture can constitute a vindication of Sarah. But the victory comes at a great cost in terms of Eddie's likelihood of ever being able to shoot pool again for money. Bert promises to shut him out. Again, close-ups of the two men with Minnesota Fats maintaining his middle position solidify the drama.

At the end Eddie's face enacts a living question mark of impenetrable ambiguity as well as his moment of temporary victory. Can he extend his responsibility for Sarah to another other? Can he carry his burden of responsibility to other people? How long will Sarah's lesson last? The ambiguity on Eddie's face continues to press the ethical challenge. The Great Minnesota Fats has been defeated finally, and the evil demon Bert has been forced back into his cave to wait for another day to do more of his dirty business. Part of Eddie's education has involved learning from Sarah that in fact Bert lives in his own private hell of limited imagination. He has only the capacity to live according to his cruel script.

Eddie's ethical triumph also condemns him to the endless testing of his responsibility for the other, of the priority of the other. The genius of Newman's performance involves the issue of Eddie's continuing moral struggle, which can be read on Newman's face even while showing the satisfaction of his victory against Minnesota Fats. Like Charlie Davis in the boxing ring, Eddie Felson wins the pool-hall fight, turning the billiards parlor into another space of responsibility between the hard face of reality and the look of ultimate responsibility. Eddie takes that ethical time of the pool-hall shootout with him, leaving the ultimate outcome of Sarah's legacy in question. The continuing struggle in the form of that uncertainty as written on the face of the redeemer hustler gives the movie significance as film art and ethical drama.

DENZEL WASHINGTON: THE POWER OF BLACKNESS

Denzel Washington has portrayed many complex characters who undergo dramatic transformations from immaturity, violence, and youthful self-obsession to become figures of heroic proportions. His success in these roles as he himself has matured over the years testifies to his genius as an actor. Washington's portrayal of Malcolm X, for example, goes well beyond impersonation. His performance helps explain Malcolm's place in history. Elsewhere, I have discussed the significance of Washington's work in *Malcolm X* and how, in this film, he portrays Malcolm as a man of ethical transcendence and universal purpose.[28]

Washington's portrayal of Trip, a runaway slave, in *Glory* anticipates the amazing overall achievement of his career. Perhaps more than any other black actor, he has broken a barrier in roles that render color irrelevant. Yet in *Glory* he gives a triumphal breakthrough performance in a scene that proves so powerful partly because of the dominance of blackness in the absence of whiteness.

Glory tells the neglected story of the Fifty-fourth Regiment of Massachusetts Volunteer Infantry, the Union's first black unit to fight in the Civil War, which was commanded by Colonel Robert Shaw (Matthew Broderick), a member of an elite, New England Brahmin family of activist abolitionists. Shaw was twenty-five years old when he commanded the unit. He died with his black troops after he volunteered to lead them on a suicidal attack against Fort Wagner in South Carolina, the fortress protecting the harbor.

Several factors distinguish the idea of redemption in this film from its depiction in other films in the American cinema of redemption. Of course, the profusion of black actors makes this film different. Although individual black actors, such as Canada Lee in *Body and Soul*, played characters who die or sacrifice themselves for whites, in *Glory* a whole military unit dies. Moreover, as volunteer soldiers in the Civil War, they die to help redeem the nation for the sin of slavery. They also die in an extraordinary act of courage for their own regeneration as free men.

In a remarkable scene, the black soldiers sing and pray to help prepare themselves for the next day's battle. The scene becomes a kind of double emergence for Washington. His character, Trip, achieves his identity, place, and sense of peace among the other soldiers. The scene also exhibits the achievement of true genius for Washington as an actor. In a brief speech of a few minutes of self-exposure, Washington conveys so much psychological and ethical intensity through verbal and facial expression, physical gesture, and sheer power of presence as to clearly embed himself as an outstanding figure in American film.

Just as the singing, clapping, and music of the soldiers create a vibrant rhythm to the scene, the actors themselves establish a flow and feel that bring out the singular nature of each soldier while interweaving them together as a group. As they all sing, "Oh my Lord, Lord, Lord!" Sharts (Jihmi Kennedy) rises to speak. His presence before the group entails a statement of great change in itself. Stuttering and shy, his appearance to speak before the men constitutes a sign of maturity and self-confidence. He now belongs. He speaks first as a symbolic gesture of the progress already achieved by him and these men. With Jesus and the Bible, he says, "I have no fear."

Then Morgan Freeman, as Sergeant John Rawlins, speaks, the voice of stability, maturity, strength, and self-confidence. The senior sergeant of the group, Rawlins intensifies the emotion of the scene. He has the deepest awareness of the historic significance of all that has happened, meaning the end of the years of slavery in the current fight for freedom, and the greatest appreciation for the price he and the other soldiers will soon pay to create a new history with the sacrifice of their lives in battle. As his speech quickens, his words inspire the aroused men. He articulates the meaning of events for them, and he places their lives in the context of their coming redemption. He offers the group a kind of poetic prayer: "If tomorrow is our great getting-up morning, if tomorrow we have to meet the judgment day, oh heavenly Father, we want you to let our folks know that we died facing the enemy. We want them to know that we went down standing up, amongst those who are fighting against our oppression. We want them to know heavenly Father, that we died for freedom. We ask these blessings in Jesus's name. Amen!" Rawlins then calls on Trip to speak.

Sharts and the sergeant have prepared the scene for the special, personal intensity Washington brings to the gathering. Sharts offered a simple introduction to the event by indicating what he already had gained from this brotherhood. Rawlins's powerful rhetoric puts their situation in a historic and religious context. But Washington, as Trip, contributes a depth and intensity of emotion to the scene that personalizes the unfolding historical events. He brings the immediacy of pain, anger, and anguish to the situation of impending battle and death, making abstract ideas of the cost and meaning of freedom and regeneration concrete.

Invariably a loner, a fighter, ironically a "rebel," and a negative force, Trip speaks in a way that makes him part of this community to such an extent that he becomes its symbol of redemption. The speech becomes a profound act of ethical commitment of the self to the other. Sergeant Rawlins urges him to speak, "to say what you feel." Trip nervously looks at the sergeant and moves his arms with equal discomfort. He scratches at his shoulder and says, "I ain't much about no praying." He hesitates nervously. "I never had no family," he says and times it perfectly with a long pause as the words sink into his own mind and the scene. "Killed off my momma," he says. His tension sparks a quick, defensive laugh. The honest simplicity of that moment when he breaks down and confesses that he feels funny after what he just said about family and mother, speaks for itself of the hopelessness of being a slave. In his awkward confusion he suggests unfathomable depths of suffering.

Whereas both previous speakers dealt simply and directly with their thoughts, Trip quickly engages in a more complicated form of dialogue with himself, as well as with his brothers in the war. He projects a forced smile and a look of fearful uncertainty that enter into a kind of visual exchange with each other. Thus Washington injects a pronounced degree of intelligent verbal and visual complexity into the scene, complexities that indicate deeper levels of feeling and meaning for his character. Trip tells Sergeant Rawlins he is not used to talking, and the nervous smile on his face conveys embarrassment and fear that relate to much more than just the particular moment, representing a culmination of his whole past and the history of the men he addresses. The silences in his speech mix with his words and carry their own resonance of meaning in the absence of definite sounds. His face expresses an ineffable yearning, as though appealing for love, understanding, redemption, and a life that has been denied him as a black man and slave.

Trip hesitatingly maintains the effort to speak, and sentences get smothered in his mouth and buried in his emotion. A hint of tears of suppressed emotion glimmers on his face in the light of the fire. His lips purse as he still tries to speak. His voice cracks like a child's. "You all is the onlyest family I got," he says, still fighting back tears. He takes a deep breath to speak as men cry out to him with encouragement. "That's alright," they say. He looks into some uncertain, mysterious mental distance and space beyond the men in the enclosure of the war camp.

Trip's hesitations and pauses continue to be perfectly timed with close-ups of Sergeant Rawlins and other soldiers encouraging him. Throughout the speech Trip finds himself leading the men as his emotion generates a steadily intensifying rhythm of singing and responding, a constant pulling back and forth between Trip, the individual, and the group. Meanwhile, Freeman injects his resonant voice into the exchange of sounds between Trip and the soldiers, helping to prompt the rhythm of the group that encourages individual distinction and group coherence. Similarly, camera movement, cutting, editing, individual close-ups, and group shots establish a visual rhythm in conjunction with the sound. Sound and vision proclaim individual difference within shared blackness.

Nearing the end of the ordeal of his triumph of a speech, Trip says, "And yuh, I love the Fifty-fourth." After more pauses, Trip says, "It ain't much a matter what happens tomorrow," and he looks this time at the assemblage before him. "We men, ain't we," he says. And says it one more time and again pauses and ends his testimony with a muffled "Shh" sound and a gesture of dismissal before the group erupts into spontaneous, joyful emotion.

Even as he walks off, Trip displays a variety of emotions that ultimately defy description. His face has been a visual ensemble of feelings, conveying hesitation, fear, repression, anxiety, uncertainty, and finally love, faith, and resolution. He turns his back to the camera while Sergeant Rawlins looks on him with fatherly pride. When Trip finishes his turning motion and his face appears again, the slight suggestion of a tear now can be seen quite clearly on his cheek.

Trip's speech of so few completed words and sentences frees what has been frozen within him. He visually emanates and sends forth to the men a fusion of emotion, energy, faith, and spirit powerful enough to energize a new community of men. Trip's face not only manifests his personal, individual redemption; it signifies a power that takes the whole Fifty-fourth Regiment along with him. A face of redemption, he exudes a revivified ethical subjectivity that engenders a new reality for himself and the other men.

As a setting of prayerful testimony, the scene evokes an ambience of spirituality. Thus, the intensity of blackness as living social and cultural history combines with blackness as spirituality and religious devotion to give the scene a special power. Through the singing, testifying, and praying of the scene, the historic reenactment of injustice and oppression in *Glory* enters a different ethical dimension to make a profound promise of redemption.

In her discussion of Levinas's resistance to representation and his warning against reducing concepts and ethics to images, Cooper emphasizes the need for relating the physical face and the Levinasian *visage* to "encounters with difference" based on race "along with cultural and historical specificity."[29] Washington's power as an actor and his charisma as a presence—his aura—fully mobilize the energy in the scene that comes from the break between the face and *visage* in the context of the "difference" of blackness, with all the ethical, political, and cultural meanings associated with blackness. With the history of slavery and racism, the color black gives the ethical transcendence of the *visage* another dimension.

A centuries-long history of ultimate violation and abuse engenders an excess of ethical demand. The tension between the power of the physical image of Washington's face and the transcendent meaning of *visage* becomes concentrated in the actor's facial expressions, speech, language, physicality, and gestures. The moral and ethical concentration of Washington's performance infuses the dynamic of the blackness of the scene so that Trip and his brothers in arms form an explosive combination of ethical power. Trip and his brother soldiers create a seething blackness of moral outrage that interacts with the power of transcendent ethical demand to exceed the capacity for containment by the scene. Under this pressure the scene erupts in visual and physical blackness.

A wave of black love, loyalty, and brotherhood emanates from the men, engulfing yet uplifting them. The atmosphere grows blacker in the sense that the men's relationships to each other help them form a distinct community as men and as soldiers. The images of the scene convey a new context of black empowerment before the transcendent ethical demand for justice in the face of the history of racism. All these forces intersect in the encampment, and they are internalized in Washington's performance and transformed into a moment of redemption.

Stirred and directed by Trip's newly acquired power, the black soldiers literally exhibit blackness as history, religion, brotherhood, community, energy, despair, and bravery. The scene clearly comes as a culmination of individual, racial, and national narratives of slavery and war. The scene follows and then continues a historical trajectory that the film depicts. This historic trajectory structures the emotional impetus of the scene. The solid, physical basis of the scene in blackness as lived, felt, and shared provides a cohesive foundation in historical experience.

Washington's acting and presence in this scene help to create a black film aesthetic of great ethical weight. His performance as Trip turns a powerful historical narrative of free, fighting former slaves into a moment of ethical transcendence. He presents a new face of redemption as the crossing of the social and physical face of blackness with its transcendent meaning. His work imbues the face with an excess of meaning beyond the purely physical image.

Washington, in *Glory*, like so many other actors, shows that the face can change from being its own mirror reflection of special, private concerns into a face for the other. Levinas could be discussing Washington's speech when he says:

> To speak is to interrupt my existence as a subject, a master, but to interrupt it without offering myself as a spectacle, leaving me simultaneously object and subject. My voice brings the element in which that dialectical situation is accomplished concretely. The subject who speaks does not place the world in relation to himself, nor place himself purely and simply at the heart of his own spectacle, as does the artist, but in relation to the Other. This privilege of the Other ceases being incomprehensible once we admit that the primary fact of existence is neither the *in itself*, nor the *for itself*, but the "*for the other*"; in other words, human existence is creature. By the proffered word, the subject that posits himself exposes himself and, in a way, prays. (*Outside the Subject*, 149)

The rhetoric and performance of Washington's speech constitutes such an act "*for the other*" that resounds with powerful meaning for its melding of religious confession and political address, a form of expression that goes back to the country's origins. The speech stands as an act of courage and community even in the precariousness of the men's situation on the brink of annihilation. In their readiness to sacrifice themselves, they repossess themselves, taking back what no one had the right to take from them. As slaves they were dispossessed of their bodies, their identity, the time of their being. As freedom fighters they face another kind of temporal incommensurability that gives them access to a new time of justice that supplants the time of oppression. Facing certain death, the black soldiers commit to a time beyond being. Washington's speech defines manhood for himself and for the others in terms of the strength of that commitment.

CHAPTER 4
SEX, ART, AND OEDIPUS
The Unbearable Lightness of Being

Inspired melding of ethics and transcendence often motivates the films in the American version of the cinema of redemption. In other films in the cinema of redemption, however, the journey tends to follow a more circuitous path into an imbroglio of ambiguity. In these films the extremism of Levinas's ethics frequently confronts the nihilism and disillusionment, the oppression and violence that many deem the modern condition. These films consider how such elements of modernity influence the search for redemption. More specifically, in these films such aspects of the modern condition color the construction of Levinasian "ethical subjectivity" in the relationship with the other.[1] The films delineate the engagement in the search for redemption between, on the one hand, the Levinasian demand for transcendence and alterity and, on the other hand, counter impulses of immediate, immanent experience that impugn the struggle for transcendence. Thus, Levinas says that "the history of philosophy" involves, at least in part, "the destruction of transcendence" and "the affirmation of immanence," considering immanence as concerning "a pure part of the world."[2]

Moreover, as Simon Critchley's phrase the "aesthetic screen" implies, film can prove valuable for gaining insight into the ethical encounter between transcendence and immanence.[3] Questions of time, death, and being persist on this aesthetic screen in the context of modernity. While the severity of the Levinasian ethical demand often exacerbates the trauma of modern existence, it also joins other forces in the construction of the ethical subject, such as sublimation, abjection, and the feminine.

Philip Kaufman's *The Unbearable Lightness of Being* (1988) provides a provocatively informative example of the construction in the cinema of redemption of Levinasian ethical subjectivity under conditions of modernity and immanence. The film elucidates the commingling of processes of social and psychological organization that help form the ethical subject. In delineating the complexity of this organizing activity, the film also offers an in-depth examination of the challenges presented by the modern condition to achieve what for Levinas constitutes the intersubjective relationship to the other. Kaufman's film version of Milan Kundera's novel (1984) becomes a journey of individual transformation in the search for such redemption. Recent revelations that Kundera, at age twenty-one, in 1950, may have compromised his integrity by informing about a potential spy to communist authorities in Czechoslovakia adds to the complexity of ethical issues in his novel and in the film.[4]

In Levinas and the cinema of redemption ethical subjectivity means thinking beyond thought, beyond the self, beyond being. To be ethical requires an interconnection of the human and the infinite. For Levinas ethical subjectivity finds "the glory of the Infinite" inscribed "in the relationship habitually called 'intersubjective'" ("Ethical Subjectivity," 162). Levinas's phrase "the curvature of intersubjective space" metaphorically suggests the asymmetry of ethical subjectivity that insists on the inequality of radical responsibility for the other.[5] For him the subject becomes a "hostage" to the infinite responsibility for the other: "The subject as hostage is a referral to a past that was never present, to an immemorial past, that of its preoriginal affection by another" ("Ethical Subjectivity," 162). *The Unbearable Lightness of Being* can be viewed as a story of going from immersion in the self-obsessive immanence of modern existence to becoming "the subject as hostage" through the recognition of a temporal dimension that supersedes conventional time and goes beyond being to absolute ethical responsibility for the other.

Part of what makes *The Unbearable Lightness of Being* impressive as an important modern ethical drama in the cinema of redemption involves its reexamination of the forces that usually go into the development of ethical being. Thus, *The Unbearable Lightness of Being* studies the interplay of psychological, sexual, and social forces of modernity that participate in the formation of ethical subjectivity. But the film also goes beyond its own original synthesis of classic Freudian and Marxist insights into rethinking the ethics of psychosexual and social structures. It depicts a drama of ethical growth before profound ethical crisis that parallels the Levinasian narrative for achieving ethical subjectivity. The film's trajectory of ethical and political maturation includes a movement from political oppression, Oedipal desire, and castration anxiety to what Tina Chanter in another context describes as an alternative to fetishized sexuality in a situation of abjection.[6]

Much of the exuberance of the narrative and character development in *The Unbearable Lightness of Being* comes from what Kaufman and others clearly intend to depict as the sheer pleasure of the hero's sexual journey. The hero, Tomas, is a Prague brain surgeon played brilliantly by London-born Daniel Day-Lewis. Tomas's sexuality becomes an extended exhibition of Don Juanism that unfolds as continuous self-centered exploitation. The journey of sexual conquests, however, also becomes a quest that takes Tomas and the film into some of the key issues of our times, including considerations of sexuality itself, freedom, art, love, ethics, and power. The film can be studied as a tour of contemporary insight into these subjects from interrelated psychoanalytical, social, political, and feminist perspectives.

Sexuality in the film becomes a Mississippi of adventures as it structures the film's meanderings into episodic events that dramatize the life of the modern mind as well as the body. The Soviet invasion of Czechoslovakia as described in Kundera's novel and in the film provides a special context for the consideration of these issues.

While time in *The Unbearable Lightness of Being* tends to unfold in a coherent narrative linearity, in the film's innovative beginning, the time of apparently unrelated events operates as cinematic time-frames of being that question traditional temporal representation, as in David Wood's theory.[7] The film delays until the end its most powerful expression of transcendence with a challenging, new ethical temporality.

Before detailing this story of the search for redemption in *The Unbearable Lightness of Being*, however, a brief detour can place in somewhat sharper relief the challenges confronting the struggle for ethical subjectivity in modern times. Carol Reed's *The Third Man* (1949) takes a radically different position on ethics, one that would propose the futility and even the intellectual dishonesty of how the cinema of redemption views the world. This film makes a strong counterargument against the Levinasian ethics of the cinema of redemption. *The Third Man* questions the value of the ethical assumptions behind the cinema of redemption for understanding the modern experience.

SHADOW OVER EUROPE:
NIHILISM AND DESPAIR IN *THE THIRD MAN*

In *The Third Man* Carol Reed and the screenwriter Graham Greene provide powerful testimony for a potential case for the inadequacy of the Levinasian argument for ethical responsibility in the world their film depicts. From the point of view of *The Third Man*, the cinema of redemption could be considered an intellectual fraud in proposing the possibility of ethical transcendence in the modern world.

Reed and Greene perspicaciously indicate what the future holds in terms of the nihilism, cynicism, and destruction that will confront the impulse toward redemption in much of the world and cinema after the mid-twentieth century. Their protagonist, Holly Martins, brilliantly played by Joseph Cotten, seeks desperately in his prolonged adolescence to justify his existence and prove his worth as a man, a hero, and a lover by living up to his own romanticized values of the American frontier that he writes about with some seeming success in pulp-fiction westerns.

Reed, Green, and Cotten turn Holly into an emblem of American moralistic bloviating, bullying, and self-centered interference. They make him into a frustrating personification of the danger of blind arrogance based on naive, emotional idealism. In spite of flashes of Holly's cultivated charm, affectionate nature, and good intentions, for much of the film he stands as unaccountable for his silly, irresponsible innocence. His impulsive, self-righteous moral superiority damages those associated with him.

Filmed with a noir sensibility, the action in *The Third Man* often occurs on and around the rubble and ruins of the horrific destruction of postwar Vienna and even descends into the city's sewers. Such filming makes *The Third Man* a literal visualization of the end of Western civilization. The ominously pessimistic tones of Matthew Arnold's poetry, which for generations signaled the beginning of a dehumanizing modernism, acquire bleak validation from the bombed-out sites and criminal *Unterwelt* of the film. *The Third Man* provides a mise-en-scène of a mental condition of nihilism and dramatizes a world that "Hath really neither joy, nor love, nor light, / Nor certitude, nor peace, nor help for pain." Arnold's imagery here in "Dover Beach" of a place "Where ignorant armies clash by night" reinforces his equally powerful description in "The Grand Chartreuse" of the modern soul "Wandering between two worlds, one dead, / The other powerless to be born."[8] Both poems anticipate the world of this film.

Orson Welles, who portrays Harry Lime, the black-market racketeer whose diluted penicillin cripples and kills the children who use it, famously personifies the values of this world of death through his embodiment of a vulgarized Nietzschean philosophy. On the Great Prater Ferris

Wheel in Vienna he gains a lofty perspective on humanity. He trivializes conventional bourgeois morality as being of no greater significance than the Swiss invention of "the cuckoo clock." Opening the door of the carriage he shares with Holly, he gestures toward the people below and asks, "Would you really feel any pity if one of those dots stopped moving forever?" Harry refuses to concede the ethical superiority of Holly's facile idealism or of the British Major Calloway's (Trevor Howard) function as an agent of the law.

Indeed, *The Third Man* to a considerable degree not only glamorizes Harry as a kind of sacrificial superman to be crucified for defiantly mocking conventional middle-class morality. The film also suggests moral equivalence between the postwar role in the world of the United States and other powers, especially the triumphant Soviet communists who share the occupation of Vienna. For individuals and nations everything rests on power, state-sanctioned or criminal violence, and manipulation.

Anticipating the fascination of such contemporary philosophers as Critchley and Tina Chanter for Sophocles' *Antigone*, in *The Third Man* the female lead, Anna (Alida Valli), Harry's girlfriend and the object of Holly's obsessive infatuation, tends to assume the position of ethical authority.[9] According to Rob White, however, the film in its portrayal of Anna, really follows Jean Anouilh's *Antigone* (1944). White proposes that "Anna is like Antigone—in spirit if not degree." Like Anna in *The Third Man*, Anouilh's Antigone, White says, "isolates herself completely, cutting any tie that may compromise her—refusing any entreaty, with an inviolable 'no.'" Similarly, Luce Irigaray says of Antigone, "she has always been drawn, withdrawn, toward one side alone."[10] Anna lives in such complete isolation without any pretense or even the desire for her own or others' redemption. White notes that Anouilh's "version" of Antigone "makes no appeal to religious observance." In her stony indifference to the opinion of others and her cold beauty, Anna epitomizes absolute ethical independence as she follows her own perversely rigid moral direction. Consistent with the film's moral skepticism, *The Third Man*, as White says, declines to offer "a moral reckoning" for its characters and leaves any such judgment to others.[11]

The Third Man encapsulates a certain modernistic sensibility that seemed original to audiences at the time. The self-conscious art of the film, including Robert Krasker's cinematography, intensifies the innovation of its presentation of characters, as well as its philosophy. Such artistry includes the use of canted framing and the provocative zither music of Anton Karas to reinforce the creative intelligence of the film's direction and script.

The ruins of war and the corruption and waste of sewers become external representations of a cultural mind-set that challenges the impulse toward ethical transcendence. The film denies the relevance, perhaps even the possibility, of a transcendent ethical temporality of absolute responsibility for the other. *The Third Man* suggests that such a temporal domain exists only in the illusions and the existential bad faith of self-serving egoists like Holly. In its cynical estimation of human nature and its nihilistic view of the hope for ethical renewal, *The Third Man* dramatizes the challenge to the Levinasian vision of ethical transcendence, a challenge that resides not only in the actual conditions of human existence but also in the direction of ethical thought and in the state of the human heart.

The Third Man presents an alternative ethical view that the cinema of redemption must engage as it continues on the Levinasian ethical adventure. The nihilism, alienation, and disillusionment of this film describe a modern state of mind that the cinema of redemption must confront, especially given the objectives of this cinema to revivify the argument for ethical transcendence. In a variety of ways the modern ethical crisis in *The Third Man* also obtains in the struggle of the films of redemption to dramatize the argument for putting the other before the self. The nature of the engagement with these issues on all levels—psychological, social, intellectual—helps distinguish *The Third Man* from the cinema of redemption.

The Third Man also helps set the stage in terms of film art, as well as ideology, for how several generations of cinema treat issues of ethics, responsibility, and human relationships. The film exemplifies a noir style of characterization and cinematography, vigorous editing, dynamic composition, and modern music to sustain its modernist perspective on human affairs.

THE DEATH OF SPRING: LOVE, ETHICS, AND POLITICS IN THE COLD WAR

The search for ethical transcendence as espoused by Levinas has persisted over many decades in international films that constitute a vigorous cinema of redemption in a modernist context of ethical challenge. The journey toward redemption continues in *The Unbearable Lightness of Being* as the film explores the full range of complexities involved in the quest for transcendence.

Thus, in one of the more perceptive reviews of the film, Pauline Kael suggests in the *New Yorker* that the achievement of "redemption" through love constitutes one of the major objectives of the film.[12] Such redemption for Tomas, the womanizing, charismatic doctor and hero of the film, involves a detailed journey through several transforming stages that include psychological, political, social, and ultimately philosophical change.

Interestingly, as in *The Third Man*, complex love relationships in *The Unbearable Lightness of Being* take place on a world stage of disaster. Just as the destruction and occupation of Vienna help to determine the mood of *The Third Man*, so the invasion of Czechoslovakia by the Soviet Union on August 21, 1968, becomes a defining moment for the characters in *The Unbearable Lightness of Being*. The invasion crushed the short-lived mood of hope during the famous Prague Spring, when music, cinema, intellectual diversity, and dissent briefly emerged and began to thrive. As an anniversary retrospective of the invasion indicates, such developments had led some in the West to hope that there was room for liberal change with expanding civil liberties under Soviet domination, what many thought of as "socialism with a human face."[13] With a stellar international cast and an outstanding international group of people for the writing, cinematography, music, and editing of the film, the American director Philip Kaufman understood the Soviet invasion in democratic cold war terms. Kaufman's overall work generally takes a basic American view of the world—what Kael calls "an exuberant American temperament" ("Take Off Your Clothes," 69)—in such films as *The Wanderers* (1979), about teenage life in the Bronx, and *The Right Stuff* (1983), the popular film about the space program based on Tom Wolfe's book. About Kaufman's American identity and *The Unbearable Lightness of Being*, Terrence Rafferty writes, "We never stop being aware that this movie is an American artist's effort to understand a profoundly European sense of life, because the film is at every moment reminding us of the heartbreaking distances that separate people's imaginations, of the enormous difficulty of seeing the world through another's eyes."[14]

In their commentary on the DVD of *The Unbearable Lightness of Being*, the Americans Kaufman and Walter Murch (the film's editor) and the French screenwriter Jean-Claude Carrière form a kind of united Western front in agreeing on the Soviet action as an invasion by an "ogre" or a "monster." They describe an atmosphere of Cold War fear that persisted while making the film during 1986 and 1987, before the outbreak of Glasnost and the collapse of the Soviet Union and international communism. The producer Saul Zaentz and the entire enterprise were denied access to Prague for filming by the communist Czech regime. The Czechs considered both Kundera's book and the prospective film to be anti-Soviet and anticommunist. *The Unbearable Lightness of Being*, therefore, was shot in Lyon, France, a city resembling Prague in many respects. Actors and other members of the production with ties to family and friends behind the "iron curtain," however, believed their work on the film placed such friends and families in genuine danger. This apparently included the Polish actor Daniel Olbrychski. Olbrychski plays an Interior Ministry official who tries to convince Tomas to acquiesce to the authority of the Czech regime in order to continue his practice as a surgeon. Almost twenty years after the invasion of Prague, danger pervaded the atmosphere surrounding the making of *The Unbearable Lightness of Being*, a film about the historic times of such fear.

IN THE BEGINNING: "A RIBALD FAIRY TALE" AND A CINEMATIC POEM

Interesting commentary has gone into the extraordinary opening scenes of *The Unbearable Lightness of Being*. Consistent with Kaufman's own description of the opening as "a fairy tale," Vincent Canby wrote in the *New York Times* that the film "begins with much promise, as if it were a ribald fairy tale."[15] The beginning of the film can be compared to the imaginative opening of Martin Scorsese's *Raging Bull* (1980), a remarkable work that also makes redemption a major theme. In the Scorsese film, redemption concerns a genuinely unattractive figure, the middleweight boxing champion Jake LaMotta.[16] Both films use suggestive abstraction in their opening scenes. In *Raging Bull* Scorsese concentrates on a smoky, artistic rendering of a lone boxer in an imaginary ring shadowboxing to the beautiful sounds of orchestral music from Pietro Mascagni's great opera *Cavalleria Rusticana* (1890) about rustic life in Sicily, while film credits flash on the screen. Scorsese's framing and scenic construction suggest an inner mental mood and a situation of lonely isolation rather than a photographic representation of actual boxing. In addition, to balance the artistic abstraction of this opening, Scorsese uses titles that establish some temporal linearity and coherence in the organization of the narrative and the history of events.

Kaufman develops this kind of artistic, abstract beginning for *The Unbearable Lightness of Being* with a series of visual narratives without a conventional, continuous, causal narrative story line. Relying heavily on the music of the Czech composer Leos Janacek, among others, Kaufman and his collaborators offer this opening as a prologue to the film, a kind of film-within-a-film. The opening becomes a synecdoche in an abstract, suggestive form of *The Unbearable Lightness of Being* in its 171-minute entirety. The initial sequence of shots condenses and foreshadows the whole film.

Carrière, the French writer who collaborated with Kaufman on the screenplay, which received an Academy Award nomination, describes on the DVD the film's opening as a "musical symphony" that required titles because of the highly intellectual nature of the film's source. Carrière (who also shared screenplay credit with Luis Buñuel for *Belle de Jour* [1967] and *The Discreet Charm of the Bourgeoisie* [1972]) thinks of the music in *The Unbearable Lightness of Being* as displacing the authorial voice of Kundera in the novel. Along with the film's editor, Walter Murch, Carrière and Kaufman note on the DVD that after the opening sequence the film departs from the nonlinear narrative structure of the novel to tell the story in conventionally ordered narrative.

Both Carrière's and Kaufman's respective descriptions "musical symphony" and "fairy tale" for the beginning of *The Unbearable Lightness of Being* understate somewhat the significance of the provocative visual images in creating an opening sequence of intelligent aesthetic power. Scorsese's sense of film as a kind of visual opera actually comes closer to describing the uniqueness of the opening of Kaufman's film. Scorsese describes the movie camera in general as working with and becoming part of the music, as though the two kinds of rhythm and temporality enmesh to create something thoroughly original: "Camera movement is dance, lighting is painting. Camera movement is also a lot like painting—and like music. I feel it's always a combination of lighting, camera movement, the use of music and the impact of the actors on the screen."[17]

Scorsese's words aptly describe the cinematography, editing, writing, and direction of the opening of Kaufman's film. Even more than Kundera's philosophical peregrinations and the nonlinear structure of his novel, the innovatively abstract, nonlinear form of the opening of the film compel the use of written titles or texts to inject greater coherence into the situation. When the film assumes a more linear, traditional narrative structure, the need for such titles ends.

Accordingly, the extended opening sequence of shots in *The Unbearable Lightness of Being* works as a kind of cinematic poem of visual images set to music. The creative force of these shots establishes the tone for the whole film, the remainder of which constitutes an extremely intelligent, sophisticated development of the themes set forth in this opening. The sequence of scenes that Kaufman and company offer in a nonlinear narrative form unleashes a semiotic hailstorm of multidimensional, audiovisual signs that convey complex possibilities. Thus, in an intellectually challenging, critically complicated analysis of the film as a study of film adaptation, Patrick Cattrysse writes that "the search for semiotic devices" in the film "often leads to a complex set of norms and models."[18]

Significantly, what Cattrysse calls this array of "semiotic devices" in the opening of the film dramatically challenges immediate understanding. Instead, the opening shots provoke questions that charge the critical imagination. Thus, the opening credits for the film first appear on an unfamiliar brownish, rough surface that in itself challenges description. It could be a wall, a door or panel with a square handle, a work of art, or just a rough, uneven surface. The laughter of one woman or perhaps more can be heard, deepening the sense of visual obstruction created by the surface. Something worth laughing about or giggling about must be occurring behind or near the surface. Without ever quite clarifying the nature of this surface, the film then cuts to the first of several titles or texts on a black background. Even after this text and the subsequent titles appear, and after seeing and hearing the brief stories in this opening sequence of scenes, the significance of the characters in the thrust of the fragmented narrative remains unclear. The title reads: *"In Prague, in 1968, there lived a young doctor named Tomas . . . "*

A SEXUAL ODYSSEY: THE BODY, THE SELF, AND THE OTHER

That simplicity of the opening language on the screen reflects the characterization by Kaufman and others of the story as a kind of fairy tale. The playful, teasing music of Leos Janacek's *Fairy Tale: Third Movement* fittingly reinforces this mood. As Cattrysse notes, "It is a cheerful violin concerto that accompanies the scenes about Tomas's sexual adventures" (228). The next cut begins to confirm the connection between the music and sexuality, indicating that the fairy tale will have something of a bawdy quality to it. The camera focuses on hands lighting a wooden match and then tilts up to a close-up of an attractive woman lighting a cigarette. The camera pulls back and Daniel Day-Lewis, Tomas the doctor, enters the dressing or locker room of a hospital after apparently performing some exhausting surgery. The woman looks up and then away as he tosses a towel in a bin and sits down and covers his face with another.

The woman gets up and walks offscreen and Tomas whispers through the towel, "Take off your clothes!" These words become a kind of joking, sexual motif throughout the film, a male fairy tale of sexual conquest. Women indeed will invariably take off their clothes for him. This woman, who wears a cap that suggests she is a nurse or an assistant to Tomas, turns and says with surprise, "What?" Tomas repeats: "I said take off your clothes." After she teasingly says, "But you saw everything, last night," the camera cuts to a shot from an adjoining room. Two other doctors and a patient, who actually rises up from a sick bed, can see Tomas and the woman through a frosty glass partition. Their excited voyeurism indicates that Tomas acts out their collective fairy tale as the woman complies with Tomas's request to be naked, but, she says, "only for three seconds." She unbuttons her blouse, revealing her breasts to Tomas. One doctor mutters, "Bastard," and wonders, "How does he do it?" After a low-angle shot of the woman, who tauntingly says, "One, Two, Three," the film cuts to a second title on a black surface.

The new title reads, "*But the woman who understood him best was Sabina...*," and the film prepares to introduce the second of the three major figures in the film. At this point we should recall that Kaufman and his collaborators also consider the opening of the film as the beginning of an "odyssey" for Tomas. The opening scene provocatively proposes that sexuality, the body, voyeurism, and pleasure will constitute important elements of this odyssey. The sexual odyssey for Tomas and the viewer, then, begins immediately and no doubt involves considerable sexual adventurism. This excursion also helps provide the structure for the film's narrative and character development. Sexuality becomes part of the film's serious articulation of issues of contemporary life. The scene that introduces Sabina also deepens the discussion of sexuality through the insinuation of important visual and verbal signifiers. The brief scene resonates with meanings that will continue to pertain throughout the rest of the film.

After the title about Sabina the camera cuts to a close-up of Swedish actress Lena Olin, who plays Sabina, the thoroughly independent artist and solitary spirit who also happens to be Tomas's primary lover and best friend. Lying on her back, she holds a key signifier, a Chaplin-style bowler hat, her hat, with her right hand so that it covers the right side of her lovely face. In slight shadow, the left side of her face glistens and her left eye stares pensively back at the camera. She raises the hat, bathing her face in light, and begins to lower the hat toward Tomas whose head rests on her chest. They clearly are relaxing after making love. It is a beautiful two-shot that includes his impressive chest and pecs and the soft features of her face with the bowler hat now between them. She then proceeds to feed him some important lines that will grow in significance as the film develops. In answer to her questions he admits that he never stays overnight at a woman's place and finds an excuse to be left alone if a woman visits him. She then asks, "Are you afraid of women, doctor?" and he tellingly responds, "Of course!" Given their situation and their obvious intimate affection for each other, Tomas's answer makes her laugh. The scene oozes with warmth, comfort, and sexuality. The joy and freedom of their lovemaking that concludes the scene show how much Tomas indeed loves women, sex, and especially Sabina.

The bowler hat, however, remains a crucial element in the scene and relates to Tomas's simple "Of course!" about fearing women. In both the novel and the film the hat plays an important role, becoming a major stimulant in their very active and acrobatic sex life. In a later scene, after Tomas and Sabina have been separated, Tomas meets up with her in Geneva. She says that she has met the best man of her life, Franz (Derek De Lint), a highly rational, conventional, liberal professor in Geneva who considers the hat distracting but finds joy in participating vicariously in "The Grand March" of the great causes of history. In fact, Franz had been with Sabina just before Tomas's arrival and had put the hat aside. So Sabina confesses to Tomas that only one thing troubles her about Franz. She says, "He doesn't like my hat." Tomas says emotionally, "Your hat! Your hat makes me want to cry, Sabina." Sabina puts the hat on and boldly looks at him, making his intended departure from the apartment to return to his new wife, Tereza (Juliette Binoche), impossible.

So Tomas clearly both loves and fears women, and the hat fetish represents his relationship to all women, at least until he meets Tereza. This ambivalence suggests the importance not just of his love for women but how he loves them in a way that requires distance. In his discussion of the work of the fetish, Freud in *Three Essays in the Theory of Sexuality* (1905) says the fetish occurs when "the normal sexual object is replaced by another which bears some relation to it, but is entirely unsuited to serve the normal sexual aim." What Freud calls "a fetishistic condition attached to the sexual object" helps to describe the complex mixture of compulsive attraction and hidden fear in Tomas's relationships with women.[19]

Also discussing the fetish and men's fear of difference, Chanter writes, "The fetish is produced in an attempt to ward off the threat that this difference presents, and to rein in its significance not by canceling it out, but by allowing it to co-exist: I know that women are castrated, but by producing the fetish I can deny it" (Chanter, *The Picture of Abjection*, 12). Fetishes function, in Chanter's terms, as "coping mechanisms" that help explain the "scopophilic practices of voyeurism and fetishism" of the opening scenes of *The Unbearable Lightness of Being* (ibid., 173–74). Similarly, Irigaray discusses the fetishization that Sabina dramatizes as a kind of encirclement that women experience because "woman cannot mime, pretend, any relation to *her own* sex organ(s)" as a result of being "cut off from any access to idea, ideality, specula(riza)tion, and indeed a certain organic 'reality.'" She says that given "the monopoly on value" of the male organ, woman must prove "particularly good at acting 'as if' she had it, at 'making believe' she has it." Irigaray argues that this situation of fetishization compels women to insist on securing "an increase in her price" and to disguise her lack through various strategies of deception.[20]

The defense against a fetishizing system of dissimulation that emotionally invests in, sexualizes, and commodifies objects would be, for Chanter, an alternative system of abjection that discards on a basis of misplaced disgust, beginning most usually, with bodily functions and the separation from the mother. She describes a "logic of abjection" and ponders, "How might abjection refigure the univocal meaning enshrined in the trope of fetishism?" (*The Picture of Abjection*, 11–12). She writes, "A dynamic is set up whereby new forms of fetishization spawn new subjects who are placed in relation to abjection, new dejects" (10). So creative abjection counters fetishization.

Armed with her natural beauty, intelligence, brilliant smile, athletic agility, and joy, Lena Olin as Sabina adds the bowler hat and the engineering of her artfully constructed underwear to her strategy for countering Tomas's fetishizing with her penchant for abjection. She appreciates Tomas's fetishizing as a form of distancing that safeguards her freedom, although such freedom comes at a cost. On occasion, her facial expressions suggest conflicting tensions between suffocating love and lonely isolation. Conflicted herself, Sabina responds creatively to his fetishizing with her abject reformulation of the body. As an artist Sabina goes through phases of artistic expression, including one important form that Terrence Rafferty leaves out. Rafferty explains: "In Prague, her paintings are elegant, suggestive abstractions with an ominous sexuality reminiscent of Georgia O'Keeffe. In Geneva, her art is constructed of dagger-like shards of mirrors: her apartment/studio is like an Expressionist changing room, in which a visitor, undressing, is constantly surrounded by splintery images of himself. In California, Sabina spray-paints seascapes for elderly buyers: the paintings are blandly serene, as if the sea (as in Baudelaire) has become her mirror but she doesn't quite see herself in it" (Rafferty, "Llastooks," 208).

Even given this creative versatility that Rafferty describes, however, Sabina, it could be argued, also works as an artist of sex and the body. At least until her last destination in California, whatever material she works in and whatever form her art takes, she also remains committed to rethinking and reshaping the body, partly in response to male fetishization, especially Tomas's. Mirrors in the lovemaking scenes with Tomas, including their first scene, become standard equipment for what Chanter calls "the corporeal mapping of the body." In Sabina's fusion of art and sex, "the process of abjection opens up the imaginary terrain of mapping the body" with the reconstruction of body images in mirrors (Chanter, *The Picture of Abjection*, 51, 38).

At the end of the initial scene between Tomas and Sabina the vigor of their return to lovemaking indicates the pleasure they find in each other. The thrust of his body as he joins her, the tightening and constriction of her extended legs around him, and their sounds of pleasure demonstrate and celebrate their lovemaking. Yet the reflection of their image in the mirror clearly also plays an important part in their relationship. Sabina's use of mirrors in her art and in her life, especially the sexual part of her life, suggests a response to the fetishization of women and the body. For Sabina sexuality and art come together in the world of the mirror. The mirror provides the scene to gain creative control of her environment. Sabina seeks in the mirror the images and space for her art and her identity. She searches for her place not only with men but also with women, as a photo-shooting scene with Tereza suggests. The proliferation of sexual mirror images reinforces what Irigaray calls woman's "multifaceted" sexuality, engendering for Sabina a sense of empowerment and the opportunity to choose. Irigaray writes, "For the sex of woman is not one. And, as jouissance bursts out in each of these/her 'parts,' so all of them can mirror her in dazzling multifaceted difference."

FIGURE 4.1. Daniel Day-Lewis and Lena Olin in *The Unbearable Lightness of Being* (1988)

Thus, Rafferty's description of one of Sabina's art forms as "dagger-like shards of mirrors" resonates with Irigaray's discussion of feminine sexuality when she says "this protean pleasure can be broken down into shards, pieces of a mirror" (Irigaray, *Speculum of the Other Woman*, 239).

Moreover, Tomas shares Sabina's fascination with the mirror. In the opening scene Tomas pushes some furniture aside so that they will be able to see their reflection as they make love. In other scenes he sets up and adjusts multiple mirrors that complicate the visual order of their bodies and that prove as interesting to him as to her.

Tomas's answer to a question from Sabina in another love scene perhaps helps to explain the meaning of his shared fascination for the mirror image. Sabina asks, "Are you searching for pleasure? Or is every woman a new land whose secrets you want to discover?" One possible answer to that provocative question could be that he appreciates women as a reflection of himself and of his self-centered imagination. For Tomas the mirror image of himself with Sabina becomes a space of representation of sameness, of sublimated sexual body power, of the assertion of male domination in a sexually charged environment that contains the potential for greater ego inflation. The mirror image for some can restore threatened phallic power.

Accordingly, Irigaray's use of the mirror metaphor includes the drama of male domination of culture and vision and pertains to Tomas in his mirror scenes with Sabina. Irigaray writes, "For relations among subjects have always had recourse, explicitly or more often implicitly, to the *flat mirror*, that is, to what privileges the relation of man to his fellow man. A flat mirror has always already subtended and traversed speculation."[21] Irigaray elaborates on the male control of the mirror and woman as the domination of "the one": "The other must therefore serve to mirror the one, reduplicating what man is assumed to know already as the place of (his) production. 'She' must be only the path, the method, the theory, the *mirror*, which leads back, by a process of repetition, to the recognition of (his) origin for the 'subject'" (*Speculum of the Other Woman*, 239).

Irigaray's notion of the male in the exploitive flat mirror that leaves no room for difference or the other captures Tomas's self-obsession and immanent way of being. It also indicates the male compulsion for domination that impels the drive in a figure like Sabina for escape and freedom through her art. Sabina must repel the male's sterile flat mirror of sameness for, as Irigaray says, "the curves of the mirror," a different kind of "living mirror" that finds "in the depths of the abyss of the 'soul' a mirror" that waits for "her reflection and her light" (*Speculum of the Other Woman*, 238, 197). In contrast to the flat mirror, the curves of the mirror suggest multiplicity and intersubjectivity.

In fairness to Tomas, he certainly fixates on and enters the mirror, so to speak, for pleasure seeking but also as part of his own soul seeking. The exploration of the physical and symbolic new land of every woman becomes part of the journey of self-discovery. For most of the film women facilitate that journey. The film clearly focuses primarily on his needs, placing secondary importance on the women's journeys of discovery. Even so, the film strives throughout to render the perspectives of Sabina and Tereza in pointed detail.

As the focus of the film and what used to be called the central consciousness, Tomas can be seen to move from a situation of immanence, an obsession with his own being, to one of ethical transcendence and alterity. In this journey, rethinking embodiment becomes key to his maturation. Tomas ultimately experiences what Jacques Derrida terms "transcendence in immanence."[22] In the end he learns to achieve what Ziarek calls "the ethical significance of the sexed body." He bridges, as Ziarek says, the "separation of ethical responsibility from the sensible life," thereby enjoying one of Levinas's later breakthroughs in *Otherwise Than Being* by departing "from his earlier insistence in *Totality and Infinity* that the ethical experience transcends sensible life."[23]

From Ziarek's feminist Levinasian perspective Tomas's obsession with sex and his Lacanian mirror image could instigate rather than impede the development for him of an ethics of the body. By attending to the body and the flesh in his later work, Levinas, Ziarek says, suggests that the body becomes a condition of the ethical relation to the other. Thus, Ziarek argues that "perhaps the most original contribution of Levinas's work to the contemporary debates on the body lies in the fact that it enables the elaboration of the ethical significance of flesh and, by extension, opens a possibility of an ethics of sex" (Ziarek, *An Ethics of Dissensus*, 54). Tomas, especially as he matures in the film, probably could serve as a convincing model for Ziarek's Levinasian notion that "an ethical body is, in other words, a passionate body." She writes, "For Levinas, carnality and passion are in fact the only analogues capable of conveying the anteriority of responsibility to freedom" (57).

In his sexualized journey toward what ultimately will become a position of ethical responsibility, Tomas moves over terrain that could be a setting for the dramatization of Levinasian theory, as described by Ziarek and Irigaray, as an "oscillation between sublimation and the exclusion of eros from ethics." According to Ziarek, the "desexualization of Eros" through a "specific form of sublimation" makes imagining "an ethics of sexuality" difficult for women while elevating men: "Levinas's male lover eventually turns toward the transcendent God while the woman is plunged back into the abyss of the nonhuman," meaning sexuality and the body to the point of irrationality through the "nonsublimated form of eros represented by feminine sexuality" (Ziarek, *An Ethics of Dissensus*, 59). Although Tomas clearly does not become a transcendent God, his journey toward ethical responsibility for the other does occur through much of the film at a great emotional and personal cost to the women closest to him—his lover, Sabina, and his wife, Tereza—both of whom undergo their own journeys of growth and transformation.

For Sabina the mirror image contains at least the potential for becoming a scene of resistance for revisioning the world. Such revisioning also occurs, however, outside of mirrors, with photography as an instrument that can be employed to feminize the space between her and Tereza, who will become Tomas's wife. Thus, in one scene, after asking Sabina to help educate Tereza about photography, art, and seeing, Tomas, the solitary male and sudden outsider of the group, becomes visibly shaken by his irrelevance to the new situation of the female alliance. His male authority collapses so that even a fetishized sock of his that testifies to a previous time with Sabina hangs in mock ridicule of him.

In another scene of vision and representation between the two women in Geneva, the camera becomes an extension of envisioning the naked female body as a means for breaking the phallic order of looking and authority. When the two women are interrupted by the entrance of Franz, Sabina's new lover, after they have been photographing each other in the nude, Sabina says that Tereza comes from Prague, "another crazy Czech." Such craziness, however, really constitutes a breaking down of the male fetishized world that the camera usually projects, empowers, and institutes. In the women's hands the camera enlists gender to reimagine the powerful potential of the female body.

Thus, for Sabina, the artist of the remapping of the body, art means in part responding to the fetishized structuring of male control by manipulating it with a Chaplinesque bowler hat and erotic undergarments or discarding such control in a process of abjection that can include escape from men. For both Tomas and Sabina, however, the enclosed circle of sameness and immanent being of their mirrors ultimately will crack so as to require a negotiation with the rest of the world that both will find difficult.

A premonition of such a breakthrough of disruption and reimagining occurs in the very brief scene between Tomas and Sabina early in the film. At one moment in this scene, the camera reveals a vision of Sabina that easily could be missed at the regular speed of projection and viewing. Lying with Tomas, Sabina rests behind him, but as they move, her beautiful face fully emerges from behind his shoulder, her deep, rich, dark hair providing a kind of natural background for her. The graceful balance of light and shadow on her face adds to the intensity of her expression. The shot turns this powerful, provocative, sexually aggressive woman into a figure of ambiguity, mystery, and introspection.

That portrait of Sabina in this shot matches her later description of herself as a girl who found it impossible to march in step with other communist children during forced exercises. The shot also suggests the face of a woman with the depth of character and strength of a natural rebel who turns the word *kitsch* into a fighting word. As suggested by a comment she utters to Tomas, the famous word *kitsch* becomes Sabina's way of defining herself and her battle with the world.

In this same scene, when Tomas confesses that he refuses to spend the whole night with a woman even after lovemaking, Sabina admits how much she likes him. She says, "You are the opposite of kitsch. In the kingdom of kitsch, you are a monster." With those words she laughingly opens herself to him as he says, "What am I—a monster?" in something like a fake, fairy tale monster growl.

In his novel Kundera explains kitsch in detail and how it relates to shit. He argues that although "'Kitsch' is a German word born in the middle of the sentimental nineteenth century," the origins of its meaning go back centuries to philosophical and theological debates about God, the human body, and creation.[24] In a world created by God, he maintains, human defecation becomes a problem: "You can't claim that shit is immoral, after all! The objection to shit is a metaphysical one. The daily defecation session is daily proof of the unacceptability of Creation" (248). Kundera's logic is that if shit remains unacceptable in human relations, "then we are created in an unacceptable manner." He writes, "It follows, then, that the aesthetic ideal of the categorical agreement with being is a world in which shit is denied and everyone acts as though it did not exist. This aesthetic ideal is called *kitsch*" (248). Kundera continues that "repeated use" of the word "has obliterated its original metaphysical meaning." He writes that "kitsch is the absolute denial of shit, in both the literal and the figurative senses of the word; kitsch excludes everything from its purview which is essentially unacceptable in human existence" (248).

Thus, in the film Tomas stands as a hero for Sabina because he epitomizes the battle with this "aesthetic ideal" of kitsch that refuses to recognize or deal with anything deemed disturbing. Also, to sustain such resistance to unsettling difference, kitsch must cultivate smug, self-serving complacency about maintaining the current state of conditions. The sentimental illusions that nourish kitsch are anathema to both Tomas and Sabina. Kundera succinctly describes this attitude:

Kitsch causes two tears to flow in quick succession. The first tear says: How nice to see children running on the grass!

The second tear says: How nice to be moved, together with all mankind, by children running on the grass!

It is the second tear that makes kitsch kitsch.

The brotherhood of man on earth will be possible only on a base of kitsch. (*The Unbearable Lightness of Being*, 251)

For Sabina, rebellion against kitsch becomes a crucial element in her life. Kundera says that as a Czech living under Soviet rule, "Sabina's initial inner revolt against Communism was aesthetic rather than ethical in character" (248). The universality of kitsch, however, crosses boundaries, cultures, and ideologies. So Kundera writes that

> whenever a single political movement corners power, we find ourselves in the realm of *totalitarian kitsch.*
>
> When I say "totalitarian," what I mean is that everything that infringes on kitsch must be banished for life: every display of individualism (because a deviation from the collective is a spit in the eye of the smiling brotherhood); . . . every doubt . . . all irony . . . (252)

In the film Sabina's revolt against totalitarian kitsch remains largely aesthetic and takes her from Prague to Geneva and finally to northern California. In Prague she and Tomas encounter Soviet-style totalitarian kitsch of varying degrees of repression. For example, during a gathering in a dance hall that becomes an occasion to celebrate the first publication of Tereza's photographs of Prague during the high-spirited days of the Prague Spring of 1968, partying communist officials stifle the music and the dancing. They resist the new freedom of the Beatles, jazz, and rock and roll, which ultimately overcome their lugubrious nationalistic dirges.

One of Sabina's most interesting encounters with oppressive kitsch occurs, however, in Geneva after she has fled from the Soviet invasion and first meets Franz. They go to an expensive, fashionable restaurant, where she becomes offended by the piped in, insipid music and artificial flowers. The waiter and manager are pale, lifeless, dehumanized figures in the artificial setting.

This scene in the restaurant becomes the one place in the film where Sabina uses the word *shit* in the general sense that Kundera uses it in his book. In this scene she becomes the voice of Kundera in the fight against kitsch. Sabina rails against the music that is "noise" and sounds like "dirty water." She hates the plastic flowers that are placed in real water. She sees in the restaurant the continuation and extension of the "uglification of the world" as evidenced by the buildings outside. Beauty only exists now where its "persecutors" have overlooked it. She says it has become a "planetary process." When told that the customers like the music, she answers, "How can they eat food and listen to shit." Here the word basically has the same meaning that Kundera gives it but with a nuanced connotation and perhaps could be put in quotation marks. For the film and a popular audience, she means "shit" in the sense of manufactured artificiality and waste. In this situation the basic meaning of *shit* remains and implies living, even thriving, with the refusal to recognize the ontology and the implications of the unacceptable.

Prague and Geneva force confrontation for Sabina with the great difficulty of expressing aesthetic freedom without also articulating a program of politics and ethics. Outside of possibly achieving her own personal independence as a woman and artist in northern California, Sabina never quite creates or seems to live a philosophy of life that enables the aesthetic to carry or incorporate the ethical and the political. In her escape to California she continues her battle against kitsch in her work and lifestyle but not, as far as we can tell, in her public and intellectual life. She succeeds with her own art of abjection that resists being forced into a condition of dependence. Indeed, in her initial meeting with Franz in Geneva, after they hastily leave a gathering of Czech exiles, she exclaims how she hates politics and the fighting and the bitterness that it involves.

Tomas, as Sabina's "monster" Golem, who in legend and myth was to protect Prague, also engages in the battle against kitsch but more directly confronts issues of politics and ethics. Intellectual and analytical, Tomas studies Sophocles' *Oedipus* for a model of the interaction between politics and ethics. At the previously discussed gathering in a dance hall with Tomas and his circle of intimate friends and colleagues that includes Sabina and Tereza, soon to be his wife, Tomas expatiates on the meaning of Oedipus. Not far from Tomas's group, the partying communist comrades wine and dine at their own separate elevated table. Interestingly, the scene opens with a shot of a poster at the dance hall that shows the Golem as a theme for the evening.

As Tomas talks, Sabina happily listens to him pontificate on how the meaning of Oedipus relates to the present political situation as represented by the smug, self-satisfied party bureaucrats in their gluttony at their nearby table. Tomas and his friends all agree that the leaders of the Soviet oppression of the East were "scoundrels." Tomas, a brain surgeon, then proceeds with a different form of brain examination as he tries to explore the inner depths of the psyche to understand the nature of such evil. To help bring light to such exploration of the psyche, Tomas notes how in Oedipus the shame of his crimes of "unknowingly" sleeping with his mother, killing his father, and causing the infliction of plagues on the people was so great that he blinded himself. He could not stand to look on what he had done. In contrast, Tomas and his friends say, the communist scoundrels not only refuse to accept responsibility for their monstrous crimes against humanity, but they proclaim their own innocence and "stayed in power." But, Sabina notes, "They should have plucked their eyes out."

Tomas's interpretation of the play emphasizes the search for ethical authority as opposed to the sexual and incestuous aspect of the story. He seems in search of his own internal moral compass. Laughing with his friends, he claims, "All I'm saying is that morality has changed since Oedipus." He really seeks a means for understanding the contemporary ethical crisis and his place in it. He sees the need for establishing some mechanism for constructing a system of meaningful values. His focus on Oedipus indicates his wish for personal and social moral authority. Characteristically, through the Oedipus myth he seeks both the power and knowledge of moral truth. Interestingly, his lack of attention to the sexual aspect of the Oedipus theory, which Sabina finds perversely entertaining, perhaps provides some insight into his own sexual ambivalence. His view may go back to the allusion to his fear of women, as he had previously expressed to Sabina, and his overcompensation for his hidden insecurity by compulsively adding to his string of sexual conquests.

Ironically, by the end of *The Unbearable Lightness of Being* it becomes clearer that Tomas's search into interior psychic spaces constitutes an early phase of a journey that must go beyond the limits of his own subjectivity. Since his sexually compulsive behavior manifests deeper psychological trauma, the direction of redemption for him begins with interiority but must extend to what Levinas terms the "exteriority" of transcendence in the concern for the other. His search must involve not just exploration for secret truths in the inner reaches of the deeply layered human mind or in his cultivated self-obsession with narcissistic mirror images but in a reconsideration of relationships that place absolute priority on the other.

OEDIPUS OR THE OTHER: FREUD AND LEVINAS

Early in his relationship with Tereza, Tomas, like Oedipus, finds himself at a distressing crossroads in his life, one that he does not quite understand until literally the very end of his journey. Given the surprising depth of his devotion to Tereza, which leads him to totally uncharacteristic feelings for her of possessive jealousy, he must decide about giving up his philandering ways to be faithful to the woman he fears losing and therefore marries. He must control his sexually predatory nature and renounce his wish for immediate sexual gratification to build a traditional relationship of fidelity to one woman. This rather mundane issue has deeper implications in the film, however, than just the development of character and narrative.

Tomas's position with Tereza places him between two conflicting possibilities about sexuality, the body, the feminine, ethics, and politics. One possibility entails a classic Oedipal journey, as delineated by Freud, of sublimation, masculine identity, the internalization of guilt, the strengthening of the individual superego, and the concomitant suppression of the maternal and the feminine. The other possibility involves a more unconventional path toward a Levinasian argument of love that commits to transcendence, alterity, and responsibility to the other. Both possibilities would require recognition of the feminine to overcome the sexism that has been the focus of much criticism of both Freud and Levinas over the years. On the second path of alterity and the other, transcendence supersedes immanence. The self operates through sacrifice to the other. The Levinasian path requires countering egoism with a new ethical phenomenology that demands rethinking the relationship of the individual self to the other. It requires rethinking time and death based on a greater love for the other.

The classic metaphor of an internal journey into the psyche in the form of a reevaluation of one's life still pertains to Tomas in *The Unbearable Lightness of Being*. For much of the film Tomas fails to appreciate that his search for meaningful ethical and moral structures also must involve such an internal journey for himself that would require a reconsideration of his way of loving and being in the world, most especially including the aggressive narcissism of his sexuality.

Tomas starts that internal journey to a new understanding of the importance of the relationship to the other without realizing it during a trip, an external journey that at first seems perfectly ordinary to him. Both the internal and external journeys take us back to the sequence of scenes that starts Kaufman's film. So returning to the opening sequence of scenes for *The Unbearable Lightness of Being*, the third and final title says, "*Tomas was sent to a spa town to perform an operation.*" The film then cuts to Tomas driving in the country. He wears sunglasses that help give him the lean, gaunt, gangster look of a hustler, suggesting a figure reminiscent of Jean Paul Belmondo. Later, Tomas explains that a colleague had an accident that resulted in his assignment to the country.

At first the spa scene seems simply quaint and oddly charming in its Old World, Eastern European ambience. Soon, however, it becomes a scene for continuing the focus on the body that began with the scenes with Sabina and the hospital episode. At the spa a stream of people appears in a variety of therapeutic and recreational activities. Their naked flesh draws attention to the generally poor condition of their bodies. Illustrating bodies in various stages of deterioration, the film thus addresses the paradox of the ephemeral body as the necessary condition for ethics. The fragile body provides the foundation for the mind and spirit. Tomas, the brilliant surgeon, perceives his limits.

And then Tereza happens. As she dives into the spa pool, Tomas observes her, obviously intrigued by her as a hint of something different, an unspoiled beginning. The strength and vitality of her body as she swims contrast radically with the questionable health and well-being of others at the spa. The musical shift to a soft, sentimental piano accompaniment helps to introduce her and to create a change of mood from playfulness to a more serious feeling of longing. The music contrasts with the initial violin concerto of the scene and could be considered her theme. Tereza's innocence, total lack of pretense or guile, modesty, and shyness all contrast radically with Sabina. The women appear to be dramatic opposites.

The book Tereza reads while working at the spa's restaurant, Tolstoy's *Anna Karenina*, anticipates the film's conclusion when Tomas and Tereza settle on a farm with their pet dog, dubbed Karenin, and live a simple agrarian life that Tolstoy advocated. In contrast, the book Tomas reads and keeps at his bedside is Sophocles' *Oedipus*. At this point Tomas epitomizes a phallic, patriarchal assertion of male authority and justice that contrasts with the strategy of abjection that Sabina and Tereza tend to employ.

When Tereza arrives unexpectedly from the spa at Tomas's Prague apartment, she ends up staying overnight with him, immediately breaking one of his prime rules about women. Apparently her innocence, spontaneity, and energy prove irresistible. When Tomas awakens to go to the hospital, she remains asleep, snuggled warmly against him and clutching his hand like a child. He replaces his hand in her hand with his copy of Oedipus in order not to disturb her sleep. A charming, innocent gesture of affection, this action has deeper connotations. The Oedipus story, with its manifest and latent meanings of guilt, repression, and difficult male and female maturation, has become domesticated and softened with Tomas's caring gesture. The book becomes a virtual caress. As we have seen, Diane Perpich considers the

Levinasian caress as described in his early writings "as an incessant recommencement of the movement toward the other" and the suggestion of a "perfect model of transcendence."[25] This move by Tomas offers a first intimation in the film of his potential for seeking a relationship that can go beyond the immediate immanence of the self. Here he begins a process of breaking the burden of his own being.

Indeed, much of the rest of the film, especially in regard to Tomas's relationship to Tereza, will involve Tomas's maturation in light of this initial Levinasian caress. Levinas learns, Perpich says, that the erotic invariably relapses into immanence and therefore necessitates a broader program for transcendence and alterity. So like Levinas, as Perpich understands him, Tomas must take a path that includes but goes beyond the caress and eros. Tomas synthesizes the differences between Ziarek and Perpich on the relationship in Levinas of sexuality and embodiment to transcendence. Ziarek concentrates on the importance to ethics of the sexed body, a body that makes ethics possible. The flesh, the senses of the body, and ethics remain fused for her. In contrast, Perpich proposes a movement in Levinas from the caress and the body to an emphasis on language.[26] Tomas, of course, could never be accused of abandoning his passion for sex and the body for language, but he does find the words as he grows to suggest the achievement of a new relationship of love and responsibility to the other.

Before such achievement, however, Tomas asks Sabina to help Tereza find work in Prague, since she lacks the experience and sophistication to find such work on her own. He tells Sabina that Tereza is not "qualified for anything." Tereza, therefore, operates as a kind of clean slate that will see and do things for the first time. Rather than a mirror image, she becomes an open lens, a living camera eye that catches and records everything around her. Fittingly, the camera becomes her instrument for her education and her interaction with the world. Her character develops with her art.

The camera also becomes a vehicle for Tereza to gain a measure of her own independence. As she acquires skill with the camera, she gains a degree of artistic credibility. Significantly, the major events in her life that relate to the camera occur independently of the influence Tomas has on her. The first event concerning photography occurs after her initial introduction to the camera and the photographic image by Sabina when the two women bond in a way that excludes Tomas. In this period of her work she gains technical proficiency, and Kaufman quite brilliantly shows the evidence of her progress by alternating her black-and-white photographs of Prague with the film in color. Her work exemplifies the "street photography" movement of the time. The alternation between black-and-white still photographs and the moving images in color occurs with a musical background of the Prague Spring and provides a vital if brief portrait of the excitement of the people in their moment of freedom before the Soviet invasion.

Another advance in her work occurs when Tereza uses her camera to document the invasion. This sequence in the film becomes a living work of art in the form of documentary filming, a significant cinematic achievement for Kaufman and his collaborators. Kaufman brilliantly integrates Tomas and Tereza into actual documentary footage of the invasion that was shot by many photographers and filmmakers in Prague at the time. Many of these people worked and studied with Czech filmmakers Jan Nemec and Josef Skvorecky, who eventually made their own film of the event, *Oratorio for Prague* (1968).[27] In *The Unbearable Lightness of Being* this sequence becomes a film-within-a-film, an original documentary narrative told through dynamic visual editing and marvelous musical accompaniment. The editors mix close-ups, establishing shots, and dramatic sequences to reenact this historical event. Using her camera as a weapon for visual truth, Tereza becomes a freedom fighter during this sequence while Tomas functions mainly as an observer. At the end she suffers defeat with the rest of the Czech people.

The documentary sequence with Tereza also serves as a lesson about the camera and modern surveillance. Freedom fighters film the event to have the footage taken out of the country while communist agents spy on the filmmakers. At the end the secret police use photographs of photographers that can be used for prosecution and persecution. Kaufman cuts to a close-up of a mouthy, fleshy communist official asking, "Have you gone mad?" as though personally pained by the rebellion. He says, "Don't you realize that we love you—that we always loved you. That we came to protect you?" Tereza cries out, "To protect! To protect from what?" The word *love* in this context constitutes a painful mixture of sexual and totalitarian politics. Love means conquest, suffocation, and death.

In this documentary sequence the camera images function as powerful instruments of control. A third event involving the camera, however (already mentioned above), occurs in Geneva between Tereza and Sabina. In this scene Tereza and Sabina exchange the use of the camera to photograph each other. Tereza has been told by Swiss editors that they need photographs of nude women rather than her photographs of the communist oppression of Czechoslovakia, which has become old news, even though the oppression continues unabated with protests that go unreported in the West.

In the photographic exchange between Tereza and Sabina, the camera is not a force of intimidating domination but an instrument of human ethical connection. As their exchange concludes, their nudity works as a complex, paradoxical artistic expression of both human separation and relationship. In their mutual nudity, exposure, and vulnerability they approach a Levinasian condition of responsibility. The camera in this scene suggests an aesthetic quality that goes beyond representation and documentation; it educates vision in suggesting the difference and humanity of the other.

A close-up of Sabina from a position of power on Tereza while photographing her in her nudity reveals a transformation in Sabina, even in both of them, that suggests Sarah Cooper's notion of the space of responsibility. Sabina's facial expressions and body language change from aggression to spontaneous playfulness, to manifesting empathy and affectionate concern. Toward the end of the scene Sabina, without saying a word, indicates a recognition of responsibility for this other woman as a human being rather than as just another figure in her life and in Tomas's personal story of sexual adventure. In her relationship with Tereza as the object of her camera eye, Sabina evidences signs of seeing the female body and her relationship to it differently.

The film soon enters a final phase that involves the transformation of Tomas's and Tereza's relationship. Marginalized in Geneva, Tereza feels compelled to return to the land of the oppressed, where everyone lives in isolated fear. She shares her pain with others in Prague. Similarly, Tomas in Geneva becomes just another hustler, an oddity on the prowl for women. He misses the power he had in Prague as a doctor and a rebel.

Moreover, Tomas witnesses the failure in both the East and the West of his Oedipal story of ethical encounter. Under communism repression cripples and dehumanizes in the process of destroying liberty. Sublimation serves the state. In Geneva, however, Tomas also finds what could be described as a living example of what Herbert Marcuse in the radical days of the New Left termed "repressive desublimation" and "'institutionalized desublimation.'"[28] In Geneva Tomas discovers an economy of money, comfort, artificial needs, and the fetishistic commodification of the body. Sexual and instinctual liberation flowers in a culture that makes such freedom meaningless. It becomes a culture of kitsch.

After Tomas and Tereza return to Prague, the narrative moves toward an extremely creative, even an unforgettable, conclusion. To summarize: Tomas fails in his attempt to resume his work as a brain surgeon at his old hospital. He refuses to acquiesce to the current regime's insistence that he disown his article of earlier times on Oedipus and the atrocities of the regime under the Soviet dictator Joseph Stalin. Consequently, not allowed by the communist authorities to practice medicine as a surgeon, he becomes a window cleaner and a living legend in Prague for his rebelliousness, but he remains unfaithful to Tereza. In turn, driven to distraction by Tomas's continued infidelity, Tereza also commits a sexual indiscretion that leaves her depressed enough to consider suicide out of fear of reprisals by the police for her compromised position with a possible informer.

At perhaps the lowest point in their lives and in their relationship, they make a radical decision at Tereza's instigation to take their dog, Karenin, and accept the standing invitation of a farmer, one of Tomas's favorite former patients and friends, to move to the country and live with him and his comical and charming pet pig, Mephisto. In this agrarian setting they all actually become a family.

Ironically, without access in an occupied country to personal and political freedom, Tomas, through his relationship with Tereza, finally breaks the self-enclosure of narcissism that has defined his existence. The film in this phase dramatizes the recrudescence of the couple's relationship into one of responsibility and love. Simply put, they each become more concerned about the other than they are about their individual selves. Interestingly, the culmination of that level of commitment occurs with the death of their dog, Karenin, who is as important to Tereza and Tomas as the dog Bobby was to Levinas when he was a prisoner of the Nazis. In their feeling for this dying animal that cannot be held responsible for itself, they get closer to achieving absolute responsibility for each other. This investment of emotion in the other, as represented by the dog, as opposed to the self saves the film from becoming in its conclusion its own example of dehumanizing kitsch. Tomas and Tereza have had this dog since Tomas bought it for Tereza on their wedding night. The dog was with them during the invasion, stayed with them through Geneva, and then returned with them to Prague. He has become the living emblem of their relationship.

Accordingly, regarding Tereza and Karenin, Kundera writes, "It is a completely selfless love: Tereza did not want anything of Karenin; she did not ever ask him to love her back. Nor had she ever asked herself the questions that plague human couples: Does he love me?" (*The Unbearable Lightness of Being*, 297). With Tereza at Karenin's side Tomas watches the dog suffer and die as the object of Tereza's unqualified "selfless love." It becomes a growing experience for him on how to love.

The film ends with an extraordinary ploy that in a way forces the viewer's involvement in the couple's death, as well as in their redemption as individuals, lovers, and man and wife. Kaufman uses an epistolary device to forewarn the viewer about events yet to unfold in the film's narrative. The viewer will know the future before the characters but will be unable to stop time or alter the outcome. This device insinuates a certain sense of dreaded, existential awareness on the spectator for the unfolding of events. The narrative thereby invites a kind of Heideggerian anxiety for the spectator about the end of time that dissimulates what will constitute an education about another attitude toward time and death that more closely follows Levinas.

Kaufman carefully structures this conclusion to achieve a powerful yet subtle impact. After a marvelous montage of their country life on the farm, the mercy killing of the cancer-ridden dog, and Tomas's intervention as a doctor to help relieve a farmworker from the severe pain of a dislocated shoulder, they all go to a country inn, including Mephisto the pig and his master. In the midst of the inn's joyful, communal environment, Tomas's visual expression of awareness of Tereza becomes a true look of love. As Tereza dances happily and spiritedly with the farmer's young cousin, Tomas looks at her with a touch of wonder and awe, clearly seeing in her an expression of a power of love beyond his own physical being.

The film then cuts dramatically to a close-up of Sabina in northern California as she looks distractedly at the magnificent beach and the breaking waves of the Pacific Ocean, with horses galloping on the sand. Sabina's expression creates the impression that she is thinking of her friends thousands of miles away, but a bit of a smile forms on her lips as she also sees a dog and people playing on the beach. Her face clears of a momentary look of concern. Back at work in her studio, she receives a letter that causes her to nearly faint with its announcement that Tomas and Tereza have died in a truck accident following their night at the country inn. After some more moments with Sabina and her friends, the camera goes back to the country inn and back in time to visit Tomas and Tereza during their last hours on earth.

This move constitutes Kaufman's startling experiment with time and death that makes Tomas's and Tereza's redemption through love come alive in the film. The letter to Sabina and then the return to the country inn means a return to the story after it is over. It forces a confrontation with death, the very opposite of a kitsch romantic, escapist Hollywood ending. When Tomas and Tereza decide to stay over at the inn that night to drink, party, and love one another rather than drive home, Kaufman has the couple go to their room upstairs at the inn in an original, loving, and charming way. She walks in front of him, slowly, rhythmically to the music of the musicians below, a light, romantic tango mixed with a Hungarian folk flavor played on a country violin and piano. With her back to Tomas, she walks ever so gracefully, lightly, seductively. He follows. The camera focuses on their feet, and Tereza positions herself like a young child on Tomas's toes and feet as he lifts and walks her step by step to their room, still moving softly to the music. He covers her eyes with his hand so she cannot see until they get to room number six, the same six that was his room at the spa where they met and the same six o'clock when she could get free from her shift so they could get together.

The next morning, as they drive in the rain, the camera shows them through the windshield of the old farm truck. The music now is Tereza's theme that has played throughout the film. She smiles and moves toward him and kisses him and says softly, "Tomas, what are you thinking?" As the truck advances slowly toward the blinding whiteness of death where brakes fail, Tomas says to Tereza, so near the end after so many years, "I'm thinking how happy I am."

The absence of surprise in the knowledge of the couple's imminent death forces a confrontation for the viewer with death. Instead of death being an end, what Levinas considers a Heideggerian annihilation, the film now makes it part of life. The experience of the film's conclusion proposes that we no longer think of time as ending with death but of death in the context of a new understanding of time. For Tomas and Tereza their time has come, and they can deal with it together. With each other they are ready.

Tomas and Tereza have achieved a love that entails the merging finally of body and soul, sexuality and tenderness, eros and ethics. If Tereza as a woman once again proves the vehicle of redemption for Tomas, they still travel that road together. At the end he also has held and carried her. In the novel Kundera refers to their time at the end as "the last station": "The sadness meant: we are at the last station. The happiness meant: we are together. The sadness was form, the happiness content. Happiness filled the space of sadness" (313–14).

In their last days and hours Tereza and Tomas evince the transcendence through their love for each other that for Levinas constitutes an ethical relationship capable of engaging infinity. For Tomas and Tereza, modern alternatives to ethical transcendence, such as a kind of "resurrection of the body" through the liberation of eros or a transformation of reality through a redirection of instinctual drives and sublimation, have little relevance to their lives together as portrayed in the film.[29]

While not the novel of ideas that Kundera wrote but a completely different art form with its own aesthetic demands, the film of *The Unbearable Lightness of Being* constitutes an intellectual tour de force as it pursues the idea of redemption through the complexities of modernity. It entails a visual and audial articulation of the challenges of the search for ethical transcendence in modern times. In contrast to Sabina's various experiments with different art forms, the film engages ethics and politics in the search for redemption.

The film does not resolve the paradox of its title, the heaviness of the lightness of being. It does suggest that the burden of being only for the self proves greater than carrying the load for another with love and respect for the other. The impossibility of handling the fragile responsibility of life becomes bearable when it involves the giving and bearing of life for another through love.

CHAPTER 5
FELLINI AND *LA DOLCE VITA*
Documentary, Decadence, and Desire

FELLINI AND THE CINEMA OF REDEMPTION

Love and redemption in *The Unbearable Lightness of Being* differ from the triumphant form of regeneration found so often in the American cinema of redemption. Redemption for Tomas and Tereza occurs in isolation from other characters in the film and in distinct separation from both Prague under Soviet control and Geneva at the apex of modern capitalistic cultures of "conspicuous consumption" and commodification. Tomas achieves redemption in part by refusing to acquiesce to communist intimidation. He undergoes a form of internal self-exile in the country with Tereza in their personal sanctuary of idyllic love that makes redemption possible. Accordingly, Tomas's journey of redemption contrasts with the sense of justification, success, and closure that often characterizes the films in the American version of the cinema of redemption. *The Unbearable Lightness of Being* also differs from another body of films of redemption, one of considerable cultural importance that comes from another country with a different cinematic history: films by Federico Fellini.

In the context of Fellini's amazing overall canon, especially including what has been deemed his own series of films with his distinct focus on redemption, *La dolce vita* (1959) stands out as a uniquely transitional work. As Peter Bondanella says in his most recent study of Fellini, "*La dolce vita* represents more than just a significant step in the evolution of Fellini's cinematic style. Like such films in America as *Gone with the Wind*, *Casablanca*, or *The Godfather*, *La dolce vita* transcended its meaning as a work of art and came to be regarded as a landmark pointing to important changes in Italian society as well."[1]

Fellini's use of a journalist's documentary vision in *La dolce vita* is widely considered by film scholars, such as Bondanella, to be innovative. This vision is inspired by the filmmaker's wish to expose the conditions of life during his times. Fellini's background informed his journalistic-documentary sensibility. During his early years in Rome he acquired experience in journalism, film, and popular culture. Media and journalism obviously represent a major preoccupation of *La dolce vita*, as evidenced in part by the film's introduction to the general public of the phenomenon of a new kind of photojournalist dubbed paparazzi after the name of such a figure in the film, Paparazzo (Walter Santesso). Also, the protagonist of the film, Marcello Rubino, famously played by Marcello Mastroianni, works as a gossip columnist and celebrity reporter. Although Fellini recreates many of his settings in Rome's famous Cinecittà studio, from beginning to end, the director clearly intends to give a kind of documentary filmmaker's view of the new world of celebrity and media culture that he witnessed in the Rome of the Via Veneto, the street that became notorious throughout the world for attracting the famously glamorous to its nightlife.

The revelation of the decadence at the core of this culture of the Via Veneto helps bring Fellini's camera to life. A moral sensibility regarding the spectacle of this environment provides considerable impetus behind the energy of his camera. Fellini's cinematic exploration of the social and cultural terrain of the Via Veneto records events that frequently were considered shocking for audiences at the time of the release of *La dolce vita*. The sexuality, self-indulgence, materialism, and narcissism of the Via Veneto dramatically challenge traditional middle-class standards of behavior and conflict with conventional social norms, values, and beliefs. The events and people under scrutiny become part of a broader system of social and cultural signs that Fellini's camera structures in the lens of his artistic vision. His camera dramatizes what one scholar, speaking about another film, terms "classic Fellinian symbology."[2]

At times the effort to accentuate for dramatic purposes the radical difference between the people of the Via Veneto from the people who pay to watch *La dolce vita* as a spectacle tends to eschew ambiguity in the film. Moral ambiguity can prove unaccommodating to dramatic graphic illustration.

It also should be noted, and will be discussed in greater detail later, that Fellini himself, as well as some Fellini scholars, at times denies any moral outrage on his part in his presentation of this corrupt culture.[3] Regardless, however, of the stated intention of the director, the exposure provided by the camera remains clear. Moreover, throughout *La dolce vita* Fellini exhibits media at work while also demonstrating media's power in constructing reality.

The difference within *La dolce vita* between journalistic documentary revelation and the probing questions of values achieves cohesion in the film's narrative structure. Just as Fellini's documentary eye explores a sick culture of decadence, it also searches for a story of redemption. It seeks to locate a special place for a renewal of belief and faith, as though hoping to locate something tangible, identifiable, and real to propose as proof of the possibility for redemption. It wants a program or plan for redemption. The moral thrust of the film indicates a yearning for not only such a program but also for a person to serve as a redeemer in the body of an intellectual friend, a movie star, a lover, or an innocent young girl. In fact, the search for this redemption narrative amid the corruption becomes the narrative of the film, the thread that keeps the loosely structured episodic story line together.

In effect, Fellini, like any city editor, sends Marcello the protagonist-reporter on an assignment to find the story of redemption in the face of utter decadence. A kind of dialogue occurs between the decadent world Fellini presents to Marcello and Marcello's quest on behalf of the film, his society, and himself. In this way the film anticipates the self-reflexivity of Fellini as a director in his later work, especially *8 ½* (1963).

Thus, the emergence of a double vision in *La dolce vita* through the introduction of the point of view, story, and journey of Marcello Rubino complicates the film's moral perspective. Marcello's faltering, quixotic search for meaning, identity, and redemption transforms the moralistic impulse behind the camera's probing powers of empirical and sociological observation into a phenomenological project of existential significance. The film presents the documentary view along with Marcello's fractured identity, debilitated moral vision, and crippled moral character.

Marcello insinuates into the film's exploration of the urban environment another kind of exploratory endeavor about the condition of the modern mind. The ethical vacancy of Marcello's vision and his world suggests the absence of resources of renewal within either Marcello's imagination or within his environment. He becomes the subject of desire in the Freudian and Lacanian sense of sexual and psychological rupture but also in the ethical sense of a search for the comfort of reassuring beliefs in the face of social nihilism. Marcello ultimately proves too weak before the decadent street. He gets consumed by the ethical vacuum of a way of life that reduces all human experience to immanence. In this situation he also reflects his society.

In general, *La dolce vita* resists the temptation to acknowledge the relevance or recognize the potential in the modern experience of a genuine, believable, and useable ethics that places the priority on human relationships based on transcendence and the other. It doubts the possibility of a transcendent temporal realm for spiritual renewal. The film follows Marcello on a quest for redemption in the domain of immanent experience. Functioning like an interior eye or internal camera to record events, as Frank Burke suggests, Marcello follows the film's aesthetic and ethical dictum that seeing is believing.[4] In this case film art and ideology cohere. Thus, Peter Bondanella notes that "the content of *La dolce vita* remains closely connected with the everyday world around Fellini and has not yet taken the decisive step beyond representation of 'real' public events."[5]

For Marcello this combination of film aesthetic and ethical position leaves him enclosed in an environment of so-called real things that becomes a living tomb. Marcello's desire for more propels him to circulate in a self-centered, self-fulfilling pattern of behavior, unable to distinguish between desire and physical need. In reaching out for love, Marcello only finds that, as Levinas says, "Love as a relation with the Other can be reduced to this fundamental immanence, be divested of all transcendence, seek but a connatural being, a sister soul, present itself as incest." Levinas proffers a different kind of love: "Love remains a relation with the Other that turns into need, and this need still presupposes the total, transcendent exteriority of the other, of the beloved."[6]

The concluding scene of *La dolce vita* does, however, briefly consider a different possibility for life than that espoused in much of the rest of the film. In both its style of filming and its ideology, the conclusion entertains an alternative for Marcello of transcendence to counter the immanent self-absorption that undermines his hopes for redemption. In this conclusion the film also proposes the possibility of an alternative temporal regime of transcendence based on the relation to the other. The film makes this proposal through the figure of the girl from Perugia, Paola (Valeria Ciangottini). Paola gestures and smiles to Marcello, instigating a challenge to him to find a new ethical subjectivity outside of himself. He should see her as the introduction of the other that requires new thinking for a new life for himself. Instead, he waves her off, and so, it seems, does the film itself.

Filming from the privileged position of an auteur director, Fellini intimates, as I have suggested, a sharply critical view of the environment that provides the context for his film. As a filmmaker, however, and as an icon himself of modern film and popular culture, he promotes this same world. This suggests a degree of complex complicity for Fellini involving his relationship with his film surrogate, Marcello, as well as the other real and fictional characters in the film.

For Fellini and the cinema of redemption, *La dolce vita* stands as transitional as it follows Marcello's faltering effort to gain some form of redemption for his life. Thus, in *The Cinema of Federico Fellini*, his comprehensive study of Fellini and his films that complements his other major works on Italian cinema, Bondanella identifies a "trilogy of salvation or grace." The films in this trilogy—*La strada* (1954), *Il bidone* (The Swindle, 1955), and perhaps most notably *Le notti di Cabiria* (The Nights of Cabiria, 1957)—constitute Fellini's cinema of redemption.

This trilogy of salvation or grace grows out of what Bondanella terms a "trilogy of character" with *Luci del varietà* (Variety Lights, 1950), *Lo sceicco bianco* (The White Sheik, 1952) and *I vitelloni* (The Young and the Passionate, 1953). These films of character, according to Bondanella, "dramatize the clash between a character's social 'role' or 'mask'—how a character tends to act in society—and the character's more authentic 'face'—represented by the protagonist's aspirations, ideals, instincts, and fantasies" (Bondanella, *The Cinema of Federico Fellini*, 73). Bondanella maintains that the trilogy of character breaks from the radical social realism that dominated the postwar Italian movement of neorealism. The films in this trilogy concentrate, he says, on an "interplay" between internal psychology and the external influence of society to develop complexity of character. Accordingly, the films of character anticipate the trilogy of salvation or grace.

While Fellini's trilogy of salvation or grace resonates as his cinema of redemption, his three films in this group differ somewhat from other films with this theme in their greater reliance on Christian imagery. As in other films in the cinema of redemption, however, Fellini carefully avoids turning his films into religious movies. Instead, the moral crises of the main characters in *La strada, Il bidone,* and *Le notti di Cabiria* compare to the challenges that confront characters throughout the cinema of redemption, including the American version. As in other films of redemption, Fellini's stories focus on the existential and ethical challenges that derive from the absence in the world of a widely accepted system of belief for a meaningful life of valuable human relations. Bondanella summarizes the common elements shared by the three main characters in Fellini's trilogy of salvation: "While each of these characters moves within a setting informed by images and concepts owing something to Christian tradition, his or her odyssey toward a moment of transcendence at the close of each of these films ultimately depends on the inner resources of the individual rather than any outside or otherworldly source" (Bondanella, *The Cinema of Federico Fellini*, 130).

La dolce vita, arguably one of the most famous movies ever made, varies from Fellini's trilogy and the overall cinema of redemption while at the same time instituting a new phase or form of it. It is a thoroughly transitional work with connections to Fellini's films of redemption that precede it but also with a definite proclivity toward his subsequent works, which take a skeptical, self-reflexive view of redemption in the modern condition. In a film from his redemption trilogy, *La strada* for example, redemption occurs as a fairly conventional act of ethical conversion based on emotional relationships of sympathy and guilt concerning the treatment of others. In *La strada* Zampanò (Anthony Quinn), a traveling strongman, comes to realize late in life the loss he has suffered through his abuse and abandonment of Gelsomina, clearly a Madonna and savior figure, who is played in a much-celebrated performance by Giulietta Masina, Fellini's wife. While Fellini introduces moral symbolism into the story along with elements of ambiguity concerning the brutality and the ultimate sorrow of the strongman, *La strada*'s power comes in part from its adherence to a simple yet classic narrative of ethical conflict and conversion.

In its own conflicted way *La dolce vita* maintains the search for redemption that characterizes Fellini's trilogy of salvation or grace and the cinema of redemption. The film takes that search into new territory, however, in the way it engages the moral and ethical, the social and psychological obstacles that frustrate the journey. As Bondanella says, "*La dolce vita* therefore continues a theme that was already familiar in Fellini's films. But now the director emphasizes the *failure* of his protagonist to experience a conversion and leaves his audience with none of the ambiguous resolutions the trilogy contained." Bondanella adds, "Religion, once offered to Fellini's characters as a possible means of escaping the meaninglessness of their anguished lives, is now represented by a series of empty images and activities and provides no solutions" (Bondanella, *The Cinema of Federico Fellini*, 146–47). More recently, Bondanella maintains even more categorically Fellini's dramatic move away from transcendence in *La dolce vita*, claiming that the film "chronicles what amounts to a major shift in Fellini's personal view of the world, for it underlines just how nearly impossible such transcendence can be to achieve, how difficult it is to receive the kind of grace that characters such as Gelsomina [*La strada*] or Cabiria [*Le notti di Cabiria*] in Fellini's earlier films effortlessly enjoyed" (*The Films of Federico Fellini*, 70).

Much of *La dolce vita*'s significance derives from its struggles with the growing disbelief at all levels of society in the potential value of a life committed to transcendence, alterity, and responsibility. Marcello's yearning for redemption for himself and for faith in others makes the film's story of loss especially relevant to the modern condition. *La dolce vita* dramatizes modern forces of nihilism, disillusionment, consumerism, and dehumanization that undermine transcendence in an existential situation of immanent subjectivity.

In addition to its importance to the cinema of redemption, *La dolce vita* warrants special attention for its many levels of cultural and historical significance, as well as for its special development of Fellini's film art. Its transitional treatment of redemption parallels the transitional nature of other aspects of the film.

Concerning the development of his art, Fellini sought in this film, says Bondanella, "a new kind of cinematic narrative that would abandon the traditional emphasis on plot and story line and concentrate on supporting the narrative by visual images and narrative rhythm" (Bondanella, *The Cinema of Federico Fellini*, 134). Up until *La dolce vita*, he says, "Fellini's cinema develops in a relatively traditional manner," but in this film, "he first explores and eventually exhausts the heritage of Italian neo-realism, a moment in film history he did so much to create as a scriptwriter" (xx).

Similarly, Burke notes that "*La dolce vita* ... served as the threshold between a renewed and heightened social realism (*La dolce vita* itself)" and other "emphatically nonrealistic" films (Burke, "Federico Fellini," 29). Other critics insist that in *La dolce vita* Fellini advances significantly in developing a modernist style that achieves a new relationship between time and space in film.[7]

While marking a transition in Fellini's film art, *La dolce vita* also achieves importance for its representation of a historic time of great change for Rome. Without perpetuating the politics and aesthetics of neorealism, Fellini in *La dolce vita* recreates, often in studio settings, the changing world in which he was immersed as a journalist, writer, and filmmaker. In this sense Fellini compares to such figures as Roberto Rossellini, with whom he worked during his formative years.

Tullio Kezich details this early developmental period of Fellini's life, and Bondanella analyzes its significance on his later filmmaking.[8] Like Woody Allen, a gag writer and story writer during an early stage of his career, Fellini transformed his verbal journalistic work and his interests in popular culture into a cinema that reflects the experiences of his background. As Kezich maintains, "In *La Dolce Vita*, set amidst the wild nightlife of Rome's Via Veneto, Fellini put characters drawn from his own world of entertainment and journalism in the spotlight. His scandalous film characterized a new sense of liberation that emerged in the Sixties and marked a radical new creative phase in Fellini's career."[9]

Similarly, Bondanella says:

> More than a major step forward in the evolution of Fellini's cinema, *La dolce vita* also summarizes an entire historical period in postwar Italy. Its lush fresco of the "sweet life" of Rome, focusing on the celebrities who frequented Via Veneto and were relentlessly pursued by gossip columnists and photo-reporters in search of a scandalous scoop, seemed to epitomize the moral atmosphere in Italy after the poverty of the immediate postwar period of reconstruction had finally ended. The country was beginning its economic boom, and its first confrontation with an emerging consumer society produced the inevitable plethora of the newly rich seeking a place in the much older aristocratic society of Rome. (*The Cinema of Federico Fellini*, 132)

Whether viewed as decadent or liberating or merely just vicarious entertainment for modern sophisticates, the fascination with the culture depicted by Fellini in *La dolce vita* has persisted over several decades, as evidenced in the media, including the *New York Times*, by stories about it and reviews of retrospective showings.[10]

A DIVIDED MORAL VISION

The passion of the moral vision in *La dolce vita* informs the film's fusing of a modernist creative aesthetic with dramatic documentary. This blending of art and documentary sensibility helps structure the film's engagement of hopes for redemption with the forces of Roman decadence. The exploitation of the inexorable connection between film and documentary generates the doubling of *La dolce vita*'s moral statement. Using actors related to real events and situations in which they themselves were involved enables Fellini to comment on both the diegetic events of the film and the society of Rome in which the events originated. Fellini turned commonly known events surrounding celebrities in Rome into fictional figures and moments in his film. One such event involved Anita Ekberg, the Swedish star whose late-night bath in Trevi Fountain was photographed, publicized, and internationally distributed. The event was then "immortalized" through its dramatic reenactment in *La dolce vita*. Other celebrities associated with creating this atmosphere for the film include the actors Lex Barker, Ava Gardner, and Anthony Franciosa (Bondanella, *The Cinema of Federico Fellini*, 137–38). Fellini mixed documentary and drama to enable his cinematic imagination to create in a new way what he saw as the real world.

Risking a bad joke, I note that in its obsession with stars and celebrities, *La dolce vita* literally begins by taking the greatest star of all time on an aerial celebrity tour of Rome that arouses the attention of the city. In this opening scene of the film, one of the most famous in film history, a statue of Jesus dangles from a helicopter that transports it across Rome to the amusement of spectators across the city. *La dolce vita* thereby reduces Jesus to a form of kitsch that constitutes the enemy so despised in *The Unbearable Lightness of Being* but becomes the source of Marcello's livelihood and ultimately his very being (Bondanella, *The Cinema of Federico Fellini*, xx). This opening scene resonates with meaning for the entire film. Alessia Ricciardi summarizes the rather basic "Fellinian symbology" in the scene: "The exuberant aerial tracking shots of the lead helicopter hauling its freight through the sky over Rome suggest if anything, the ascendancy of human technology over the religious, rather than any portentous return of spirituality. And in its most absurd, celebratory interpretation of science as a new religion, the film seems to position itself as the latest addition to a cultural genealogy that includes poems such as Marinetti's 'The Pope's Monoplane' and Apollinaire's 'Zone.'"[11]

Indeed, the scene does suggest the dominance of technology over institutional religion. It trivializes the divine and the spiritual. To continue Ricciardi's symbolism of flight and elevation, the director, in another helicopter, lords it over everyone and everything through the power of his camera. Shots of the "freight" helicopter carrying the statue of Jesus to be delivered to the pope and shots of the helicopter in pursuit of it, with Marcello and his partner photographer, Paparazzo, indicate the higher power of the man with the movie camera. The invisibility of the director's helicopter and the invisibility of the director's camera give them a special, superior power.

Clearly, the whole scene implies the incongruity, even the incoherence, of Jesus for many in modern times. In addition to the shots from below of the dangling Jesus, other shots from above the transporting helicopter give a bird's-eye view of the city. These shots emphasize Jesus as a kind of alien figure in the modern urban setting of Rome. A shot from the ground of workers notes their surprise at what they see in the sky. More important, a shot of girls in bikinis on a rooftop, including one shot that foregrounds the backside of one of the girls and the legs of another, not only mixes the sexual and the profane with the appearance of Jesus but also adds insult to injury with the gleeful, giggling laughter of the girls in their excitement over seeing the statue. From his helicopter hovering over the rooftop, Marcello uses handwriting gestures on his palm to urge one of the girls to give him her phone number. The whole scene illustrates attitudes of the public toward religion and the sacred.

The opening scene, then, immediately establishes a powerful editorial position and voice on the part of the director. The organization of shots directs a point of view to make a statement about the condition of modern moral and ethical life. A moral vision infuses every shot, every cut. The intellectual montage of dramatically opposing images—helicopters and Jesus, bikinis and Jesus, the circuslike spectacle of animated crowds racing on the ground to follow the flying statue above—speak as loudly as Eisenstein's or Griffith's montages. The conflicting images constitute a statement on contending beliefs in Rome that the rest of the film pursues. The opening clearly projects an acute moral perspective in its exposure of these contrasting values.

As I have noted, Fellini and some of his critics profess the director's serious detachment from the moral vision that for many defines *La dolce vita*. Obviously, Fellini can claim to be describing a moral condition without proclaiming his own moral stand through the excoriation of others. As Bondanella writes, "Perhaps the most original aspect of *La dolce vita* is that its creator is absolutely not morally outraged by the world he depicts and finds it incomprehensible that others are." In contrast to any suggestion of a strong editorial position and voice that pertain throughout the film, Bondanella stresses that Fellini refuses to stand in judgment of the people in his film: "What intrigues [Fellini] about the world he has created is its vivacity, its energy, the power of its imagery, and the last thing in his mind was a denunciation or a jeremiad of the world in which he was perfectly comfortable" (*The Films of Federico Fellini*, 80).

Comments at times by Fellini support Bondanella's contention regarding the director's own moral purpose. While emphatically agreeing "with those who maintain that the author is the last to talk knowledgeably about his work," Fellini says, "But I believe I never had any specific intention to denounce, criticize, scourge, or satirize. I don't stew over protests, angers, things I can't tolerate. I'm not out to accuse anyone."[12] Such statements by Fellini and others about his putative moral distance obviously demand consideration, especially in light of a critical argument that focuses on the film's moral position.

La dolce vita's pungent editorial voice and moral vision stand in spite of these expressed reservations. Fellini's comments, however, indicate some conflict within his moral view. Such conflict may suggest some explanation for other aspects of the development of the film's ethical position. Fellini's professed detachment may dissimulate a certain reluctance or inability on his part to articulate a coherent alternative ethical position and philosophy for his film.

Fellini's pattern as a director of shockingly provocative shots, dramatic intellectual montage, and vivid images of deep emotional content persists throughout *La dolce vita*. This style of filming structures the tensions of the film's moral and ethical vision. It also incorporates into the structure of the film itself a relationship to time and movement that significantly helps to articulate the moral vision of the film.

In *La dolce vita* time tends to follow a general linear and synchronic pattern of development. While the conclusion of the film, with Paola, the girl from Perugia, breaks this pattern with its relatively long take and its insinuation of the other to challenge Marcello's ethical subjectivity, most of the film avoids the suggestion of a disjunctive or diachronic dimension of transcendence between the self and the other. The time of the Levinasian other tends not to burst open to force a reexamination of the ethical meaning of existence. In *La dolce vita*, a film that concentrates on immanent being and experience, the other usually engenders the same. Time as the regular chronological order of events tends to structure immanent subjectivity in the film. The artistic form of the film, therefore, remains consistent with its philosophical view of experience. This combination of art and ethics positions Marcello to look for redemption in the so-called real world of immediate experience, but it also constitutes a boundary of the film's artistic and ethical imagination.

La dolce vita's opening helicopter sequence presents, however, the possibility of an innovative use of time to suggest a potential challenge to spectator subjectivity. In its suggestiveness the shot anticipates to a degree the concluding Paola sequence by opening the possibility of a different understanding of time and its potential relationship to ethics and subjectivity. The opening, therefore, can be looked at in terms of the various theories of time that have been discussed in this study, theories that propose a temporal regime for difference and change as opposed to order and synchronicity, such as the cinematic time-frame based on David Wood's concept of the time-shelter.[13]

In the opening scene of *La dolce vita*, in a very long, low-angle establishing shot from ground level, the camera focuses on the two barely visible helicopters in the beautiful cloud-filled distant sky. In a vividly balanced internal frame for the shot, the ancient Roman aqueduct leads toward the horizon, forming a kind of visual runway in the sky that the chugging helicopters can follow toward the center of the frame and the camera, which lingers on this vision in a long take. With the helicopters approaching the camera and passing the aqueduct, the scene creates the possibility of finding a new temporality for considering the film's issues of ethics, morals, and human relationships. Taking place against the background of the heavens, the scene suggests a transcendent temporal dimension. The time-frame of this scene demands thought and consideration as to its meaning. It arouses a degree of what Luce Irigaray would call "wonder." To paraphrase Wood, the question of being as opposed to determined, motivated action infuses this time-frame. The time-image aspect of the scene also suggests a comparison to Deleuze, as indicated by Ricciardi in her argument about this film and Fellini's work in general.[14]

Thus, the shock of the temporal structure of the very opening shots of *La dolce vita* could initiate a sustained reexamination of one's subjectivity. The opening of the film challenges the experience of time, thought, and sensibility. The helicopter assault and its startlingly unconventional manner of presentation force a questioning of perception and sensibility and demand consideration about what amounts to an ethical encounter. The shot entails the intervention of the other. The scene contains the explosive potential of requiring a reexamination of ethical subjectivity from an alternative perspective of a different temporal and ethical dimension that could contribute to the film's representation of social corruption and vice.

The moment of the helicopter and the film goes in a different direction, however. Thus, as the time-frame continues and the helicopters pass overhead in the frame, we get a cut of the helicopters rising over the city to be followed by other cuts, which I have already mentioned, and it becomes apparent that a montage of movement-images will continue the scene in a way that establishes the film's pattern. Moreover, these cuts and edits clearly reflect representational thinking of conflicting values and explosive emotion— children running after a stunning religious spectacle, a city under construction, girls exposing their bodies rather than baring their souls. The flight of one helicopter gets recorded artfully as a shadow crawling up the side of a building like some kind of sci-fi monster of modernity. Fellini offers a dynamic composition of dramatically changing images that indicate a world of change, but he does so by indirectly alluding to time by emphasizing movement. Movement through montage dramatizes the excitement and contingency of modernity but also compels a different way of thinking than the emphasis on time proposed by Wood's time-shelter or time-frame or Deleuze's time-image. As the scene progresses, the presence of a time-frame of incessant interaction of time and being recedes before the more typical mobile frame.

Also, the statue of Jesus, with all of its connotations of irony, parody, and social criticism, can be seen as a fulfillment of Levinas's deep concerns about the shallowness of images in the absence of the clarity of critical analysis. The reaction of the people in the film to the Jesus statue supports Levinas for committing the modern-day sin of seriously challenging art and images for fear of idolatry. As Levinas proposes, "To say that an image is an idol is to affirm that every image is in the last analysis plastic, and that every artwork is in the end a statue—a stoppage of time, or rather its delay behind itself.... The immobile instant of a statue owes its acuteness to its non-indifference to duration."[15] For Levinas, a statue as "artwork" becomes, as we have seen, a lifeless representation and "caricature." The reception of the statue of Jesus in *La dolce vita* would seem to support his point.

Whereas the image of Paola at the end of the film initiates a dynamic interaction between her and Marcello that provides a temporal and ethical challenge to his being in the world, the statue of Jesus assimilates into the environment of corruption. The statue loses all potency as a sign of the infinite gap between the religious promise of redemption and the narcissism of those on the ground who stare at it, chase it, and mock it. The treatment of the statue as a spectacle dissipates its power to inspire.

When the statue of a flying Jesus first appears in the opening scene to shock and even intimidate with its quality of strangeness, the presence of the aqueduct in the shot provides a historical reference that insinuates the complexity of time and history into Wood's filmic time-frame. This notion of the complexity of time in film also recalls Paul Ricoeur's theory of the relationship between narrative and time.

Ricoeur, as I noted previously, focuses on the interconnection in narrative between fiction and history; the importance of documents or archives that bring together various temporalities; and the organization of the space of experience, or what could be termed for film the scene of experience and the horizon of expectation.[16] For Ricoeur all of these elements of the relationship of time and narrative or "the poetics of narrative" provide structure for dealing with the paradoxical "aporetics of time."[17]

In the opening scene the juxtaposition in the frame of the aqueduct as a sign of the distant past and the helicopter as the present moving steadily toward the future evokes in a stark visualization the paradoxes that Ricoeur conceptualizes as aporetic temporalities. The aqueduct serves as what he terms a "connector" to the past, functioning as an architectural and engineering archive, a physical and historical presence that suggests the mystery of history and time. It injects a sense of wonder about the past and its relationship to this force of modernity approaching from the distant horizon in the form of the helicopters. A cracked aqueduct itself symbolizes a broken historical chain that nevertheless still connects to the past. The positioning of the aqueduct within the expansive view of the sky and the horizon of infinite possibility develops the associations of time, being, and history. The mise-en-scène thus visually evokes questions about the paradox of both the discontinuity and coherence of time and the relationship of the self to time, and it suggests the power of time and history in the midst of modern technological innovation as the helicopters move ever closer.

As the scene proceeds, however, the aqueduct, like the statue of Jesus, loses much of its potency and becomes little more than a prop, a visual referent of the dead past. Its potential fades to fulfill its promise of conveying a complex relationship of multiple temporalities and being. It stands in the film and scene as a dead, ancient structure on the landscape.

With the long take in the opening scene, the possibility emerges of a temporality to challenge representational thinking and the spatial organization of time. The initial intimation of possible temporal transcendence in the scene becomes, however, a conventional view of Rome. The tracking shot along the aqueduct turns the ancient engineering feat into a border or boundary, a division that divides and subdivides time and being into spatial compartments. The shots of Rome show a city under construction, at the same time presenting the buildings as enforcing urban enclosure. Thus, in these scenes, the film operates to provide a mundane visual narrative of urban life rather than proposing a possibility of transcendence.

La dolce vita proceeds scene by scene, episode by episode in its dramatization of Marcello's deepening frustration as he ventures on his quixotic quest for hope in the face of the film's inexorable exposure of the carnality, cruelty, and corruption of the people of the Via Veneto. Through most of it, transcendence, alterity, and the priority of ethical responsibility for the other exist only suggestively through their absence. One scene in particular becomes something like a minifilm-within-the-film concerning its encapsulation of issues in *La dolce vita* about different ways of perceiving the truth, especially regarding the contrast between transcendence and immanence.

In this scene young children become overnight sensations by claiming to have seen the Madonna. The scenes that immediately precede this event, however, help to set it up for its dramatic articulation of the conflict between transcendence and immanence.

In one of the scenes preceding the Madonna-sighting scene Marcello gets to be alone with Sylvia, played by Anita Ekberg, a Swedish actress considered at the time to be a blonde bombshell and a European counter to the glamour and public sexuality of Marilyn Monroe. In a masterpiece of modern comedy Marcello, who is involved with both his fiancée, Emma (Yvonne Fourneaux), and Maddalena (Anouk Aimée), an impulsive, tempestuous, and promiscuous lover, becomes hopelessly infatuated with Sylvia. During their evening together he apparently comes to recognize his own ridiculousness as he indulges her eccentric, bizarre behavior, which includes howling in the night with the dogs of Rome, walking in the dark nighttime streets and alleys of Rome with a stray kitten on her head, and finally bathing in the Trevi Fountain. When Marcello enters the water, after his evening-long pursuit, however, the fountains stop—an obvious intimation of impotence. Marcello's adulation of Sylvia pathetically involves more than sexual attraction, however. The scene achieves its special edge because Marcello also sees Sylvia as a kind of Nordic love goddess whose sexuality and free spirit offer a promise of a form of redemption for his life. So Marcello's failure and humiliation with her occurs on several levels of his manhood: his sexuality, his profession as a journalist, his identity.

The conclusion of the scene contributes to his humiliation. Marcello returns Sylvia to her boyfriend, Robert, played by Lex Barker in a role that continues the film's mixture of fact and fiction. Barker had played Tarzan in several movies in the early 1950s and was in Europe for a long end to his career, a real-life role he duplicated in the film. The film shows him passed out in his open sports car in the early morning while paparazzi photograph him and mockingly comment that he once had played Tarzan in the movies. When Marcello and Sylvia arrive, Robert proceeds to bully and slap her in front of the paparazzi, who photograph each action, urging them both on to extend the fight to make for better photographs. The paparazzi literally make rather than simply record the news. The scene ends with Marcello doubling over and falling to the pavement in pain after being slapped and struck by a bored but avenging Robert. So this phase of Marcello's search ends as it had begun, in farce and in his failure to see a clear direction for himself for renewal.

The following scene briefly continues to visit the issue of media and develops the search for redemption. Marcello, bored and fatigued, sits reading a magazine while his photographer friend Paparazzo shoots a silly scene of a beautiful model and a horse in an apparently meaningless juxtaposition. Neither the horse nor the model makes any sense in the setting, and Marcello sardonically urges Paparazzo to put the horse on a nearby table. Media-created reality achieves surrealism every day.

Then, in a lovely shot, Marcello looks over the classic Triumph sports car he drives and observes the entrance of, as some writers have noted, an uncharacteristically modern church for Rome, a building with a design and architecture that certainly make it different from the usual religious sites and churches in the city. In the shot the figure of a person entering the church seems barely visible. It could be, as Ricciardi suggests, another woman Marcello finds attractive, or it could be Steiner (Alain Cuny), the man Marcello will soon encounter on entering the church.[18] Steiner explains the Sanskrit text in his hands as the reason for his visit to the church. The church priest had informed Steiner about it and has offered to let him examine it. Steiner then proposes to play the church organ for Marcello. Steiner is what Johnny Friendly (Lee J. Cobb) in *On the Waterfront* (1954) would call a "deep thinker."

Clearly an intellectual mentor and father figure to Marcello, Steiner, in his relatively brief role in the film, will have a profound impact on the protagonist. In their conversation in the church Steiner praises Marcello for articles that he has written and urges the obviously embarrassed Marcello to pursue his serious writing. Each man seeks recognition and value in the other's eyes. Both appear frustrated, alienated, and insecure. Writers, intellectuals, self-obsessed, ambiguously employed, Steiner and Marcello clearly yearn for meaning in their vacuous lives beyond mere success. Both will be limited by the way they seek for such inspiration and where they think they need to look for it. Steiner refers to himself as a "devil," a remark made in jest in reference to the priest's concern that he might sully the sanctity of the church by playing jazz on the organ. He does teasingly hit a few playful notes before turning to his serious Bach fugue. The remark, however, will prove horribly portentous.

The Sylvia and Steiner scenes seem to offset and counterbalance each other, the first being an example of a new celebrity culture of wasted, purposeless lives involved in endless distraction and frivolous pursuits and the second being an effort to find a deeper meaning to life through learning, music, and the church. Both scenes, however, suggest underlying self-obsession and self-indulgence. In both scenes interactions with the other only reverberate as reflections of the self. Ethical subjectivity takes little account or responsibility for the other. The scenes show individuals seemingly intensely involved with each other. From a Levinasian perspective of absolute responsibility for the other, however, the scenes reject transcendent ethical regard for the other. Subjectivity remains ego-driven for the characters as they seek a new life by focusing narcissistically on their own images. The holiness of the other as epitomized by the face goes unrecognized in preference for the false security of the self.

These scenes are shot as rather straightforward dramatic episodes in continuous narrative time. The structure of each avoids suggesting a temporality that really challenges the characters' daily lives or ways of thinking. The scene that follows Sylvia and Steiner, of the Madonna's children, dramatically intensifies such self-obsession into a social pathology.

A typical Fellini sharp cut opens on Marcello and Emma, his live-in fiancée, driving in his Triumph to another religious site, the location outside of

Rome of the alleged sighting by the children of the Madonna. Seated next to him in the passenger seat, the possessive, pestering Emma infantilizes Marcello by literally forcing him to eat an egg and a banana. This one brief interaction speaks Freudian volumes of Marcello's prolonged adolescence. "Mangia, mangia [Eat, eat]," Emma repeats. Of utmost importance, however, Paparazzo, with his camera, sits squeezed into the back of the sports car. As in so much of *La dolce vita*, the camera and its picture of reality play a key role in this scene.

The location of the alleged sighting has become a scene of bedlam. On arrival they ask for "the Madonna's children" and the precise location of "the miracle field." It has been turned into a veritable set for television and media with towers for lighting, broadcasters, and journalists. Crowds of screaming people banging pans and waving handkerchiefs in some kind of celebration, buses, and arriving cars greet Marcello's group. Marcello checks out "the miracle tree." The children claim to have seen the Madonna by the tree. The paparazzi try to track down the children, who have been sequestered by the police, while overheard conversation indicates that people are receiving money for relating their visions. Ordinary poor folk ridiculously testify for the cameras while worrying about how they look for the public. A tape recorder plays an earlier testimony by the children of their vision of a loving Madonna. For perhaps the only extended time in the film, Marcello seriously takes notes like a real working newspaperman about events around him, such as the woman praying by the miracle tree to help her ailing child. As night falls, carnival and spectacle reign over all, lit by towering, fiercely bright television lights as a broadcaster narrates events. Relatives of the children give precise times for the sightings of the Madonna. Just after Emma prays to the Madonna for Marcello to love her again and marry her, the children appear. Total panic ensues and then grows into mass hysteria as heavy rain starts. Invalids on the wet ground get trampled as the children run to and fro followed by the mob as they claim to see the Madonna. Fellini's montage of the mob scene, the crowd, the danger, the darkness, the general chaos remarkably manages to personalize the event with the reactions of individuals. The rhythm and timing of his shots, the powerful intercutting between individuals and small groups in total panic, and the tight control of the intensity of the mise-en-scène make this sequence a classic for filming group action. Brilliantly melding individual reaction with mass chaos, Fellini achieves a milestone in this scene in his study of mob psychology.

The scene ends with the children claiming that the Madonna demands the construction of a church on the site. While someone lies dying in the madness, the mob, including Emma, insanely tears apart the miracle tree in the hope of acquiring its miraculous powers.

By exposing the media's exploitation of the dishonesty of such events, Fellini's *La dolce vita* pioneers an understanding of how the media operates in modern culture. The scene demonstrates that often the media cannot claim exemption from responsibility for the crises it covers. In the Madonna scene the media perpetuates the fraud of a potential miracle. It feeds on the event for its own purposes of survival but also literally makes the event itself possible. The event becomes a media-event. Even in exposing fraud, the documentation brings the event to life. The media and the mob, including the children themselves and ultimately even Emma, seek the truth in a way that makes only one form of truth possible, the so-called real and the material.

In *La dolce vita*, journalists, photographers, and paparazzi invariably transform any suggestion of diachronicity, difference, and the other into the simultaneity of a photograph, an image, the truth of a snapshot, or a moment in time. Looking with the children for the work of the miracle tree and the Madonna, even to disprove it, entails intellectual, emotional, and psychological complicity in that truth-seeking enterprise. The exposure of the children and their families as frauds and the people as superstitious dupes still maintains the discourse. The exposure still legitimizes the effort of the search. The paparazzi and the media give credibility to the lie by continuing to seek the truth with the same mentality as the children and the mob, by insisting on tangible, empirical evidence as the ultimate, perhaps the only, truth of spiritual value.

The media's complicity in the Madonna's children scene involves more than an issue of journalism, media, and documentary. The media and the mob scene constitute a more obvious expression of a greater dilemma for *La dolce vita* as a film. The Madonna sequence illustrates a way of thinking in *La dolce vita* that speaks to some extent for the film itself about experience, knowledge, and truth. This in turn relates to the form and content of the search for redemption in the film. *La dolce vita* reduces knowing reality to a basic subjective and objective dichotomy and proposes basic structures of consciousness and perception to acquire understanding. It relies on immanent experience for knowledge.

The frantic search of the media and the people for a miracle of redemption in the Madonna's children scene mimics *La dolce vita* as a transitional film in the search for redemption. The scene becomes a kind of parody as the making of a film-within-a-film in acting out *La dolce vita*'s idea of the search for truth and redemption. Like the media that requires linearity and synchronicity in a temporality that offers clear representation of being and truth, *La dolce vita* also seeks truth in the kind of certainty that can be documented.

La dolce vita, therefore, adheres to a theory of knowing that runs counter to Levinas's thinking and the work of the philosophers he admires, such as Maurice Merleau-Ponty and Franz Rosenzweig, among several others. Levinas says they espouse an "intelligibility outside the objectifying subject." In contrast, Fellini's film in general limits itself to what Levinas calls "structures imposed upon thought by the subject-object correlation to understand the meaningful in man." For Levinas this reduces thought to "an act of knowing" that depends on "consciousness" and, as I have already noted, on "that *immanence* of being" for determining relationships with the other.[19] Ultimately, Levinas wants to challenge the limitations on knowing by the subject-object dichotomy, ontology, and consciousness to propose an alternative in the form of the transcendence of ethics beyond being. To what Levinas calls the noema-noesis relationship and the reliance on representation for truth, he proffers a diachronic temporality that trades empirical certainty for infinite responsibility. He wants a form of thinking that "does not bring all transcendence back to immanence and does not compromise transcendence in understanding it."[20]

The immanent model of mind and knowledge in *La dolce vita* helps explain the film's overall eschewal of the diachronic temporality of transcendence and alterity in favor of a synchronic temporal order for the representation of reality. The narrative structures the time of the film to serve its purpose of portraying the social chaos of moral decline. It dramatizes characters locked in an unforgiving temporal order that resists a time of Levinasian recuperation.

With this grounding in immanence for its idea of knowing, *La dolce vita* declines to present an alternative discourse for truth and ethical belief. Although in the Madonna scene a priest and an elderly woman proclaim that God and miracles can be found elsewhere than in a crude reality and should be sought anyplace where anyone seeks God, the film itself really continues the search for an easy time for redemption, a time that spells it out and empirically proves it. Like paparazzi who avoid the different time of diachronicity, the film rejects in both its style of filming and its moral argument a different temporal realm. It seeks to explore for the truth in the ontology of a situation and gets frozen into more of the same.

Fellini's apparent refusal to proclaim a "jeremiad" against his cast of characters for their corruption or to articulate a coherent ethical project as an alternative of his own seem consistent with *La dolce vita*'s rejection of the potential of transcendence for Marcello at the end of the film. This occurs, we recall, with Paola, the young innocent girl from Perugia. Paola's face in the Levinasian sense, as an epiphany of a relation to transcendence that touches the infinite, holds out the promise for a new time for Marcello. In its beauty and ambiguity Paola's face suggests the contrast in Levinas between transcendence and immanence, a contrast that Fellini avoids in the film with few exceptions.

Paola's face and her look toward Marcello suggest what Levinas describes in "God and Philosophy" as "the desire beyond being, or transcendence, not to be an absorption in immanence." Levinas writes, "It is a dazzling, where the eye takes more than it can hold, an igniting of the skin which touches and does not touch what is beyond the graspable, and burns." He describes this desire as being of a different order than the desire of the "hedonist." It is desire as transcendence in the relation to the other in a time associated with infinity: "Love is possible only through the idea of the Infinite—through the Infinite put in me." Levinas emphasizes the destructive power of such transcendent, infinite love: "The Infinite affects thought by devastating it and at the same time calls upon it." The devastation of a new time and a new way of thinking means seeing that "transcendence is ethics" and involves "a responsibility for another, a subjection to the other."[21]

Precisely such transcendence, ethics, and time prove impossible for Marcello, the film, and, most tragically, for Steiner. The dead end of immanence that Levinas describes becomes for Steiner a force behind his murder-suicide in the killing of his children and himself. Significantly, for Levinas the relationship to children exemplifies the transcendent responsibility for the other. It epitomizes his ethical argument, an argument that unfortunately but inevitably gets undermined by his deprecation of the feminine and maternity in favor of paternity and the son. Levinas's dated, counterproductive development of his position on the "alterity of the feminine" as part of his theory

FIGURE 5.1. Valeria Ciangottini as Paola, the girl from Perugia in *La dolce vita* (1959)

of fecundity has been addressed by Kelly Oliver, among other feminist scholars.[22] Thus, Oliver asks, "Should we interpret Levinas literally in his discussion of the paternal election of a son? If so, paternal election not only provides an image of the father's choice of this particular child, but it also provides the image of the father's choice of a son in particular." As Oliver suggests, for Levinas "the feminine lover" and even the daughter ultimately become "subhuman," thereby undermining his whole project.[23]

The dehumanization that Oliver describes in Levinas's project occurs in *La dolce vita* in the treatment not only of women but in the sensationalizing of gays and blacks. It reaches full horrific expression with Steiner's murder of his children and his own suicide. This slaughter constitutes Steiner's failure to uphold the transcendent command of absolute responsibility and love for the other. His murder of his children constitutes the ultimate betrayal. It also can be interpreted in this context of the film as a possible comment on the inherent danger of a deadly form of fatherhood and patriarchy that ultimately sees the other as only part of the self and the same.

La dolce vita is very much about fathers—Maddalena's, Marcello's, the priest, Steiner. Perhaps even with his difficulties with the feminine, Levinas's ethical philosophy can help elucidate the dimensions of the ethical catastrophe of the scene of Steiner's slaughter of his children and his suicide. Levinas apparently intends with his argument about the transcendent significance of parenting to concretize the idea of fulfilling the extremism of his ethical demand for the other. Levinas refers to Isaiah to make his point: "My child is a stranger (Isaiah 49), but a stranger who is not only mine, for he *is* me. He is a stranger to myself." This paradox succinctly summarizes in a personal way the heart of Levinas's philosophy of the same and the other. The child epitomizes the same as the parent but must be recognized also as ethically distinct and other. The child becomes, Levinas says, "both my own and non-mine, a possibility of myself but also a possibility of the other, of the Beloved" (*Totality and Infinity*, 267).

Thus, from a Levinasian perspective the parental relationship can be viewed as a unique example of the possibility of actually living the radicalism of his insistence on absolute responsibility for the other. Seeing the child as both the closest of human beings and a stranger attests to the ultimate unknowability, otherness, and alterity of the other. It suggests the holiness of the person. "Paternity," writes Levinas, "is the relationship with a stranger who, entirely while being Other, is myself, the relationship of the ego with a myself who is none the less a stranger to me" ("Time and the Other," 52). The child as the future also becomes the means for creating a physical link between ethical responsibility for the other and the relationship to the future and infinity. Thus for Levinas "the relation with the child" can also establish the "relationship with the absolute future, or infinite time" (*Totality and Infinity*, 268).

The passion of Levinas's argument about paternity accentuates the disastrous gap between his intention and its outcome when it concerns the feminine and women. Regarding the feminine, Levinas's oversight of so much of such importance that proves so great as to weaken his whole ethical position also informs the Steiner slaughter. Levinas's blindness to the feminine and gender speaks to Steiner's madness.

Conceivably, Steiner destroys his children and himself to strike most brutally at the wife who gave the children life. The scene of death suggests the slaughter could be a purposeful punishment that Steiner intends for his wife, the sole family survivor. Her crime in this film filled with misogyny must consist in being a woman, a wife, and a mother, and therefore the source of life that leads to an intolerable death, a death that Steiner obviously cannot face alone.

As though to prove that the point of the death scene really centers on the mother, she must undergo an added form of hell—torture by paparazzi. The cameras of the paparazzi, the eyes of the world, focus on her. The blindness of Levinas in regard to the feminine and women and the madness of Steiner in dealing with his own ethical impotence come together in the proof the viciously cruel paparazzi provide that women are visual, physical, and mental objects for abuse.

Paparazzi, as agents of misogyny, epitomize the use of the camera to objectify and degrade women, especially in contrast to Sabina's and Tereza's sensitive, regenerative use of the camera in *The Unbearable Lightness of Being*. Moreover, the paparazzi's sheer, vicious disregard for the most humane of impulses when it comes to this mother demonstrates a profound pathology as perverse as their exploitation of her pain.

Thus, in another unforgettable scene in *La dolce vita*, while Marcello and the police wait in the Steiner apartment amid the dead bodies for the arrival of Steiner's wife, she gets ensnared by paparazzi, photographing her as she walks to the apartment from her bus in ignorance of the horrific scene of death that awaits her.

The disappointments and disillusionments that Marcello confronts on his shaky road to finding a means for renewing his life and his place in the world culminate in the Steiner apartment. The scene confirms for him the impossibility of finding value for himself in life. The calamity imposes the question for him and others as to what authority other than himself gave Steiner the right to such a horrible taking of life. No twisted notion of a higher power seems to have compelled him. The answer seems to be that Steiner found that authority in himself, in his own immanent subjectivity, as he searched for meaning to his life. Marcello also must look for inspiration and belief to overcome this horror. Looking, he also finds nothing from which to gain strength.

The shock of the slaughter accelerates the desperate decline that has been Marcello's life. He went to that apartment already a figure of death. He learns there that any hope for a new life to change the sweet life died with the children and their father.

Marcello also rejects the face of Paola, with its promise for a chance at redemption. Declining yet again to be a hostage of the other in a new kind of love of responsibility, he remains a prisoner under a death sentence serving only his own time in a world that will end with him.

CHAPTER 6
ANTONIONI AND *L'AVVENTURA*
Transcendence, the Body, and the Feminine

A CINEMA OF THE INVISIBLE

A Levinasian reading of Michelangelo Antonioni's *L'avventura* (1960) as a journey to achieve redemption in terms of ethics, transcendence, and alterity also should include a reading of Levinas by Tina Chanter, Luce Irigaray, Ewa Ziarek, and Kelly Oliver, among other feminist interpreters of his work. Feminist interpretations of Levinas provide a bridge between the philosopher and the filmmaker and help measure how far Antonioni in *L'avventura* ventures beyond Levinas's own sexist limitations in articulating a case for transcendence, ethics, and the other. Their writings can help show how Antonioni contributes to our understanding of the great ethical potential of Levinas's philosophy. Together, these writers and Antonioni proffer a form of redemption for Levinas himself by rethinking the importance of the feminine to a revised understanding of Levinas.

L'avventura can be viewed not only as providing a cinematic enactment of basic Levinasian intellectual positions but also as rendering a special service to Levinas and those sympathetic to his thought by feminizing his argument. *L'avventura* dramatizes the problematic of Levinas's ethics of transcendence in the context of the feminine. In so doing the film takes Levinas to a place relating to women, subjectivity, ethics, and sexuality that the philosopher failed to venture into himself. *L'avventura* thereby makes a contribution to philosophy, as well as to cinema.

L'avventura signals the importance of the feminine with its tight framing of an attractive woman in its opening sequence. In dramatic contrast to the opening of Fellini's *La dolce vita*, *L'avventura* begins in a literally pedestrian fashion as the camera shoots Anna (Lea Massari) walking through a narrow roadway of parallel hedges that creates the impression of a kind of enclosed channel. Compared to the aerial dynamics that open *La dolce vita*, the beginning of *L'avventura* comes across as simple to the point of being mundane.

Indeed, the contrast between such apparent surface simplicity and deeper complex meaning in Antonioni has intrigued many film scholars. Antonioni's film art has challenged the critical imagination and vocabulary of such writers for years.

Seymour Chatman has dubbed Antonioni's "stylistic approach to cinema" a form of "visual minimalism" that compares to other trends toward "'de-dramatized'" cinema and "'anti-theater.'" Chatman approvingly quotes Richard Gilman that "'Antonioni's films are indeed about nothing,'" meaning a cinema that subverts conventional representational codes for plot construction, character development, and thematic expression.[1]

Accordingly, as Peter Brunette demonstrates, the apparent simplicity of the opening scene of *L'avventura* disguises considerable artistic complexity. Brunette notes that as Anna "turns the corner, the camera seems to struggle to keep her perfectly framed in the center of the image. Then it begins to track backward, forcing her, unnaturally, and in an uncanny way, to remain *stationary* in the center of the visual field, even though in actuality she continues to move forward. The effect is to turn her into an *objet d'art*, something to be looked at, perhaps admired." Comparing this action to other similar movements regarding women in the film, Brunette concludes that "the very gesture of 'framing' woman as an aesthetic object to be looked at is undermined by the forced, unnatural quality of the gesture itself."[2] Thus, whereas Fellini provides in his opening sequence an expansive perspective on society and advances that perspective through a classic montage of moving images, Antonioni tends toward a slower filming with an intense focus on a dramatic scene.

Interestingly, although Fellini and Antonioni evidence different styles of directing in *La dolce vita* and *L'avventura*, they share similar concerns about the world around them. Antonioni explores the same social life that at once repelled and intrigued Fellini. In *L'avventura* Antonioni presents his own view of a decadent leisure class in the midst of changing social and cultural environments.

In *L'avventura* Antonioni creates a new kind of cinema. He articulates an ethics of cinema, what Brian K. Bergen-Aurand terms "an ethics of the cinematic—that responds to uncertainty without making it certain."[3] This ethics of cinema puts ethics before being and before the temporal regimes of conventional film narratives. Antonioni wants a cinema that internalizes in its artistic structure the tensions of ethical and temporal relationships. As part of this new cinema, he also wants to focus on the crisis of the sexual ethics of modern life in the context of the feminine. He achieves these objectives in *L'avventura*. As Geoffrey Nowell-Smith proposes, "It is hard to overstate the importance of *L'avventura*.... The feeling that *L'avventura* was a revolution in the making was widespread when it came out."[4]

Antonioni constructs in *L'avventura* a clear example of John Llewelyn's "spiritual optics" that sees in terms of Levinas's "ethics of responsibility."[5] As in Levinas's own thinking, time in this film establishes difference and distance to articulate a dynamic of ethical tensions that demands the priority of the other. The film image in *L'avventura* projects the idea of infinite possibility in human relations. All the elements of cinematography and mise-en-scène insinuate a temporal dynamic into the drama of the film that structures the ethical dynamic.

Thus, Bergen-Aurand correctly perceives a vital link between Antonioni's revolutionary cinema and "Levinas's post-phenomenological ethics and the call of the other." In his insightful essay on Levinas and *L'avventura* Bergen-Aurand writes, "Here cinema is not the frame or window of classical and realist film theories. It is not the mirror of psychoanalytic, Lacanian theory. It is not even the address of contemporary phenomenological approaches, but an other that calls me to respond by regarding it. This is an ethics of response, not a traditional ethics of dogmatic absolutism, rational universalism, moral relativity, right conduct or subjective reciprocity. It is an ethics of responding to the otherness of the other, without grasping and reducing the other to the same."[6]

Antonioni's description in just one sentence of his philosophy as a director provides some insight into how he came to this extraordinary achievement of a new ethics of cinema: "The world, the reality which we live in ... is invisible, hence we have to be satisfied with what we see."[7] In *L'avventura* Antonioni rejects his own advice. He refuses to be satisfied as a filmmaker with the imposed boundary of the visible when the invisible reality of the lived-in world would provide a picture of greater significance. *L'avventura* suggests a vital relationship between the invisible reality of the world as lived and an ethics of transcendent, infinite responsibility to the other that goes beyond being. The invisible becomes both the artistic and the ethical challenge of *L'avventura*.

The invisible in Antonioni's film means a search that deviates from the empirical. It indicates the desire to go beyond the understanding of immediate experience. Of course, like *La dolce vita*, among other films in this study, Antonioni's *L'avventura* carefully investigates the visible, the ontology of immanent experience. As with Fellini, Antonioni's documentary sensibility directs his attention toward the study of the world of his daily existence.

In *L'avventura*, however, Antonioni refuses to acquiesce to a form of stultification by immanence, the visible, and the putatively real. In contradistinction to such immanent entrapment, *L'avventura* suggests the value of the search for another realm of understanding, one that goes beyond the certifiably known to an ethics of transcendent experience. *L'avventura* engages the possibility of achieving transcendence in immanence rather than accepting experience as confined by the visible horizon. It envisions meaningful relationships as ethical relationships that involve transcendence and the other. Cinematically and philosophically, the film suggests the possibility of going beyond one's own being to a transcendence through absolute responsibility for the other.

Antonioni's commitment to a cinema of the invisible leads logically to his formulation of another idea, that of the "abstract cinema." Such an abstract cinema, as he describes it, entails working with, exploring, and exceeding the restrictions of a world that "no one shall ever see": "We know that beneath the represented image there is an other image more true to reality, and that beneath that one, still one more, and again a further image beneath that one, until you get to the true image of reality, absolute, mysterious, that no one shall ever see. Or perhaps, one will arrive at the decomposition of any image whatsoever, of any reality whatsoever. The abstract cinema would then have its rationale for existing" (Rohdie, *Antonioni*, 155).

So in aspiring to create an original cinema of what "no one shall ever see," Antonioni injects into *L'avventura* a crosscutting of different kinds of temporalities for different journeys. The times of journeys on a boat, trains, and cars intersect with the film's other temporality of the transcendence of an ethical domain. It cinematically varies between immanence and transcendence, synchronic and diachronic temporalities, conventional representational codes of form and substance and more abstract expressions.

Accordingly, Antonioni's achievement of an abstract cinema in *L'avventura* involves the merging of different strains of thought, artistic creation, and ethical experience. Antonioni incorporates his documentary sensibility into the film's artistic structure to engage the ethical and moral crisis of his times. In this film an abstract cinema of ethical transcendence also reconsiders in a sharply original way the place of women as themselves invisible as truly liberated human beings in a sexist society.

Confronting this sexism, however, the film ironically presents women as empowered to embody ethical transcendence so as to expand, transform, and revivify the Levinasian argument. The feminine becomes a source for redemption, including redemption for women, but the feminine also becomes a field and focus for discourse over the meaning of transcendence. Antonioni's female characters negotiate between the sexual body of the feminine and Levinas's ethical language of transcendence. Antonioni turns the bodies of his female characters into dynamic scenes for the inscription of conflicts over transcendence, otherness, and redemption. As Marcia Landy says, "The core of the film presents the mystery of femininity as it involves depiction of the woman's body."[8] Similarly, in this film Antonioni contrasts the redemptive face of physical joy and love with the deadened look of despair and loss.

REDEEMING LEVINAS: THE FEMINIST WRITERS

From the beginning of the critical and public reception of his work, Levinas has been criticized for objectifying women to facilitate the dominant male as the subject in his ascension to transcendence. Throughout his writings Levinas articulates the feminine as a condition of the ethical for the male. This condition assumes the form of feminine representation of the "dwelling" as a source of maternal nurturance. The feminine makes the fulfillment of transcendence possible for the male through paternity, fecundity, and the birth of a son who enables access to the future. The son, as the embodiment of the future, concretizes the demand for the subject to assume absolute responsibility for the other.[9]

While reviewing the list of concerns by feminists who oppose Levinas, Tina Chanter also emphasizes what attracted feminists to his thought in the first place, in spite of his sexism. She describes what caused them to overcome the severity of their reservations about him. In contrast to the original arguments made by such initial critics of Levinas as Simone de Beauvoir, Chanter notes how "Levinas's notion of the feminine" works "to disrupt the primacy of totality, sameness, system, concept," thereby making room in philosophy for feminist participation in the philosophical tradition. "The problem with Beauvoir's straightforward dismissal of his conception of women as other," writes Chanter, "is that it fails to engage with Levinas's overall philosophical project, which is to elevate the notion of alterity above the notion of totality."[10]

Similarly, Alison Ainley, in an explanation worth repeating here, summarizes the importance of Levinasian thought to feminist thought:

> What makes Levinas's thinking initially appealing for feminist philosophers is the critique it provides of the structure of philosophical thinking. For Levinas, it seems that most or all philosophical thinking is determinate, if it takes others as objects and fixes them under a conceptual category. The identity of the other is thus determined relationally and placed or theorized accordingly. Levinas objects to this primarily because it appears to him to be reductive, making otherness equivalent to "the same," and recuperating alterity under the scope of representational thinking, in a way that, although it may try to make subsequent assertions of ethical legitimacy, is actually denying the possibility of anything other than its own modes of representation and relation. In this respect philosophy is apparently unable to allow for the "otherness" of others, if its thinking is by definition the elaboration of conceptual abstraction and universalizing laws. It is in this regard that Levinas shares some of the concerns of feminist thinking about the "shape" of Western philosophy.[11]

So as Ainley indicates, for such feminist philosophers Levinas stands in the forefront of the battle over challenging representational thought that inherently predetermines the place of the feminine. By insisting on radical alterity as a form of radical resistance to totalizing thought, Levinas opens the door for new thought about the ethics of the feminine.

Unfortunately however, as Chanter indicates, while Levinas's thinking "might well open up a space for the rethinking of the feminine," he fails to "follow through on this promise, but rather closes it down." She notes that Levinas suggests "the feminine as a disruption of the virile categories of mastery, domination, and self possession." This argument, she asserts, has the potential to open "up the possibility of another way of (non)being, a different mode of existence." After presenting such a potential, however, he then, she says, shuts off "the radical possibilities he opens up for feminism," focusing instead on the feminine in a way that stalls his overall project of alterity as opposed to totality. His misuse of the feminine becomes evident, Chanter says, in the "sexualized terms" and "sexualized language" that pervade his writing. Even as presumed metaphors, his language reduces the feminine to "the most traditional stereotypes" that undermine his ethical enterprise (Chanter, introduction, 16–17).

As an example of such stereotypical thinking and writing by Levinas, feminists frequently quote sections from the "Phenomenology of Eros" in *Totality and Infinity* in which sexist language abounds. There Levinas refers to "the beloved" as "irresponsible animality which does not speak true words." He writes, "The beloved, returned to the stage of infancy without responsibility— this coquettish head, this youth, this pure life 'a bit silly'—has quit her status as a person." He again compares the feminine as the beloved to an "animality" that plays "as with a young animal."[12] Obviously, such language from Levinas regarding the feminine constitutes a major challenge to the feminist philosophers who, as Chanter says, wish to give him "a charitable reading" by crediting him "with having seen the radical potentiality of the feminine to break up the categories of being, and to create the possibility of ethics" (Chanter, introduction, 17).

Feminist thinkers, including Irigaray in some of her seminal essays, strive to return to Levinas's contradictory work on the relationship of the feminine to alterity, transcendence, and otherness in order for them to reopen possibility for the feminine. Discussing Irigaray's important contribution to Levinasian studies through her work on ethics and sexual difference, Claire Elise Katz notes that "Irigaray worries that Levinas, like the philosophers who precede him and despite appearances, did not take sexual difference into account with his conception of the Other." She adds, "Irigaray is concerned that the role in which the feminine is cast, that is, as the Beloved, is a disparaging one. As the Beloved, the woman plays a transcendental role: she makes possible the man's transcendence to the ethical, while she is cast downward."[13]

Like many other feminist critics of Levinas, Ewa Ziarek believes that primarily through his focus on the importance of embodiment, Levinas opened great possibilities for rethinking the feminine but then never pursued them. She says that "perhaps the most original contribution of Levinas's work to the contemporary debates on the body lies in the fact that it enables the elaboration of the ethical significance of flesh and, by extension, opens a possibility of an ethics of sex." Ziarek quickly adds, however, that "this possibility is never realized in Levinas's own work." She also emphasizes that "the decisive difference between Irigaray and Levinas" concerns "the fact that for Irigaray . . . embodiment discloses an ethical significance of eros and the female body." For Ziarek "the radical potential of Levinas's work" in recognizing "the ethical structure of embodiment" and "the ethical significance of embodiment" gets undermined out of distaste for the feminine "at the moment it confronts sexuality." Thus, "Unable to imagine an ethics of sexuality, Levinas's male lover eventually turns toward the transcendent God while the woman is plunged back into the abyss of the nonhuman."[14]

Irigaray, according to Ziarek, works to overcome this crisis of the break between the ethics of sexuality in Levinas. She endeavors to fuse the divine and the flesh in the feminine body. Irigaray's method of addressing this problem in Levinas also pertains directly to a Levinasian reading of Antonioni's *L'avventura*.

Irigaray mounts a direct assault on Levinas's theory in her article "Questions to Emmanuel Levinas: On the Divinity of Love" by arguing that his position on the feminine ultimately subverts the otherness "of the other sex."[15] This subversion weakens his whole ethical theory, not only because of the damaged ethics of such treatment of women but also because it eliminates the possibility through the feminine of "an alterity irreducible to myself." The logic of Levinas's whole program relies on such alterity. For Irigaray the "other of sexual difference" engenders the irreducible. Significantly, sexual difference has "its roots also in the natural universe, in the body." Reliance on other sources of difference without sexual difference invites "an infinite series of substitutions" for the other, a "nonethical" proposal in its indiscriminate usurpation of identities (110–13).

Irigaray says Levinas loses the "feminine other" as an irreducible alterity, partly as a result of his disdain for the pleasure of the flesh, "that transcendence of the flesh of one to that of the other." Levinas, she says, "knows nothing of communion in pleasure." For Irigaray the porosity of the borders of the flesh enables "a unique and definitive creation." She writes, "Either pleasure is a mere expenditure of fire, of water, of seed, of body, and of spirit . . . or else it is a unique and definitive creation." By resisting such pleasure, Levinas, she says, fails to "perceive the feminine as other" (110–11).

Levinas's repudiation of the potential transcendence of the flesh relates to his substitution of "the son for the feminine." For Irigaray this reliance on the son pertains to Levinas's denigration of women while constituting a form of violation and exploitation of both the woman and the son. She believes failure justifiably awaits this substitution because "the child belongs to another time. The child should be for himself, not for the parent" (111).

Accordingly, for Irigaray, Levinas's blindness pertaining to the irreducible difference of sex denies subjectivity to the feminine and compels Levinas to formulate a weakened abstraction of the other that leads him to other dichotomies between being and the other, metaphysics and phenomenology, philosophy and theology. She suggests that only a rethinking of the ethical importance of sexual difference can salvage Levinas's quest for ethical transcendence and alterity. While "Questions to Emmanuel Levinas" presents a direct theoretical engagement with his project, in "The Fecundity of the Caress" Irigaray endeavors, as we will see, to make the word flesh by demonstrating in her sensual and metaphorical writing the power of the feminine, the body, and the flesh to engender a new ethics of sexual difference. That essay provides another valuable bridge from Levinas to *L'avventura*.

A STATEMENT OF ETHICAL CRISIS

Several decades before Irigaray wrestled with Levinas on the feminine and the body, Antonioni engaged in his own battle concerning sex and ethics. In fact, an argument for a sexual ethics suffuses *L'avventura*. Antonioni wishes in this film to confront what he perceived as a profound ethical crisis in society in the form of a pervasive sexual illness. This illness, as he understood it, directly affected the situation of women in society. The illness demanded the development of an ethical project.

Interestingly, Antonioni's high intentions for the film could not prevent the occurrence of a so-called scandal surrounding the film's Cannes opening at the Palais des Festivaux on May 15, 1960. The scandal has been widely discussed as part of modern film lore and concerns boos and catcalls that came from some members of the audience during the film's showing. As Nowell-Smith describes the incident, part of the audience became outraged over Antonioni's unusual development of the plot, the unconventional emphasis on long takes, and the early disappearance from the film's story of one of Italy's most popular actresses, Lea Massari, the woman who opens the film with her walk through the roadway. Antonioni reportedly became so upset by the response that he left the theater in tears. Like a happy Hollywood ending, however, rather than the usual ambiguous conclusion to one of

Antonioni's own films, defenders of Antonioni and his film mounted a counterattack against those who had insulted him. Such eminent figures as André Bazin put together a petition overnight praising him and persuading the festival to give him a special award for his originality (Nowell-Smith, *L'avventura*, 12–14).

Antonioni discussed the sexual crisis behind the making of *L'avventura* in his often-quoted statement at the film's premiere. This Cannes Statement expresses at least part of his motivation in constructing what can be seen as a revolutionary art form of temporal difference and ethical transcendence. The deep ethical concerns he expresses in this statement about excessive eroticism explain his search in the film for a new ethics for modern society. His statement of crisis helps show how the journey in *L'avventura* can invite a comparison to a Levinasian ethical philosophy of transcendence and the other. While Levinas deprecates, as the feminists maintain, the sexual impulse, Antonioni challenges its corruption in modern society. His ethical stand in the statement indicates the importance of ethics to an understanding of *L'avventura*.

Not only did *L'avventura* survive the "scandal" of its opening at Cannes to go on to become recognized as one of the great modern films, but the statement that Antonioni composed to describe his motivation behind the film also has survived to become an indispensable element for consideration by serious critics of the film to the point sometimes of being misunderstood or misused as a critical cliché. Explaining his hesitancy over mentioning the Cannes Statement, Brunette says, "I have held off discussing it until now because the vast majority of Antonioni's previous commentators have used it as the basis for their interpretation of the film, but in a way that has robbed it of its innovative power" (Brunette, *The Films of Michelangelo Antonioni*, 50). Brunette goes on to indicate that many commentators have misconceived or oversimplified Antonioni's statement.

Although I recognize the validity of Brunette's caveat about overuse, any analysis of the film that emphasizes ethics and values would be remiss to minimize the significance of Antonioni's statement. Thus, William Arrowsmith makes the statement an important element in his study of *L'avventura*. An esteemed scholar, Arrowsmith begins his chapter on *L'avventura* by emphasizing his own repetition of Antonioni's actual words in order to accentuate the intense passion behind the director's statement. Arrowsmith writes, "'The Malaise of Eros.' The phrase is Antonioni's, not mine."[16] Arrowsmith then immediately proceeds to give an extended quotation from Antonioni's Cannes Statement.

The Cannes Statement expresses Antonioni's concern about "this ever-increasing split between moral man and scientific man, a split which is becoming more and more serious and more and more accentuated."[17] He says "the present moral standards we live by, these myths, these conventions are old and obsolete," but we honor them nevertheless (Cannes Statement, 178).

Without specifically identifying, as Brunette notes, "these myths, these conventions" that resist much needed new ways of thinking, Antonioni proceeds to narrow his focus to the problem of "eroticism." He asks, "Why do you think eroticism is so prevalent today in our literature, our theatrical shows, and elsewhere?" He then says, "It is a symptom of the emotional sickness of our time. But this preoccupation with the erotic would not become obsessive if Eros were healthy, that is, if it were kept within human proportions. But Eros is sick; man is uneasy, something is bothering him. And whenever something bothers him, man reacts, but he reacts badly, only on erotic impulse, and he is unhappy" (Cannes Statement, 178–79).

Linking this "emotional sickness" to *L'avventura*, Antonioni emphasizes that the illness in the film "stems directly" from the sickness that pervades society: "The tragedy in *L'avventura* stems directly from an erotic impulse of this type—unhappy, miserable, futile. To be critically aware of the vulgarity and the futility of such an overwhelming erotic impulse, as is the case with the protagonist in *L'avventura*, is not enough or serves no purpose" (Cannes Statement, 179). He says that the response of "the protagonists in my film" to society's failure to update antiquated and obsolescent values "is not one of sentimentality. If anything, what they finally arrive at is a sense of pity for each other" (Cannes Statement, 178).

Antonioni further maintains that simply dramatizing this social sickness of eros by bringing the sexual pathology to light in the film will fail to cure it. *L'avventura* instigates "the crumbling of a myth, which proclaims it is enough for us to know, to be critically conscious of ourselves, to analyze ourselves in all our complexities and in every facet of our personality." He repeats that such awareness "is not enough. It is only a preliminary step" (Cannes Statement, 179).

If awareness constitutes only "a preliminary step" for Antonioni, he also remains unclear about the specific subsequent steps that could build a program for social action. He, therefore, concludes the statement with a profound sense of pessimism: "For even though we know that the ancient codes of morality are decrepit and no longer tenable, we persist, with a sense of perversity that I would only ironically define as pathetic, in remaining loyal to them. Thus moral man who has no fear of the scientific unknown is today afraid of the moral unknown. Starting out from this point of fear and frustration, his adventure can only end in a stalemate" (Cannes Statement, 179).

With all of the ambiguities of Antonioni's statement, his venture into "the moral unknown" becomes what Levinas terms "the ethical adventure" that *L'avventura* initiates as an artwork and a social and cultural endeavor. In the Cannes Statement Antonioni proposes the revivification of the modern moral imagination, in part through the complex cinema aesthetics of *L'avventura*. He does so in the hope of responding meaningfully to the sexual sickness that his film, like Fellini's *La dolce vita,* documents. It also should be noted that like Fellini, Antonioni disavows any suggestion of himself as a kind of modern-day Jeremiah castigating others for their evils. "I am not a moralist," he says, "and my film is neither a denunciation nor a sermon" (Cannes Statement, 178).

The crisis of erotic illness that he cites as the cause for his efforts for a renewal of the moral life, however, did not emerge from a vacuum. For greater understanding, the statement should be placed in a larger historical context. Antonioni appears specific in regard to his time and place in Italy, but his argument clearly applies across cultures and times. His focus on sexual sickness suggests one place to begin exploring his argument, including its application to his film: with Freud! Indeed, Antonioni's language and understanding of the malaise of eros resonate with some of Freud's theories about sexuality and social illness that were articulated during the first decades of the last century.

In his epochal work on sexuality, *Three Essays on the Theory of Sexuality* (1905), Freud notes the complex indeterminacy of the sexual instinct that for Antonioni leads in his time to deep social sickness. Freud writes that "the impulses of sexual life are among those which, even normally, are the least controlled by the higher activities of the mind."[18] For Freud the uncontrollable nature of the sexual impulses and the excessive attempt by society through parents and institutions to create controls over sexuality guarantee perpetual conflict and the kind of sickness that Antonioni observes.

In a later essay Freud's association of "psychical impotence" and "erotic life" anticipates Antonioni's concerns. Freud writes in "The Most Prevalent

Form of Degradation in Erotic Life" (1912): "If a practicing psychoanalyst asks himself what disorder he is most often called upon to remedy, he is obliged to reply—apart from anxiety in all its many forms—psychical impotence."[19] He maintains "the proposition that psychical impotence is far more widespread than is generally supposed, and that some degree of this condition does in fact characterize the erotic life of civilized peoples" (63–64). Freud attributes this sexual malady to an inability to commingle sexual impulse and tenderness toward the loved one as sexual object. He claims that psychoanalysis has "reduced psychical impotence to a disunion between the tender and sensual currents of erotic feeling" and says "this inhibition" is "an effect of strong fixations in childhood and of frustration in reality later, after the incest-barrier has intervened" (63). While for Freud "restrictions" that inhibit "erotic life" can cause psychic illness, so also "unrestrained sexual liberty from the beginning leads to no better result" (67).

Antonioni's insights into the malaise of eros echo in some ways the analytic work done decades before by Freud on the same subject. Based, therefore, on Antonioni's words and the comparable argument by Freud, *L'avventura* could be discussed as a kind of case study of the malaise of eros or psychical impotence. Antonioni sometimes talks this way in the Cannes Statement about his characters in the film.

Antonioni's language in the statement puts the illness of eros in the context of ethics and morals. His challenge to undertake a moral adventure through *L'avventura* goes beyond a therapeutic examination of the roots of the sexual disease in the psyche and childhood experience. Instead, for Antonioni, the aesthetic screen of the film, to paraphrase Simon Critchley, provides a means for the interaction in a multidimensional temporality of ethics, art, sickness, and trauma.[20] The trauma of "psychic impotence" and erotic illness and the trauma of Antonioni's implied ethical demand achieve dramatic expression in the art form of the film. *L'avventura* takes the issue of erotic illness into a domain of ethical discourse that invites engagement with the work of Levinas and Irigaray, among others.

DOCUMENTARY ROOTS

As in the case of Fellini, Antonioni and his critics deem the documentary aspect of Antonioni's work in film to be of great importance to his overall cinematic theory and practice. Like Fellini, Antonioni wishes to document the life of the people he observes. Recalling his argument in his Cannes Statement that becoming aware of the problem of erotic illness constitutes "only a first step" in dealing with the crisis, it would seem that documentary provides the means for taking such a first step. The documentary undertaking creates the public record of the story of sex and the city.

For Antonioni, however, it also could be argued that documentary constitutes the first step toward the unique challenge of filming the invisible. Documentary for Antonioni inexorably inheres in film. Documentary puts into play the visual and audial materials that provide a foundation for the experimentation, innovation, and ethical engagement of abstract cinema. "All films," he says, "are more or less documentaries. Let's say that when the subject matter of the film is contemporary, the camera documents it. In the case of period films, more violence is exercised on reality, but this is legitimate in any creative operation." Moreover, for Antonioni all films provide documentary of the director himself: "A director does nothing but look for himself in his films. They are documentaries, not of an already-made thought, but of a thought in the making."[21] As Gilberto Perez suggests, "One pull to involvement in an Antonioni film is his keen documentary sense, his strikingly lifelike rendering of the look, the feel of things."[22]

Even with his strong commitment to documentary, Antonioni just as energetically proclaims the shortcomings of a rigid, reportorial adherence to an unimaginative understanding of the visible as the standard for truth in documentary. "You cannot penetrate events with *reportage*," he says. "Today, neorealism is obsolete, in the sense that we aspire more and more to create our own reality. This criterion is even applied to films of a documentary character and to newsreels, most of which are produced according to a preconceived idea. Not cinema at the service of reality, but reality at the service of cinema" (Antonioni, *The Architecture of Vision*, 62–63).

Similarly, Sam Rohdie emphasizes Antonioni's sophisticated understanding of documentary in his filming. For Antonioni, Rohdie argues, documentary involves an unfixed notion of truth that requires creative interaction between the filmmaker and the environment being filmed. Rohdie maintains that Antonioni's idea of the impossibility of capturing reality with finality in film and documentary manifests itself in such films as *L'avventura* and *The Passenger* (1975).[23]

Accordingly, in his discussion of the documentary effort to film and construct reality, Antonioni argues for the need to go beyond the restrictions of a rigid understanding of realism. He says that in his documentaries "there had already been a tendency towards narrative, an opening out towards the intimate problems of the individual. In short, elements of storytelling were already present in my work" (Rohdie, *Antonioni*, 242). In proposing the inescapable connection between documentary and fiction, Antonioni aligns himself, as I noted earlier, with Paul Ricoeur regarding the lines separating history and fiction and documentary and history.[24] Antonioni, however, also passionately articulates his need to capitalize on this connection between documentary and fiction to express his own vision of reality and his original idea of film. He says that he is "convinced that if you want to express your own poetic world you have to transcend reality" (Antonioni, *The Architecture of Vision*, 242).

Antonioni's comments regarding documentary grew out of his personal history as a writer and filmmaker during the period of the collapse of fascism in the early 1940s. Geoffrey Nowell-Smith and Sam Rohdie have both suggested that Antonioni's experience during this period was crucial in helping to shape his approach to film.[25] It was at this time that Antonioni made some of his first documentaries. During this period he also was forming some of his basic critical ideas about film art that developed into the theories and projects of his years of cinematic success.

As Antonioni matured, his thinking on film came to blend with his perspective on the social crises of the times. Thus, his articulation of a coherent theory of documentary and the art of film seems consistent with his concern for a society in crisis. In his film theory Antonioni proposes a radical program for challenging what Rohdie calls the conventional "representational codes" that dominate how cinema communicates (Rohdie, *Antonioni*, 175). For Antonioni, representational codes involve both film art—the use of film techniques and forms to construct cinematic narrative and documentary—and film content and subject matter. The ethical crisis of a powerful social sickness compels the urgency of Antonioni's program for rethinking representational codes as a part of a new cinema.

ANNA AND HER FATHER

Levinas's name appears in the title of Irigaray's crucial essay on him, "The Fecundity of the Caress: A Reading of Levinas, *Totality and Infinity*, 'Phenomenology of Eros,'" but it barely comes up again. Rather than directly address him, as she does in "Questions to Emmanuel Levinas," Irigaray in "The Fecundity of the Caress" ingeniously works off of Levinas's bias toward women as apparently based on his doubts about the ethics of female sexuality. Irigaray proposes her own provocative program for achieving ethical transcendence for the other through sexuality. This way she supersedes the role that Levinas gives women as a platform for men's transcendence.

For Levinas, as Irigaray and other feminist writers see him, the female body initiates ethics as the embodiment of the dwelling but at the cost to the feminine of sacrificing woman's humanity to the power of the male. Levinasian ethics, as delineated in *Totality and Infinity* and his other works, turns the female body into a self-contained prison that Irigaray wishes to liberate through a new understanding of the saving power of the flesh.

In pieces on Levinas and other writings, Irigaray proposes the merger of the divine and the flesh. In contrast to the solipsism of "possession," she argues, "Sensual pleasure can reopen and reverse this conception and construction of the world."[26] Irigaray writes, "Scent or premonition between my self and the other, this memory of the flesh as the place of approach means ethical fidelity to incarnation." For Irigaray the suppression of the flesh vitiates alterity and therefore weakens "any possibility of access to transcendence" ("The Fecundity of the Caress," 217).

The dynamic between Irigaray, other feminists, and Levinas offers a vital perspective for viewing *L'avventura*, for the film provides a cinematic development of the discussion. *L'avventura* extends the exchange of ideas that occurs between Levinas and feminists on the feminine and women, sexuality in modern times, the flesh and the body, and ethics and transcendence.

Going back to the beginning of this discussion with the entrance onto the scene of Anna in the film's opening shot, *L'avventura* presents the crisis of the feminine. In the light of Irigaray's work the scene even resonates with another opening, the initial sentences of "The Fecundity of the Caress." Irigaray writes, "On the horizon of a story is found what was in the beginning: this naïve or native sense of touch, in which the subject does not yet exist" (185). Indeed, the scene with Anna suggests an absence of subjectivity, an ambiguity of identity, an uncertainty of direction.

As Anna enters the scene and walks on the roadway, a country house behind her and then an open field provide the background to her entrance. As she continues her walk, the moving frame changes the background, and the camera tracks back to concentrate in a medium close-up on her unhappy face and disgruntled expression. Going through a kind of open garden gate or door, she pauses, clearly seeking someone. Offscreen a voice that will prove to be her father's says, "Soon this poor villa will be smothered." She turns toward the voice as though the words also could be describing her situation. The expression of annoyance on her face never quite changes in this scene (or through much of the opening sequences of the film for that matter), revealing such anxiety as her general state of mind. At the words, she turns to her right, and the expression on her face becomes almost threatening as she looks offscreen to her father (Renzo Rizzi), who says, "To think there were woods here once," as Anna moves to her right. As she moves offscreen, the camera lingers briefly on the field and trees in the background that soon could be demolished by the construction the father mentions. The brief lingering of the camera in the midst of Anna's exit exemplifies Antonioni's famous style of "dead time," when he concentrates on a scene or setting after the action has moved on.[27]

The camera then cuts to the father and a worker. At first glimpse the shot seems perfectly ordinary, but closer examination indicates much about the rich, deep meaning of Antonioni's settings and film construction. In the far background in a long shot the scene provides a view of the Vatican almost in a direct line with the father's face. To the left, construction sites with workers in a field in the middle ground illustrate the change that bothers the father. The father stands on the gravel road by the fields and open landscape. He wears an expensive-looking business suit with a white handkerchief in the breast pocket that matches the whiteness of his shirt. He seems formidably formal and reserved and thoroughly out of place in the midst of the setting. His bearing is rigid as Anna enters. He turns behind him and greets Anna, who is coming toward him. He stands in line with the Vatican while her youthful white dress stands out against the dark earthy colors of the villa's house in the middle ground to the right as she faces her father. The camera stays briefly with this balanced division—his dark formality offsets the Vatican in the distance while her youth connects to the domesticity of the house and the fertility of the fields. Antonioni subtly insinuates into the scene meanings about fathers, daughters, authority, and love that will resonate throughout the film.

Clearly, Anna and her father represent contrasting principles. He suggests serious paternal authority in conflict with her daughterly distance and alienation. Their opening dialogue evidences tensions that their body language and physical separation accentuate. He indicates displeasure with her plans to leave him alone by going sailing yet berates her for failing to keep up with his notion of proper attire by not wearing a hat with the name of the yacht on it. Whatever choice she makes, he seems prepared to criticize her for it. When she moves past him to face him, with the fields and the construction behind her, he looks off to his left. In this frame the Vatican dome appears directly over his left shoulder. Several critics, including Gilberto Perez, note that *"L'avventura* links the bald head of Anna's father with the dome of St. Peter's behind him" as part of the "rather witty visual rhyme at the beginning" of the film (Perez, *The Material Ghost*, 408). Perez suggests that this self-conscious visual choreography of signifiers leaves unsettled the question of Anna's relationship to her father, the church, and society. Such themes permeate the film.

This scene also significantly dramatizes Anna's sense of entrapment, most obviously as a woman and a daughter, in a powerful patriarchal culture. Even when she switches places in the frame with her father so that her beautiful dark hair rather than her father's gleaming bald head lines up in contrast to St. Peter's in the background, she remains encircled by suggestions of masculine, lifeless patriarchy. She stands between her father and the church, ostensibly drawing fire from both, creating a situation of self-generating rebellious disaffection. The sensuous features of her face with her pronounced lips and dark, angry eyes, the voluminous dark hair, and the sense of barely suppressed, simmering anger vividly contrast with the way St. Peter's reinforces the rigidity, coldness, and austerity of her father's stance, dress, and demeanor.

The verbal exchange between father and daughter also indicates hidden secrets and guilt in their relationship that never get revealed in detail but suggest a degree of deeper mystery. He says that "after thirty years of never telling the truth" as a diplomat, he wishes to speak the truth finally to his own daughter. He feels forced "to rest, not only from my diplomatic duties but as a father." She asks in turn if there are "any more truths to tell me," and he responds, "You know it." She says, "That one I beg you to spare me: goodbye father." In the absence of a specifically stated event or act, the exchange indicates underlying guilt over secrets between father and daughter as a permanent, unresolved situation that helps determine their relationship.

THE ABJECT FATHER

This opening scene in *L'avventura* of a daughter in conflict with her father—perhaps all fathers—provides dramatic illustration of Kelly Oliver's argument about disembodied paternity and abjection in both Freud and Levinas. At first the scene with Anna's father and the papal dome suggests her confrontation as a daughter and woman with the power of traditional patriarchal authority. Anna's situation follows the classic Freudian model of patriarchal authority. Freud's paradigm, of course, starts with the father's virile dominance of a son who ultimately will internalize and supersede the father's authority. The father's power takes shape in the form of cultural, psychological, and legal authority. This masculine model places Anna as a daughter in a secondary relationship to the father.

Levinas's alternative to Freudian virility emphasizes the infinite potential of fecundity and paternity that becomes possible through the sexuality and maternity of the feminine, a feminine that remains a secondary, perhaps even a nonhuman, figure defined primarily by her animal nature. The woman enables the father's access to the infinite through fecundity and maternity. Explaining what she calls Levinas's "ontology of paternity," Oliver says, "Paternity conquers 'father time' by moving through the feminine." She adds, "Fecundity engenders the subject as desiring and therefore as an infinite subject who transcends the limits of subjectivity.... For Levinas, fecundity, associated as it is with paternity, is distinct from virility."[28]

Although Levinas breaks with the Freudian tradition of "the father's authority and virility," he repeats the problem of disembodiment, as Oliver says, largely because "of the belief that *embodied eros* is a contradiction, that feelings and passions are associated with the body that must be overcome for pure eros." Like Irigaray, Oliver sees Levinas as undermining the potential of his own project through his rejection of the sexualized body. "For Levinas," she says, "even though the father is not the virile subject, his love is not embodied. The body of the father is still absent from paternity and the father's love is still abstract" ("Paternal Election and the Absent Father," 236).

This notion of the abstract, disembodied love of the father helps to explain Anna's and her father's situation in *L'avventura*. Anna's father embodies abstract paternal authority. No less than papal authority itself seems to reinforce that authority of Anna's father through its presence in the setting. Yet the scene ultimately dramatizes the contradiction of this authority. The father's apparent lack of consistent involvement in Anna's life, his self-centered emotional estrangement from her, and his bitter sense of forced retirement in his role as a father epitomize the notion, as described by Oliver, of the "abject father," as opposed to the patriarchal figure of Freudian dominance.

Thus, while the omnipotence of the father poses a threat, the greater threat comes from the possibility of the absence of paternity. Oliver writes, "The fantasy of the father's omnipotence protects the child from a more terrifying fantasy, the fantasy of the father's impotence, which threatens not just the child's death, but the child's coming to be." Oliver emphasizes that "because seminal fluids are out of control, accidental, chancy," the inescapable question persists of the indeterminacy of paternity. The uncertainty of the relationship between bodily boundaries and such fluids dramatizes the significance of Oliver's "abject father":

> The threat of what I call an *abject father* is more terrifying than the threat of an omnipotent father. At least the omnipotent father promises omnipotence for the son who one day can take his place. An identification with an abject father, on the other hand, promises indeterminacy and contingency with regard to even life and death. In the end, both the fear of the omnipotent father and the terror of the impotent father operate within the same economy of virility, which trades on the fear of a male body. (234)

Oliver asserts that only the father's "virile will" and "the authority of his law" can separate him from "indeterminacy or chance" when it comes to paternity: "The virility of his will and the authority of his law are based on the complete evacuation of his body and its uncontrollable fluids" (236).

Interestingly, when Oliver attributes this crisis of the body, of love, and identity—what she calls "the repressed fantasy of the abject paternal body"—to the "notion of virile subjectivity, and the opposition between body and mind or nature and culture," her explanation compares to similar concerns expressed by Antonioni, Freud, and Irigaray on the split between body and psyche as a key source for sexual illness. Irigaray, especially, recalls Freud's discussion of the dichotomy in the West between the deprecation of the sexual impulse and the overvaluation of the sexual object: "Only certain oriental traditions speak of the energizing, aesthetic, and religious fecundity of the sexual act: the two sexes give each other the seed of life and eternity, the growing generation of and between them both." Irigaray writes further of the "question of the dissociation of body and soul, of sexuality and spirituality, of the lack of a passage for the spirit, for the god, between the inside and the outside, the outside and the inside, and of their distribution between the sexes in the sexual act" (*An Ethics of Sexual Difference*, 14, 15).

Oliver's brief suggestion for the beginning of an "antidote" to this situation of sexual sickness again points directly to Anna's place in *L'avventura*. Oliver says the culture both maintains and represses "the fantasy of the abject father" because it "has no antidote or counterweight for such a fantasy." She writes, "The antidote is an image of paternal eros—a paternal eros that is embodied, passionate, and that is not just channeled through the maternal body" ("Paternal Election and the Absent Father," 236). Of course, Anna's father gives no suggestion of such a radical antidote to their mutual crisis. He does not indicate a potential for offering an embodied, passionate love as a father for her as his daughter and a woman. In fact, everything about him in the scene intimates his double absence from her, not only as a father but, especially, as a father of a daughter. He epitomizes abstract paternity in his style while also clearly seeing her as less than fully human, as a kind of domestic decoration who should perform a stereotypical female role of supporting and serving him. The promise of fecundity and infinity that might exist in a relationship with a son clearly does not exist in his relationship with her. Thus, when Oliver asks, "Could the future be a daughter?" (237), the father's answer certainly would be no, at least not as long as she acts independently from him, a potential answer that soon gets fulfilled by Anna's mysterious, unsolved disappearance.

Oliver's battery of other questions about fathers and daughters that concludes her essay could be interpreted as intimating a possible suggestion for the secret between Anna and her father: "Would the father discover himself in his daughter's substance, gestures, and uniqueness? And, if the father does not, or cannot, elect a daughter, then doesn't the fantasy that she is unwanted, an accident, unloved, should-have-been-otherwise, become devastating for her? Isn't she forced into an identification with an abject father who refuses to love her?" (239).

Oliver's questions summarize Anna's plight, hinting at a possible reason why her beautiful face is such a study in dejection, sadness, and anger. The questions also suggest that the basic underlying secret between father and daughter might just be that, sadly, the answer to each would be yes. Of course, these questions apply so well to Anna in *L'avventura* because they would apply so well to other women.

Oliver's questions and conclusion highlight the central ethical dilemma and the contradiction at the core of Levinas's philosophy involving the feminine and women. "For Levinas," she says, "the future that paternity engenders is masculine. Insofar as it is masculine, it is limited. Insofar as it is limited, it is not open to radical alterity. And insofar as it is not open to radical alterity, the future is finite and must come to an end. If there are no daughters, then [there] will be no more sons" (239).

Oliver's argument constitutes a challenge to Levinasian writers to reexamine his thought to account for and include daughters such as Anna. Oliver's words also can be taken as a test of *L'avventura*'s success in contributing to this program of revision. She reframes the issue in the context of making a meaningful future possible for daughters and sons.

The tracking shot that follows the initial exchange between Anna and her father develops the question of the feminine in the film. Considering the issue of gender and "feminism" in his book on Antonioni's films, Brunette wonders "if we read" Antonioni's films in a certain way now "because feminism has altered our interpretive frame" (Brunette, *The Films of Michelangelo Antonioni*, 34). Brunette notes that attitudes were different in 1960, when the film first appeared. Antonioni's Cannes Statement testifies, however, to how seriously he was thinking about such matters at the time.

Thus, in the opening scene of *L'avventura* the cut from Anna, with her back to the Vatican, to her approach to her father continues a special interest in the scene on the situation of women in relation to men. As she moves from her position in front of the Vatican to another frame to say good-bye to her father and kiss him on the cheek, the kiss and body movement remain grudging. The annoyance on the father's face matches Anna's hostility. After kissing him, she steps in front of him for the beginning of a tracking shot. She looks off thoughtfully to her left while behind her the father proclaims of her boyfriend, "My darling daughter, that guy—he'll never marry you." He says it as though to punish her for leaving him, especially with such a perfunctory kiss. Lost in thought, with her back to him and with the continuing dark expression on her face, Anna's words confirm the vulnerability of her situation as a woman: "Up to now, I didn't want to marry him." The father responds with a remark that dismisses her with a strong indication of his visceral indifference toward her: "It's all the same difference. Good-bye dear." Both comments assert the lack of clarity about the place of women in the modern society around them that uproots suburban villas and extirpates the roots of classic family ties.

INTRODUCING CLAUDIA

While the verbal exchange between father and daughter further explains the nature of Anna's relationship to her father, the visual track, as usual in Antonioni's films, proves even more important in advancing the significance of the film. As Anna and her father exchange hostilities, Claudia (Monica Vitti) enters the frame from the upper left corner, at a rough diagonal from the father and Anna. She observes father and daughter and, in a lovely little internal dynamic, walks past them, out of the frame to await them as they walk along in the slow tracking shot. The frame demonstrates a kind of Deleuzian time set of a dynamic of internal and external meanings, movements, and temporalities. As the father says "Ciao" to his daughter, the camera tracks and catches up with Claudia.

Even in this momentary initial glimpse of Vitti, it can be imagined why Antonioni not only used her in so many of his important subsequent films but also fell in love with her. Antonioni has said of Vitti that she "has an extremely expressive face" and that falling in love with her did not interfere with working with her "because I forget about the relationship between myself and any actress when working with her" (Antonioni, *The Architecture of Vision*, 42, 164). In this scene the self-conscious, awkward smile on Vitti's "extremely expressive face" radiates her character's wish to be accepted and noticed while also indicating her recognition that she is intruding on a private moment between Anna and her father. Vitti's instant ability to convey these conflicting emotions demonstrates her brilliance as an actor. Her restrained body movements and language further indicate sensitive magnetic energy.

Significantly, the father barely notices Claudia, even failing to acknowledge her presence after he bids Anna good-bye. Such rude disdain for Claudia signals an immediate repetition of his attitude of superior indifference toward his daughter. Distracted with his own problems, he walks off. The women look offscreen to the father, who leaves through the garden gate and enters his villa, the perfect picture of abjection. He disappears as Anna herself also soon will disappear. Claudia, however, also looks at Anna looking at her father as though intuiting the tension of the family scene. Claudia's place on the sidelines dramatizes her marginality as a figure in this scene but also emphasizes the theme of feminine alienation that has marked Anna's dealing with her father throughout the film's opening moments.

As the film advances, Claudia moves steadily toward the center of the story as the dominant figure, bringing with her two important themes that have been at the heart of our discussion of *L'avventura* from the beginning. From both a Levinasian and a feminist perspective, the great challenge for Antonioni involves showing that these forces can move together. One theme thrusts Claudia forward on her journey toward the ethical challenge of transcendence, alterity, and responsibility for the other. The second theme for Claudia requires reconciling the ethical challenge of transcendence with the immanence of the demands of her own sexualized body. As indicated in Antonioni's Cannes Statement about *L'avventura*, and as articulated by Irigaray and others, the failure to meld these two movements of ethics and the body leaves both in perverted conditions of incompletion in a sexually sick society. This duality relates to the distinction Irigaray sees in Levinas between the descriptive phenomenological approach toward understanding the ontology of the feminine and the metaphysical demands of ethical relationships, what Stella Sandford calls "the metaphysics of love."[29]

Claudia's journey in the film to reconcile these forces of transcendence and the feminine body will involve encountering multiple forms of the sexual sickness that Antonioni describes. Her position as an outsider gives her a special perspective on those crises and the strength to engage them. In contrast Anna, from the beginning, walks into the trap that has been set for her from birth under the gaze of her absent but powerful father, who has admitted to years of deception. Anna has been defined in a way that takes away her options as a person, leaving her with little direction on how to escape to create a new life for herself. Anna yearns for such escape but does not know where to go, whereas Claudia's search opens possibilities for her of imagining a different kind of life, one that can meld transcendence and love.

Antonioni's double perspective on transcendence and the sexual feminine body helps structure his ethics of cinema in sequences that follow the film's introduction of Anna, her father, and Claudia. The drama of the ethical crisis of the body comes first.

THE BODY AND THE DWELLING

The importance that Levinas places on the body and enjoyment has helped make his work of value to feminist writers who wish to empower women through the tangible immediacy of the feminine. He says, "Only a subject that eats can be for-the-other, or can signify. Signification, the one-for-the-other, has meaning only among beings of flesh and blood." This power of the body inspires him to emphasize physical enjoyment and what he terms "sensibility": "The immediacy of the sensible is the immediacy of enjoyment and its frustration." Levinas uses the term *proximity* to convey the ethical relationship to the other involved in such physicality and sensibility: "The proximity of the other is the immediate opening up for the other of the immediacy of enjoyment, the immediacy of taste, materialization of matter, altered by the immediacy of contact."[30]

As we have seen, however, the feminine changes the meaning of the body and enjoyment for Levinas. The feminine body for Levinas becomes important primarily for what it can do in aiding the male to achieve ethical transcendence. Accordingly, Levinas compares the feminine to the dwelling as home and as necessary for the nurturance of the ethical. In *Totality and Infinity* he says that "within the system of finalities in which human life maintains itself the home occupies a privileged place." He describes this "privileged role of the home" as the "condition" and the "commencement" of "human activity." He then associates this "condition" with the woman. Comparing the woman to the dwelling, he says that "the primary hospitable welcome which describes the field of intimacy, is the Woman. The woman is the condition for recollection, the interiority of the Home, and inhabitation" (*Totality and Infinity*, 152, 155). For Levinas this condition of the home that the woman represents clearly serves the interests of men.

In the sequence in *L'avventura* that follows the opening garden scene with Anna and her father, Antonioni maintains the association that Levinas proposes between the female body and the dwelling. He develops this connection in a sequence involving a shot of a vestibule and an apartment scene that suggest why attitudes about such a connection of the dwelling, interiority, and the feminine need more thought. Antonioni relates the interior space of the dwelling to the feminine, but he also adds a powerful tone of critical irony to the association that emphasizes the problematic nature of this so-called condition for women.

Running late, because of Anna's meeting with her father, Anna and Claudia take a car driven by Anna's chauffeur to meet the male protagonist of the film and Anna's lover, Sandro (Gabriele Ferzetti), and stop at a small plaza or square. After dismissing the driver, Anna becomes more impulsive, surprising Claudia by telling her that she no longer wishes to see Sandro, in spite of her extended separation from him. Just as she decides to leave, thereby disappointing Claudia by ending the plans for a cruise, Sandro calls from the window of his apartment. A low-angle shot appropriately positions him between both women. Anna then lightly touches Claudia and proceeds to enter the building through the door and hallway.

The film cuts to an interior shot of the hallway as Anna enters the door. The shot from the end of the hallway signals a change to feminine space. What seems to be the simplest and most obvious of shots of an ordinary entryway proves, in fact, to be a transformational visualization of the feminine. Anna moves over the threshold into the interior feminine space to take her place as a woman with a man she often wishes to leave. As she walks through the hallway toward the camera, her shadow follows her on the wall to the right, as though an aspect of her identity separates from her but also watches over her. Continuing toward the camera, Anna veers slightly to her right; her head disappears from the shot so that only her midsection—her thin waist—and arm appear in the shot. The shot would seem to suggest, therefore, a decapitation, with a close-up of her body at the precise time when her body and the space of Sandro's apartment building enter into an important representational relationship. As she passes before the camera, in the middle of the screen on the outer side of the threshold, Claudia appears in the light, walking away from the door.

With Anna walking into the building and Claudia walking away into the sunlight, the shot captures a beautifully simple but profound bidirectional action, a clear pull in opposite directions by both women. The threshold of the door becomes a kind of visual fulcrum, a center of the action. This literal threshold is equally symbolic, reifying Levinasian contradictions so central to Irigaray. For Irigaray a threshold conveys the mind-body opening of the struggle of the feminine to overcome patriarchal sexism in the search for transcendence. The word *threshold* appears repeatedly in her essays. At times the word signals the beginning of a descent into a surrender of the female body to the demands of the male. At other times *threshold* passionately evokes the potential for spiritual renewal through the interaction of flesh and fluid with the lover. Anna crosses a threshold into a kind of hell by handing herself over to an unappreciative, insensitive lover, who will epitomize the rampant sexual sickness that Antonioni decries in his Cannes Statement.

Thus, in their different ways Irigaray and Antonioni use the idea of the threshold to structure a complexity of meanings. Irigaray writes in "The Fecundity of the Caress" that "profanity always designates a threshold" (188). Anna enacts in *L'avventura* such profanation with her surrender to Sandro. In fact, Irigaray could be thinking of Anna when she writes, "She is placed under house arrest, lacking the will and movement of love" ("The Fecundity of the Caress," 199). Under such "house arrest," in essence turning herself in, "she becomes," in Irigaray's phrase, "part of the male lover's world. Keeping herself on the threshold, perhaps" (206). Failing to carry through on her self-protective impulse on the plaza to leave without seeing Sandro, Anna gives up body and soul. Once again, Irigaray's words pertain to Anna: "She divests herself of her own will to love in order to become what is required for his exercise of will. Which assigns her to the place of nonwilling in his ethics. Her fall into the identity of the beloved one cancels out any real giving of self and makes her into a thing, or something other than the woman that she needs to be. She lets herself be taken but does not give herself. She quits the locus of all responsibility, her own ethical site" (198–99).

Without a sense of possession of her own dwelling place and ultimately of her own body and identity, Anna lives in what Irigaray in "Love of Self" calls "*internal exile*" (*An Ethics of Sexual Difference*, 65), perpetuating such a relationship that clearly originated with her absence of place in her father's home.

The scene that follows painfully enacts a process of possession of Anna by her lover. As the other for Sandro, she experiences "a transformation of the flesh of the other into his own temporality," as Irigaray says, rather than the creation of something new and regenerative for the both of them.[31] This relationship undermines any possibility for Anna of achieving Irigaray's idea of "an ethics of sexual difference." As Irigaray says in "Sexual Difference," "in order for an ethics of sexual difference to come into being, we must constitute a possible place for each sex, body, and flesh to inhabit" (*An Ethics of Sexual Difference*, 17–18).

The powerful visual and psychological pull between Anna and Claudia will continue both to connect and separate them when Anna enters into Sandro's room to make love. Anna enters the room with the same look of glaring hostility and the same physical intensity that have characterized her actions from the beginning. Seeing her mood, Sandro tries to entertain her with a silly pose that only aggravates the situation. She walks around the room without smiling, staring at him until she moves below an iron bar that divides the room, a bar that a builder or an architect such as Sandro would have occasion to find. With her back to Sandro and the camera, she begins to unbutton her dress. Sandro moves closer and says, as she turns toward him, "Your friend is downstairs, waiting." The iron bar literally covers her forehead right above her eyebrows, visually dividing her head. Meanwhile, Anna's facial expression and body movements continue to show no affection toward Sandro, only division and angry hostility. Her attitude about sex seems professional. She answers him: "Let her wait." The remark seems rude regarding her close friend. As she enters the bedroom and lowers herself onto the bed, an ornate, imposing bed frame makes a diagonal across the screen, partially enclosing her.

At this point Antonioni makes a marvelous cut to Sandro's back and Anna's face as they kiss. The new shot helps to explain the apparent callousness of Anna's remark about Claudia by continuing the tense visual and physical pull between the two women that began in the vestibule. The shot of Anna and Sandro kissing extends in a visual line from the kissing couple in the interior of the apartment through an open window above a window guard to Claudia, who is in the plaza and who looks up at the window. This repeats the dynamic tension of the vestibule shot, with Anna inside in relative dark and Claudia in deep background in the light of the plaza. The window guard has something of the same ornateness as the bed frame, thereby visually continuing the idea of enclosure. The open window, the guard, and the frame constitute another threshold.

For Anna the visual line to Claudia constitutes a kind of lifeline. She wishes to expose herself to Claudia, not in an exhibitionistic act of self-indulgence but as a revelation of her desire and vulnerability. The expression on Anna's face throughout the scene displays a state of utter desperation. As Sandro draws the drapes, Anna again is shown enclosed by the bed frame. Claudia on the outside plaza sees Sandro draw the drapes, and in the next shot a narrow opening between the drapes from the apartment shows Claudia looking up. The shots dramatize the separation of and bond between the two women, leaving Anna alone with Sandro.

On the bed Sandro, paying serious attention to Anna for the first time, asks, "How are you?" Her expression underscores her answer: "Awful."

When he asks, "Why?" she grows angry, repeating his question several times through clenched teeth with a bitter facial expression and a voice that grows increasingly frustrated. She says, "Perché? Perché? Perché? Perché?" while striking at him with her fists. Laughing, he gets excited by her emotion, oblivious to the significance of the word. Anna's "Why?" expresses protest not just over Sandro's possessiveness but the difficulty of comprehending the situation of her life.

In contrast, Claudia goes into an art gallery on the plaza that seems to be directly below the apartment. Tourists chatter in English about the art. The choice of an art gallery for the scene could seem random on Antonioni's part. But when Claudia walks from the gallery, she turns and looks up at a window. The scene cuts to Anna's face as Sandro makes love to her. The back of his head momentarily covers her face and then moves off. Her face appears in a tight close-up. In the midst of her lover's grasp and their lovemaking, her face reveals absolute anguish.

Again in sharp contrast, the cut back to Claudia in the gallery shows her in a beautiful low-angle, fully lit shot, her face radiant. The contrast between the close-ups of the women suggests the setting of the gallery, rather than being random, may indicate the importance for Claudia of creative independence in life as in art.

Toward the end of the sequence a cut to the apartment and Anna's face provides another powerful contrast with Claudia's close-up. As Anna and Sandro kiss, the shot steadily focuses on the look of distraction and pain on Anna's face. Her mouth indicates not passion but a kind of self-consumption, her lost identity and being.

In the final cut of this sequence the interior camera shows Claudia pausing at the door to the vestibule. She looks in the vestibule as though searching for her friend and pondering the significance of this interlude. She closes the door. The vestibule seems to have the last word. In Antonionian dead time, with no major action in the scene, the shot compels self-reflection on its meaning. A superimposed shot of the closed doors of the vestibule on a car on the road ends the sequence as all three drive off for their cruise.

The sequence in Sandro's apartment, which seems at first to be about an innocuous episode in the lives of three ordinary people, turns out to be a complex, carefully constructed portrait of one woman's despair intersecting with the presentation of the beginning of another's journey. The apartment scene dramatizes the feminine as a dwelling, a place, a scene to be possessed joyfully by the male. The apparent simplicity of Claudia as the outsider and Anna on the inside betrays the deeper meanings of the scene and the challenge confronting Claudia.

JOURNEY TOWARD REDEMPTION: CLAUDIA'S STORY

Following the apartment-vestibule sequence, the drama on the interior side of the threshold of the surrender of the feminine body as the dwelling for the male slowly shifts to Claudia's journey, a quest for a form of redemption that incorporates both Levinasian ethical transcendence and feminist sensibility regarding the sexual body. It begins with the cruise she takes with Sandro and Anna, and it synthesizes a sexual ethics and transcendence.

Claudia's quest for renewal also demonstrates Antonioni's effort to examine the invisible in the film. Roland Barthes' important statement on the genius of Antonioni helps to explain this aspect of Antonioni's filmmaking. Barthes compares Antonioni's aesthetic to the artist Henri Matisse's effort "to paint the void." He says that "there is a way in which your art is also an art of the interstice." Antonioni, in a manner of speaking, films the invisible by compelling the opening of the imagination to the invisible. He directs attention to the interstices, to the difficult meaning of what cannot be seen; he "approaches truth at an angle; his world is truth seized indirectly."[32] Thus, in the opening scene Antonioni only hints at the harshness, and perhaps even abuse, of the father toward Anna by emphasizing her reactions to him and what occurs between them rather than directly filming blatantly cruel behavior.

Similarly, in Sandro's apartment the artistry of Antonioni's organization of shots brings to life the relationships of the characters by often leaving unsaid the implications of what appears in the scene. Sandro's indifference manifests itself partly by what he fails to do and see. Also in the apartment scene, the ultimate significance of Claudia's relationship to Anna suggests itself indirectly through what remains unspoken and intimated through visual expressions and physical gestures.

At the same time, Antonioni, like Fellini, could carefully document the life around him of such concern to his ethical sensibility. Thus, on the cruise that follows the scene at Sandro's apartment, the characters on the yacht become interesting in both their singularity and typicality as part of a wealthy leisure class whose lifestyles exemplify Antonioni's concerns about sick sexuality. Licentiousness, flirtation, animosity, and boredom characterize their attitudes, behavior, and interactions, although some of them also, as Nowell-Smith says, exhibit redeeming qualities "of insight and compassion" (Nowell-Smith, *L'avventura*, 37).

The documentation of erotic illness provides motivation for the search in *L'avventura* for new ethical and moral meaning to modern experience. As Brunette says, "men chase women throughout the film." He then delineates in detail many examples of erotic sickness that characterize the culture that confronts Claudia on her search—a mob scene in Messina of "thousands of crazed males" chasing an actress-prostitute, Gloria Perkins (Dorothy De Poliolo), with a torn dress in a role comparable to Anita Ekberg's in *La dolce vita*; "hordes of glowering men in Noto," who menace Claudia to the point of seriously suggesting the possibility of a gang rape; a "sex-crazed" pharmacist, uninhibited by his sexual addiction even in front of his wife (Brunette, *The Films of Michelangelo Antonioni*, 32–33). To this incomplete list of obsessions and obscenities we can add the farcical mutual seduction between a middle-aged Giulia (Dominique Blanchar) and Goffredo (Giovanni Petrucci), a seventeen-year old artist who disguises his embarrassing obsession with nude women with his paintings and explains himself to Giulia by telling her that "no landscape is as beautiful as a woman."

In this context Claudia embarks with Anna and Sandro and several other people on a crowded yacht for a shared adventure on the seas north of Sicily by the Aeolian Islands. In the opening shot of the cruise the stark, massive rocky face of the volcanic island of Basiluzzo looms rather ominously in the distance, foreshadowing events to come. Before they arrive at the island of Lisca Bianca, Anna creates a commotion, first by spontaneously diving into the sea for a swim, causing others to join her, and then by concocting a story about seeing a shark.

Drying off and donning fresh clothing in the cabin below deck, Anna and Claudia engage each other in a sweet, intimate manner of friendly gestures and looks that comes closest to giving credibility to Brunette's claim that a "strong undercurrent of homoeroticism" exists between the two women (Brunette, *The Films of Michelangelo Antonioni*, 34). Smiling profusely and genuinely, they exhibit great pleasure in each other's company as Anna urges Claudia to try on Anna's black blouse. Anna actually bounces slightly with joy watching her friend try on the blouse. Claudia moves left and steps up to the bathroom mirror to check out how she looks. When she turns around with the mirror over her left shoulder, she looks down as Anna enters from the right with her back to the camera, creating a multiple-mirror effect. They look at each other, seeming to mirror each other except for the stark, symbolic difference that Anna is dark and Claudia blonde. Anna urges her friend to keep the blouse and then moves right, facing the wall with her bare back toward the camera as she continues dressing. Claudia soon joins her, facing the wall with her bare back to the camera. Faceless, they are the same yet different, the self in the other. After Claudia leaves to return to the deck, Anna's look follows her offscreen with a pensive, self-reflexive expression. A cigarette protrudes from her mouth as she thinks. She stuffs the black blouse into Claudia's bag. The gift of the blouse signifies not only intimacy and affection but an intimation of the forthcoming transfer of identity between the women.

Perhaps motivated in part by her intimacy with Claudia on the yacht, when the people disembark on the island of Lisca Bianca and break up into different groups, Anna tells Sandro that she thinks they need to separate again. As they argue, they are situated on a ledge of rough rocks with the open sea in the background. Sandro insists that since they plan to be married, their disagreements will take care of themselves. Giulia and her partner, Corrado (James Addams), pop up theatrically in the background on the rocks. Their appearance constitutes a symbolic gesture, suggesting the likelihood of a rough future for Anna if she stays with Sandro.

In their argument, Anna's and Sandro's movements and the camera's movements reinforce the tortuous nature of their conversation as further confirmation of their tortured relationship. She reveals that the thought of being without him makes her want to die, but she says, "And yet I don't feel you anymore." In a two-shot, with both of them facing the camera, Sandro moves toward her on the rocks, touching her hair and asks if she felt that way "Even yesterday, at my place, you didn't feel me any more." She turns, facing him, so that the sea and coast are behind her. She stares fiercely into his eyes. Seeming to forget her own bitter state of mind at the time, she says angrily, "You always need to vilify everything." A deep look of sorrow replaces her anger. Scratching at rocks and gesturing with annoyance, Sandro turns and walks behind her toward the sea, tosses a pebble and moves on to lie down on a ledge. Anna stays in the foreground, leaning against a rock, turning her cheek, and resting her face on her hand. Sandro looks at her sullenly from behind. She turns back toward him as he stretches out to fall asleep, perhaps an indication of what marriage would mean to him. The shot of the two of them dissolves slowly, unevenly to the rough, dangerous cliffs and the sea.

Even on an island, miles away from Sandro's apartment and her father's villa in Rome, Anna remains in a state of her own perpetual exile, on the threshold between profanity and love. The jagged, protruding rocks and careful filming of the scene dramatize Anna's continuing sense of entrapment. In spite of her efforts to leave, she cannot escape, at least not in a conventional way. So she disappears! Ready to return to their yacht, the group realizes Anna is gone.

The rest of *L'avventura*, by far the longest part of the movie, becomes the adventure of Claudia as the driving force in a search for the lost Anna. In fact, Anna's trauma can be seen as prefatory to the ethical crisis that confronts Claudia as the film proceeds. Anna's existential struggle for her own identity evolves into Claudia's ethical adventure. The ontology of the feminine moves into the realm of ethics and the other, including the realm of Irigaray's ethics of sexual difference.

For Claudia, the ethical responsibility of her relationship to Anna sharpens after Anna's disappearance as it conflicts with her developing affair with Sandro. She sees herself in terms of her relationship to Anna while at the same time having to deal with Sandro, whose behavior and character remain basically unchanged with both women. It becomes an engagement of ethical subjectivity and the other.

BODY AND SOUL

In her love for and devotion to Anna, Claudia cannot escape her body. Equally important, she does not want to escape it. Almost immediately, Sandro will begin transferring his affections to her, an act of shared disloyalty to Anna that will haunt Claudia and ultimately return to strike her when Sandro, at the end of the movie, cheats on her with Gloria Perkins, the actress-prostitute from the earlier Messina mob scene. Before that, Claudia will find it almost impossible to resist him. Indeed, as the story advances, Claudia's fear that Anna will reappear and take Sandro away from her grows steadily. This conflict obviously confounds her ethical position. Thus, Brunette thinks the film in the end emphasizes "the possibility of redemption" for Sandro (Brunette, *The Films of Michelangelo Antonioni*, 49). It would seem at least equally reasonable, however, that the primary focus belongs on Claudia's search for redemption.

Claudia must transform the ethical and sexual energy that goes into her conflict of body and soul into a means to satisfy both impulses. The pull of immanence and the body and the effort for a transcendent ethics toward the other must join forces to develop a new sexual ethics that will play out both on the body and in the soul. This melding in Claudia constitutes an advance on several fronts, including the feminine, ethics, sexuality, and Levinasian thought.

Claudia does, indeed, enact the call for the power of the body and of sexuality that feminists such as Irigaray propose. She must find, to use Irigaray's term, an "economy of love" that may "indeed lead to despair" or to something else that involves "the woman as subject desiring *along with* man as subject." Irigaray writes, "It is possible to live and simultaneously create sexual love. Here would lie the way out from the fall, for in this case, love can become spiritual and divine" ("Questions to Emmanuel Levinas," 115). The achievement of such a love as Irigaray describes becomes Claudia's objective.

Claudia's steady but difficult struggle toward a new economy of love that retains Levinasian transcendence without the enclosure of irreversible immanence advances during the search for Anna on Lisca Bianca. The complex visual detail of the search sequence artfully sets up challenging natural and social environments. The remark by a sailor from the yacht that the group should leave the island because of the incoming weather and rough seas introduces a touch of danger into the situation. As the members of the group look for Anna, Antonioni films the island from high-angle shots to extreme long shots of the sea. He shoots the rough rocky landscape, frightening crevasses, and steep ledges. From high points on the island he emphasizes the sense of its isolation on the sea. Pounding waves and the boiling ocean roar and resonate. Through it all Antonioni vividly diagrams the efforts of the members of the party in their search. With almost no dialogue, each member participates in the search in ways that dramatize their individual character and their relationship to the others. Giulia never stops thinking about herself, could care less about Anna, and worries and pouts only about how Corrado treats her. Corrado rises to the occasion with a genuine awareness of the seriousness of the situation. Sandro dutifully searches every part of the island and then takes the yacht to search around the island. Worried about Anna, he appears both stoical and annoyed over this crisis, obviously thinking of the whole affair as another example of Anna's unpredictable, impulsive moodiness.

Claudia's fierce loyalty toward Anna manifests itself in the intensity of her commitment to the search for her friend. She walks the island, crawls on the rocks, explores the crevasses. Her every movement emphasizes her dedication to the search and her pain over Anna's absence.

Shots of Claudia on the search show her endangering herself on ledges as the water below churns and pounds the island's edge. In one shot a huge boulder tumbles down the rough cliffs. The camera shifts to the left revealing the top of Claudia's head and shoulders from behind her as she looks precariously over the edge with her arms before her. She looks to her right at the falling boulder. The camera brilliantly shifts to a close-up shot from just in front and on top of her head. She rises so her head disappears out of the frame leaving just her arms and hands, a cinematic metonymy that accentuates anxious disconnection.

To Sandro's annoyance, she insists on staying on the island with him and Corrado when the search and the group break up, with others leaving for a neighboring island to inform authorities about events. Claudia exhibits devotion to her friend in a way that differs radically from the concern of the others, including Sandro.

Throughout the search on the island Antonioni's famous long takes suggest the precariousness of the situation. In one long take dark clouds form in the distance while a waterspout erupts from the sea below. The whole scene suggests prolonged uncertainty. In fact, the search for Anna on Lisca Bianca can be seen as a kind of dramatization of Levinas's concept of the "*there is*" of anonymous being, what Kelly Oliver terms "raw being" and Levinas describes in *Existence and Existents* as the "horror of being and not anxiety over nothingness, fear of being and not fear for being."[33] In a sense both alive and dead during the failed search for her on Lisca Bianca, Anna remains invisible but present as the other for Claudia. Thus, Antonioni shoots this search with a strange sense of time. He presents an extended series of cuts, shots, and movements but without a clear sense of ordinary, organized time. Interestingly, a conversation between Corrado and the old man of the island dramatizes confusion about the precise temporal order of various events during the period of the group's visit to the island. In sharp contrast, Sandro's mixture of impatience, annoyance, and genuine concern clearly suggest his time of a regular chronological order.

Claudia's time of the search comes closer to Antonioni's filming as a duration without traditional linear temporal breaks. Such duration suggests the power of existence that compels an ethical response of a different order of time, a diachronic time of infinite ethical responsibility to the other. Claudia never checks her wristwatch. Instead, for Claudia, looking on Lisca

Bianca for Anna in the midst of the *il y a* of endless, intimidating existence suggests the relation of the finite, searching individual to a time of infinity. Thus, toward the end of the first phase of the search, when Claudia calls out "Anna!" from a barren, high spot on the island plateau to the empty air and open space, the time of day makes no difference because her call constitutes a gesture toward the infinite. Her cry goes beyond being to an intensity of commitment that does not end with the time of her being.

THE MYSTERY OF ANNA

The unresolved mystery throughout the film of Anna's disappearance further intensifies the ethical crisis for Claudia. Considering that Anna's friends stop looking for her "about halfway through" the film, Brunette recalls the French critic Pascal Bonitzer's remark that the great shock of the film concerns "'the disappearance of the disappearance of Anna,'" suggesting scandalous attitudes for the people in the film. Brunette also notes Antonioni's own difficulties with this aspect of the film at the time of its release: "This double disappearance creates a gaping hole in the film, an invisibility at its center, which suggests an elsewhere, a nonplace, that remains forever unavailable to interpretation and that destroys the dream of full visibility."[34] This center of "invisibility" concerns, as we have seen, a major paradox for Antonioni in his pursuit of filming the invisible. "Full visibility" ironically would be a loss for Antonioni in that it would stifle the force of the search for the invisible, including the unseen psychological drama of Claudia's ethical journey.

Arrowsmith proposes that Anna's "disappearance is unresolved because this serves Antonioni's purpose here—the impotence of human affection and reason in the presence of this vast landscape, with its revelation of a violent mystery at the heart of things." Antonioni's greater "purpose" in *L'avventura*, however—which Arrowsmith does not find in the filmmaker's body of work until *The Passenger*—involves what Arrowsmith calls "the transcendental impulse." This means transcendence in the form that Arrowsmith denies in *L'avventura*, "transcendence in the philosophical sense" and also, it could be argued, in the Levinasian sense of the relationship to the other.[35]

All of the concern for the drama of Anna's disappearance depreciates to a certain extent the point of Anna's nonexistence. From the opening scene she has been denied her own place of existence. In a sense she has never been there. Thus, she dramatizes Irigaray's argument that woman as place, as home for the existence of others, must find her place. Referencing Zeno and Aristotle, Irigaray argues "*'everything that exists has a place,'*" so where does woman find a place? "As for woman, she is place. Does she have to locate herself in bigger and bigger places? But also to find, situate, in herself, the place that she is" (*An Ethics of Sexual Difference*, 34–35). Anna's disappearance confirms her absence and lack of place from the beginning.

TRANSCENDENCE

Antonioni's regard for Heidegger and Camus, among many other philosophers, and his expressed interest in transcendence also suggest that such themes are consciously implanted in *L'avventura*. He says, "I'm convinced that if you want to express your own poetic world you have to transcend reality" (Antonioni, *The Architecture of Vision*, 242). Accordingly, while images of the immanence of her surroundings as enclosure, entrapment, and possession help describe Anna in *L'avventura*, the images of Claudia on Lisca Bianca as she searches for her missing friend mark the beginning of a new vision, not just of Claudia but also of ethics and the feminine. A turning point occurs with Claudia's refusal to leave Lisca Bianca with the others while Sandro and Corrado stay, watching over the island for Anna and hoping eventually to solve the mystery of her disappearance. Both men directly suggest that Claudia leave. Sandro speaks to the point of rudeness, blatantly suggesting that she "might get in the way" of the men, who intend to use a small hut on the island as their only shelter.

After announcing that "I'm not leaving," Claudia moves off by herself, facing the camera, with Sandro, Corrado, and Patrizia (Esmeralda Ruspoli), one of the women on the cruise, behind her. The shot beautifully sets her off against the group, establishing her independence. She exudes confidence and determination. She turns her back to the camera and without saying a word moves forward toward Sandro and then turns right and goes up the rocky, rough path toward a higher elevation and the hut, leaving everyone behind. She ascends with the sure footedness of a mountain goat. Sandro and Corrado follow, while the others leave for the yacht.

A slow dissolve opens with a beautiful high view from the island's edge. The shot shows the sea, other islands, and a blazing sky. Thunder indicates an incoming storm. Claudia looks at the view from the center of the frame and then turns to face the camera.

This facial shot of Claudia on the edge of the island provides a vision of her as a new force in *L'avventura*, fulfilling the symbolism of her independent stance, her ascension from the men, and the light from the sky above and beyond her. Her expression evinces unqualified determination. At this point Claudia starts a new phase of her ethical adventure. She stands by herself in the intensity of her commitment to Anna, the woman as "other" in the story, while also starting a new story of her rapidly developing relationship with Sandro. From the elevated position of this scene, flooded in light, it seems clear how closely she embodies the merging of forces of her mission of transcendence and sexual fulfillment that Irigaray describes.

Antonioni, however, also brilliantly dramatizes the obstacles that await Claudia on her journey toward redemption. They appear almost immediately and, ironically, are similar to those forces that overwhelmed Anna. As the action moves from the exterior of the Lisca Bianca search to the small, primitive hut of the old man of the island, the matter of the significance of a dwelling again takes center stage. Claudia enters the hut with Sandro and Corrado. Soon the old man joins them, surprised but not upset to see they have entered his little home.

In this setting, with Anna gone, Antonioni makes clear how quickly Claudia comes to replace her as the center of Sandro's attention. Sandro exposes like a physical wound his sense of guilt over Anna's disappearance, and Claudia exploits his feelings of culpability by suggesting he wasn't thinking enough about Anna. She even suggests he was misdirecting his attention toward her rather than Anna, something the film itself does not absolutely support, thereby hinting at Claudia's own unconscious desires. As the tense recriminations mount between Claudia and Sandro, the old man talks on about a lamb of his that also once had disappeared and fallen off the rocks behind the house. He remains oblivious to the impact on Claudia of his words that connect Anna with the lamb. The drone of the man's voice becomes unbearable. Claudia breaks down and runs from the hut into the rain, calling Anna's name. Corrado brings her back.

THE ARCHITECTURE OF THE BODY

The incident in the old man's hut reignites the tensions surrounding the meaning of dwellings and the home as the place of the feminine. The challenge for Claudia of the possession of her own body becomes a crucial factor in her adventure. Significantly, Sandro's work and self-image as an architect give even stronger focus to this theme of the dwelling. Claudia's mission of redemption compels a notion of body architecture that must contrast with Sandro's violation of his artistic and professional ideals. Sandro fails to live up to his own expectations of creative artistry as an architect. He sells his services to commercial builders by giving them estimates for their artless projects. His self-loathing and frustration over such failure erupts in one scene when, out of envy, he knocks over a bottle of black ink onto a young man's architectural sketch, as though hoping to start a fight with him.

"Architects are needed," Irigaray proclaims in "The Fecundity of the Caress." Sandro's corruption provides special relevance to Irigaray's words on the relationship of architecture to the body as a dwelling for transcendence. She writes of "architects of beauty who fashion jouissance—a very subtle material." She talks of "the threshold" of "the house of flesh" that must provide a "dwelling" for the "heart." Irigaray's call for an architect to construct such a dwelling directly counters the architecture of forms of entrapment associated with Sandro. Irigaray wants "a kind of house that shelters without enclosing me, untying and tying me to the other, as to one who helps me to build and inhabit. Discharging me from a deadly fusion and uniting me through an acknowledgment of who is capable of building this place. My pleasure being, in a way, the material, one of the materials" (*An Ethics of Sexual Difference*, 214).

Elsewhere Irigaray discusses the "subtle material" of "jouissance" that composes this human "house of flesh" as pleasure, "my pleasure with the lover of my flesh" ("Questions to Emmanuel Levinas," 111). Of special significance, Irigaray describes this pleasure as "pleasure transcendent and immanent to one and to the other." In stark contrast to Levinas, seeing both transcendence and immanence in the pleasure of the flesh, Irigaray hopes to "recognize God in carnality." She asks, "And who is the other if the divine is excluded from the carnal act? If these gestures of ultimate relations between living humans are not a privileged approach to God, who is he?" She wants to know when and how God withdrew "from the act of carnal love." Irigaray refuses to separate God from the senses, from "his presence, as nourishment, including nourishment of the senses" (ibid., 111, 116).

Ironically, the filmmaker considered to be the creator of an "architecture of vision," Antonioni constructs in *L'avventura* the character of an architect who fails to see and to cherish what Irigaray considers the house of flesh of the feminine.[36] Claudia must be able to propel her achievement of independence on Lisca Bianca into a program of her own design, architecture, and construction of the feminine. In a moving moment later in the film, Claudia seems to achieve such jouissance with Sandro, a mixture of sexuality, flesh, and the transcendence of the other.

In dramatizing this effort of Claudia's to achieve such a union of transcendence and love, Antonioni, it should be noted, was part of a tradition that is at least as old, as Irigaray argues, as the Song of Solomon and cultures that celebrate the feminine.[37] Some tendency in this direction also can be found in modern writers who can be compared to Antonioni. Critics have noted with great interest that Claudia finds copies of the Bible and F. Scott Fitzgerald's *Tender Is the Night* among Anna's belongings as part of the search for her. Noticing that Claudia wears the blouse that Anna tucked away for her, Anna's father hopes the Bible indicates that Anna would not try to kill herself. Critics see the hero of *Tender Is the Night*, Dick Diver, as an example of the sexual sickness that concerns Antonioni and that Sandro exemplifies.[38] As Dick Diver turned out to be a failed doctor, so Sandro is a failed architect, both of them subject to similar weaknesses. Fitzgerald writes of Diver, "He was in love with every pretty woman he saw now, their forms at a distance, their shadows on a wall."[39] Antonioni admired Fitzgerald and probably realized that Diver's sexuality in *Tender Is the Night* actually could not be isolated from all the other themes that went into this complex novel and character.[40] As many have argued, Diver's sexuality is part of a greater study in the novel of the modern crisis of love, spirituality, and ethics.[41] Fitzgerald's very sentence, like one of Antonioni's images, compresses the complexity of the relationship of sexuality and the body to the mind and spirituality. Fitzgerald's words, "forms at a distance, their shadows on a wall," could describe Claudia's form in the distance and Anna's shadow on the wall of the vestibule at Sandro's apartment. Fitzgerald and Antonioni capture in their different ways the sense of how time and spirit suffuse desire. Author and director are also both as much about transcendence as painful desire.

Sandro persists in his predatory role even on the search for Anna. The morning after the night in the hut, Sandro's concentration on Claudia grows more intense. A series of two-shots frame Sandro with Claudia, slowly connecting their images in anticipation of the merger of their relationship. Then, only three days after Anna's disappearance, as Claudia guiltily asserts, Sandro aggressively pursues Claudia, trying to convince her that with Anna gone it becomes pointless for them to sacrifice their own feelings as a gesture of loyalty to her. Always ready to rationalize his behavior, Sandro, later in the film, thoroughly perverts the meaning of a key term in the popular existentialism of the day to argue that the "absurdity" of their situation relieves them of responsibility. Claudia, who on her own had visited neighboring islands looking for Anna, still resists him—barely—and forces him to leave her to continue her train trip.

Claudia and Sandro, however, soon reunite, following rumors and bad leads about sightings of Anna. Coming from Troina, where they encounter the sexually obsessed pharmacist, and on their way to Noto, where men surround Claudia like sex-crazed vultures, they stop by a completely deserted town and a beautiful but vacant church. In the distance Sandro mistakes a cemetery for a village, a symbolic confusion of the living and dead. Antonioni's filming here of beautiful but lifeless architectural structures repeats in another way the suggestion of the difficulty of raw being, the Levinasian *il y a*, he conveyed in his images of the sea. The scene also maintains the architectural metaphor of dead as opposed to vital forms. The dead time of the lingering long take of Antonioni's camera on the village and the church without people and life sets up the next scene.

THE HILLSIDE

Leaving this deserted place of lifeless spirit and on this strange travel itinerary, a sharp cut shows the couple on a hillside making love. Especially impressive about Antonioni's art of filming in this scene, he refuses to be shocking or sensationalistic either in getting to the scene or developing it. The scene, a powerful contrast to all the sexual obsession that precedes and follows it, contrasts most profoundly with the agony on Anna's face during her moments of lovemaking with Sandro. The scene becomes stronger in the absence of typical, artificial cinematic emotionalism. The hillside scene could have been ruined easily with excess instead of Antonioni's wonderful understatement.

The scene can be interpreted, I think, as an exemplification of Irigaray's notion of jouissance, of pleasure in lovemaking that opens to transcendence. As opposed to the anger, hunger, and violence of the film's other scenes of love and sex, this scene of the interconnection of transcendence and immanence resonates with joy. This scene concerns something other than what occupies the pharmacist, Giulia, and the mobs of men glaring at women.

Brunette also comments on the unique quality of this scene: "The camera dwells on their love-making for the longest time, prolonging it well beyond the normal length of such scenes, which has the uncanny effect of making it more emotional and more sensual even though the sex actually 'shown' is not very explicit." Antonioni's close-ups of the lovers, their smiles and their kisses, suggest an experience for Claudia that goes beyond the kind of physical gratification and sexual aggression of other scenes to achieve a quality of transformative transcendence, which explains Brunette's puzzlement over the scene's "strange, but difficult-to-specify feelings" (Brunette, *The Films of Michelangelo Antonioni*, 40).

These feelings in the scene that challenge specific description can be imagined as the transforming pleasure of the flesh that goes beyond the ordinary. Rather than feeling consumed like Anna, Claudia grows empowered, repeating "mia, mia, mia, mia . . . mine, mine, mine, mine." Hands, lips, murmurs, smiles, hair, moans, laughter, cheeks, fingers, giggles, teeth, looks, and more smiles rapturously intermingle in the scene under a blaze of beautiful sunlight on an expansive field and landscape.

To underscore that this scene depicts a mutual invasion of the flesh by the lovers to reach, especially for Claudia, previously unfelt and unknown places and feelings, Antonioni cuts to an extreme long shot of a train coming from the right through the field with the sea in the background. The camera follows the smoke-belching train by panning to the left until it disappears into the landscape through an underpass or hidden line.

The camera then cuts back to the lovers. After a bit of a time lag, the train comes again, this time from the opposite direction, the left, thereby violating a basic film principle of perspective and position to create a starkly disjointing effect, a disjuncture of time and space and of the mind and senses. The train's violation of cinematic spatial and temporal relations raises questions about the location of the lovers. In a continuation of the sexually suggestive action, the train, now quite close to the lovers, passes by with a rumbling roar and disappears again into a crevice in the landscape. While Hitchcock uses a train and a tunnel as a sexual joke in *North by Northwest* (1959), Antonioni exploits the same idea to change the meaning of the act to a transformative moment that suggests the regeneration of the senses, emotion, and love.

As Brunette recognizes, the initial shot of the train suggests the point of view of the lovers. As the scene advances, however, with subsequent shots of the train and the lovers, it becomes clearer, as Brunette says, "retrospectively," that the long shot had been from Antonioni's objective, distant camera. The change in the direction of the train causes the viewer to be "momentarily disoriented" in a manner that also sustains the change occurring in Claudia's sensibilities, as dramatized by her actions, expressions, gestures, and voice.[42] The train's opposing movements problematize the issue of time and the order of events. Antonioni's filming disrupts ordinary temporality.

This altered, disorienting perspective of time and space insinuates another temporal regime into the scene of ethics and the diachronic. By injecting a different temporality into the scene, Antonioni opens the possibility for reimagining ethical awareness of responsibilities and relations, again achieving an ethics of cinema. Antonioni enacts the program that Irigaray proposes in "Sexual Difference" when she says that "we must reconsider the whole problematic of *space* and *time*." "The transition to a new age," she says, "requires a change in our perception and conception of *space-time*, the *inhabiting of places*, and of *containers*, or *envelopes of identity*" (*An Ethics of Sexual difference*, 7). She asks, "Perhaps we are passing through an era when *time must redeploy space*? A new morning of and for the world?" (18).

Especially in the context of Irigaray's idea of a new temporality for a reconsideration of space, in *L'avventura* the outdoor setting for the couple's lovemaking suggests Claudia's transcendence over the masculine domination of the interior spaces of the feminine as home and dwelling. Still an outsider, Claudia's exteriority enacts Irigaray's program for a transformation of the feminine as a place for the male only. The sexualized body of flesh, pleasure, and joy in the scene becomes the instrument for the transcendence of the body over the enclosed circle of immanence.

TIME OF WONDER

Following Irigaray's argument, the portrait of Anna in *L'avventura* illustrates the need to open temporal regimes that imprison and to free the places of habitation and containment that become stultifying enclosures of immanence. The film dramatizes the possibility for the redeployment of time for engendering new ethical relationships. *L'avventura*, most especially in the hillside scene, places Claudia at the center of the frame and at the center of the struggle for a new ethical and temporal regime.

In the scene Claudia looks up in what Irigaray calls "the first passion: *wonder.*" Irigaray is thinking of Descartes when she writes in "Sexual Difference" that "this passion has no opposite or contradiction and exists always as though for the first time. Thus man and woman, woman and man are always meeting as though for the first time because they cannot be substituted one for the other. I will never be in a man's place, never will a man be in mine. Whatever identifications are possible, one will never exactly occupy the place of the other—they are irreducible one to the other" (*An Ethics of Sexual Difference*, 12–13).

On this open field in *L'avventura* that stretches out to the beyond of the sea, Claudia experiences for the first time, to recall Irigaray again, "the horizon of the divine, of the gods, of an opening onto a beyond, but also a *limit* that the other may or may not penetrate" (*An Ethics of Sexual Difference*, 17). For Irigaray sexual difference makes the "mark" of this "limit of a place, of place in general" (17). In contrast to Anna, who gets consumed as an internal exile on the threshold of the body, Claudia undergoes, in Irigaray's phrase, "a remaking of immanence and transcendence, notably through this *threshold* which has never been examined as such: the female sex" (18).

Thus, for Claudia, in the relationship to the other through sexual difference, the vital threshold of the lips and the body provides access to experience beyond the body. Irigaray emphasizes that "the borders of the body are wed in an embrace that transcends all limits—without, however, risking engulfment" (18). In their opposition, limits or thresholds and transcendence safeguard each other from dissipation and engulfment. In *L'avventura* Claudia withstands the "engulfment" that consumes Anna.

Perhaps Antonioni's self-confessed fascination for women helps explain how *L'avventura* interconnects so readily with radical ethical feminist thought. In attempting in his film to advocate for the position and condition of women, he has created a work that apparently finds resonance with such thought. He writes:

> I especially love women. Perhaps because I understand them better? I was born among women, and raised in the midst of female cousins, aunts, relatives. I know women very well.

> Through the psychology of women everything becomes more poignant. They express themselves better and more precisely. They are a filter which allows us to see more clearly and to distinguish things.
>
> I have always given great importance to female characters since I think I know women better than I do men.... They are more instinctive, more sincere. (Rohdie, *Antonioni*, 183)

As an exploration of women in *L'avventura*, the transcendence and jouissance Claudia experiences still must engage the sexist world that Antonioni questions. Thus, following her special time, literally a reimagining of time through the transcendence of the flesh with the other, Claudia once again encounters ordinary, chronological male time.

On the road again with Sandro, Claudia returns to a temporal regime of linear time and chronological order with a man, her love, who knows only that realm. Sandro proves repeatedly throughout *L'avventura* that for him adventure means the search for ontological certitude. For him knowledge is power—total power. His comment to Claudia back in Noto that existential absurdity relieves them both of ethical responsibility constitutes his basic approach to life. Trying to explain to her about their new life together, he says, "It's better if it's absurd. It just means there's nothing we can do about it. Do you understand?" In his bitterness toward the young artist whose ink drawing he ruins, Sandro indicates that he thinks of the time of his own life and of his lost opportunities as lost possessions he would like to regain as lost dollars or investments. Evincing a similar attitude toward Claudia that replicates the rapaciousness of other men throughout the film, he comes close to forcing himself on her in a moment of angry frustration.

With this combination of conflicts as their background, Claudia and Sandro arrive at the San Domenico Palace Hotel in Taormina for the justifiably famous if ambiguous conclusion to the film. Sandro goes to the hotel for a meeting to conduct exactly the kind of business of estimating costs that he has wanted to give up to pursue more serious architecture. Tired, Claudia decides not to join him that evening with his friends and business associates and stays in the hotel room to sleep. But as the night passes without Sandro's return and the morning sunshine slowly comes through the windows, she becomes restless and scared and tries to find him. At that early morning hour she finds the rooms, dining halls, and corridors of the hotel totally deserted.

The men who turned to look and leer at her the day before have gone, like Sandro. As she becomes increasingly anxious, she races down a long corridor and back through it after checking with Patrizia about Sandro. Her footsteps echo and the sound reverberates through the corridor, emphasizing her own emptiness. Continuing her search, she goes through a large dining room that is in a state of disorder from the events of the night before. The disorder indicates the lack of restraint of the people at the hotel. Finally she finds Sandro having sex on a couch in the public room with Gloria Perkins, who looks up at her with extreme annoyance and then whiningly insists on payment from Sandro for her services after he rises to try to catch up with the retreating Claudia. Gloria asks for "only a little souvenir" and then gathers the money he throws down at her with her feet.

Outside the hotel Claudia races to an open square near the San Domenico church. She cries sorrowfully. All of this action and detail build up to Claudia's final gesture toward Sandro. Sandro finds her, walks past her, too ashamed to look at her, and sits by himself on a nearby bench, slumped over in obvious humiliation, weeping pathetically. Claudia walks to him and puts her hand on the back of his head.

Her gesture can be read in obviously contradictory ways—as her act of submissive acceptance of his behavior or as a generous sign of forgiveness. Antonioni clearly intended for it to be ambiguous. In this final scene Antonioni creates a kind of split screen that visually dramatizes the conflict. The blank wall of a stolid architectural structure fills the right half of the screen, Sandro's half, as though suggesting a dead end, a potentially meaningless, lifeless future. On the left side, Claudia's side, in the far background, Mt. Etna looms over the scene in all its majesty, perhaps signifying a promise of something better in the future for the couple. Antonioni himself describes the possible meaning of this conclusion for him:

> On one side of the frame is Mount Etna in all its snowy whiteness, and on the other is a concrete wall. The wall corresponds to the man and Mount Etna corresponds somewhat to the situation of the woman. Thus the frame is divided exactly in half; one half containing the concrete wall which represents the pessimistic side, while the other half showing Mount Etna represents the optimistic. But I really don't know if the relationship between these two halves will endure or not, though it is quite evident the two protagonists will remain together

and not separate. The girl will definitely not leave the man; she will stay with him and forgive him. For she realizes that she too, in a certain sense, is somewhat like him. Because—if for no other reason—from the moment she suspects Anna may have returned, she becomes so apprehensive, so afraid she may be back and still alive, that she begins to lose the feeling of friendship that she once had for Anna, just as he had lost his affection for Anna and perhaps is also beginning to lose it for her. But what else can she do but stay with him? (*The Architecture of Vision*, 34–35)

Antonioni's last sentence in the statement suggests an absence of choice and a lack of options for Claudia, thereby perpetuating the worst kind of entrapment for her as a woman. Antonioni's verbal summary of the film's conclusion takes much of the ethics, as well as the adventure, out of the journey, reducing Claudia to Anna, a woman trapped by her situation within the restrictions of a sexist, patriarchal society. This scene, however, involves greater complexity than Antonioni's own words indicate. Claudia's gesture of forgiveness, her extension of her arm, her Levinasian caress, cannot be separated from what the film already has shown of Claudia's growth. Her act entails a Levinasian moment of transcendence for the other but also involves her embodied sexuality.

The faces and body movement of Claudia and Sandro in this final scene dramatize the change that has transpired between them. A low-angle shot of

FIGURE 6.1. Monica Vitti and Gabrielle Ferzetti before Mt. Etna in *L'avventura* (1960)

Sandro reveals him in tears and humiliation, a man reduced to complete abjection, as described by Oliver. He has been exposed as the same as the prostitute he was with on a couch in a public place. In this shot a chimney over his right shoulder stands in phallic isolation. The cut to Claudia standing over him thoughtfully, reflexively shows strength returning to her face. She does not exhibit vindictiveness or triumph or false empathy. Significantly, she stands above him at the upper position on the screen. Behind her shoulder stands the San Domenico church.

The scene recalls the opening sequence of the film, with the Vatican dome in the background reinforcing Anna's entrapment and her father's power. In the final scene the church still shows signs of wartime bombing as a testimony to the historic failure of violent patriarchal authority. Now, however, Claudia determines love, forgiveness, and the future. Indeed, in the close-up of Sandro's face as Claudia stands before him, his closed eyes and lowered head intimate an act of prayer. His eyes open, and he wipes away a tear; but his nose continues to run, indicating his extreme abjection, sense of loss, and remorse and perhaps even the potential for change.

The cut to Claudia above him casts her in a Madonna pose with her downcast eyes and her blonde hair forming a kind of halo. But this figure of redemption does not project the kind of disembodiment or holy sublimation that so concerns feminist critics such as Chanter, Oliver, Ziarek, and Irigaray. She brings her body and her history with her, including her time with Sandro and the transformative love that helps her continue her relationship with him. She remains both physical and spiritual.

In the final cut the long shot shows Claudia standing with Sandro, a figure of strength comparable to the extraordinary mountain peak in the far background. Sandro remains seated on the bench in a crumpled position, appearing emotionally if not physically crippled. Claudia lowers her head toward him in a motherly gesture of encouragement, as she might deal with a child, and gently strokes his head. The rising strains of music, with its dissonance and broken melody, reinforce the ambiguity of the scene, suggesting both movement toward climactic resolution and continued uncertainty.

Claudia's stance at the end of *L'avventura* anticipates her continuation rather than the conclusion of her journey. A pregnant question in the film remains how far Sandro will go with her along a path that necessarily involves pioneering the kinds of changes about sexuality and ethics that a history of sexism, patriarchy, and, to paraphrase Antonioni, sexual obsession demands. The film suggests that in his arrogance, self-absorption, and latent violence, Sandro stands in for all men, making it pointless to leave him for someone else but important to work for his redemption as a hopeful sign of greater change. Levinasian ethics of transcendence and the other, as feminist critics maintain, fails by itself to insinuate that change, primarily for the sacrifice it requires of women for the transcendence of men.

Instead, Claudia's adventure in *L'avventura* enacts a powerful case for making the sexed body a force for transcendence for the other through, as Irigaray repeatedly proposes, the mutual transformation of the flesh in a new program of ethics based on sexual difference. Similarly, Ziarek's case for ethics, dissensus, and sexuality could prove helpful to Claudia and Sandro for clarifying their journey of achieving, in Ziarek's phrase, the "entwinement of thought and carnality." Ziarek argues against "transcending the sexed body," as Levinas proposes even as he advocates ethical embodiment. Instead, she emphasizes that "erotic creation consists in the transformation of the flesh, in the rebirth of the lovers bestowing on each other life." She says, "In such an act of creation, lovers give each other time and future" (Ziarek, *An Ethics of Dissensus*, 50, 61).

From the beginning, time and the future have been key for Levinas, his feminist critics, and Antonioni. Perhaps the ultimate adventure in *L'avventura* has been its place in the cinema of redemption in articulating the need for a new time and future for a rebirth of love. Levinas says that "the relation with the Other alone introduces a dimension of transcendence" (*Totality and Infinity*, 193). Somewhat later, however, he switches this emphasis from ethical transcendence to love: "Philosophy is this measure brought to the infinity of the being-for-the-other of proximity, and is like the wisdom of love." He repeats, "Philosophy is the wisdom of love at the service of love" (*Otherwise Than Being or Beyond Essence*, 161–62). Levinas's use of "love," as we have seen, disturbs some critics such as Stella Sandford. Thus, Slavoj Žižek says, "Love that suspends the Law is necessarily accompanied by arbitrary cruelty that also suspends the Law."[43] Without settling questions of the law, immanence, and finite structures that concern him as much as his critics, Levinas's commingling of philosophy with the infinite and love pronounces his priorities. Well aware of such insuperable challenges as the tensions between law and ethics or love and eros, Levinas remained convinced that any search for answers to these dilemmas that excludes the ethical transcendence of the face, the other, and the infinite would lead only to a place of immanent enclosure that denies access to sources of renewal. Levinas's argument with such critics becomes, in other words, the difference between seeing Mt. Etna in the distance as supporting a horizon of the limitation of being or as a vision of infinite time and possibility.

Claudia's vision and our vision of her as she stands next to Sandro before Mt. Etna project Levinas's idea of the merger of love with ethics. Levinas says, "The fact that in existing for another, I exist otherwise than in existing for me is morality itself" (*Totality and Infinity*, 261). Similarly, Antonioni creates in *L'avventura* an ethics of cinema with the embodied sexual love and transcendent ethics of Claudia. The question in *L'avventura* remains: in extending herself to Sandro, does Claudia stand alone?

NOTES

INTRODUCTION

1. Emmanuel Levinas, *Existence and Existents*, trans. Alphonso Lingis (Pittsburgh: Duquesne University Press, 2001), 36–37.
2. Tina Chanter, *Time, Death, and the Feminine: Levinas with Heidegger* (Stanford, CA: Stanford University Press, 2001), 247.
3. See Salomon Malka, *Emmanuel Levinas: His Life and Legacy*, trans. Michael Kigel and Sonja M. Embree (Pittsburgh: Duquesne University Press, 2006), 67.
4. See Emmanuel Levinas, *Difficult Freedom: Essays on Judaism*, trans. Seán Hand (Baltimore: Johns Hopkins University Press, 1990), 152–53.
5. Jacques Derrida, *Specters of Marx: The State of the Debt, the Work of Mourning, and the New International*, trans. Peggy Kamuf (New York: Routledge, 1994), 26.
6. See Emmanuel Levinas, *Time and the Other*, trans. Richard A. Cohen (Pittsburgh: Duquesne University Press, 1987). Subsequent references to this work will be cited parenthetically in the text.
7. Simon Critchley, *Infinitely Demanding: Ethics of Commitment, Politics of Resistance* (London: Verso, 2007), 57.
8. Emmanuel Levinas, *God, Death, and Time*, trans. Bettino Bergo (Stanford, CA: Stanford University Press, 2000), 194. Subsequent references to this work will be cited parenthetically in the text.
9. Emmanuel Levinas, "God and Philosophy," in *Emmanuel Levinas: Basic Philosophical Writings*, ed. Adriaan T. Peperzak, Simon Critchley, and Robert Bernasconi (Bloomington: Indiana University Press, 1996), 129–48, 141. Subsequent references to the essays and lectures in this work will be cited parenthetically in the text under the volume title *Emmanuel Levinas*.
10. Slavoj Žižek, "Neighbors and Other Monsters: A Plea for Ethical Violence," in *The Neighbor: Three Inquiries in Political Theology*, by Slavoj Žižek, Eric L. Santner, and Kenneth Reinhard (Chicago: University of Chicago Press, 2005), 134–90, 150.

11. However, in making the case for ethics, the Levinasian project also must contend with the skepticism of critics who see a debilitating confusion in Levinas between the relationship of ethics to love that accounts for the tension in his philosophy between eros and ethics. Thus, Stella Sandford argues in *The Metaphysics of Love: Gender and Transcendence in Levinas* (London: Athlone, 2000) that Levinas subordinates "the phenomenology of eros," meaning the feminine and the sexual, to a "metaphysics of love" or a sensibility of ethical transcendence (5, 91, 139). She says he fails to adequately explain how to achieve transcendence this way or what is to be gained, especially for real, empirical women, by placing such a priority on ethics before ontology. Sandford proposes, instead, "the co-conditionality and equi-primordiality of metaphysics and ethics, the necessity of the relation between transcendence and its appearing—the necessity of their simultaneity—the transcendence, to be intelligible, would be *finite*" (131). On this theme of the wisdom of love in Levinas see also Roger Burggraeve, *The Wisdom of Love in the Service of Love: Emmanuel Levinas on Justice, Peace, and Human Rights* (Milwaukee: Marquette University Press, 2002); and Corey Beals, *Levinas and the Wisdom of Love: The Question of Invisibility* (Waco, TX: Baylor University Press, 2007).
12. The concept of the "face" and the "face-to-face" occurs throughout Levinas's work as his expression of ultimate ethical responsibility to the other. See Emmanuel Levinas, *Outside the Subject*, trans. Michael B. Smith (Stanford, CA: Stanford University Press, 1993), where Levinas says, "the face is meaning of the beyond." He continues: "The face is alone in translating transcendence. . . . A Transcendence that is inseparable from the ethical *circumstances* of the responsibility for the other." Levinas goes on to assert that "the epiphany of the face" engenders the "uniqueness of self" (94–95). Thus, Tina Chanter claims, "The face to face is a relationship that exceeds the categories of being and nothingness" and "For Levinas, the face to face founds language" (Tina Chanter, *Ethics of Eros: Irigaray's Rewriting of the Philosophers* [New York: Routledge, 1995], 181, 189).
13. Simon Critchley, *Ethics-Politics-Subjectivity: Essays on Derrida, Levinas and Contemporary French Thought* (London: Verso, 1999), 152, 243.
14. See Joseph Campbell, *The Hero with a Thousand Faces* (Cleveland: Meridian, 1956).
15. A partial list of other directors in the cinema of redemption would include Carl Dreyer, Robert Bresson, and Yasujiro Ozu (who have been studied in terms of transcendence by Paul Schrader), as well as Guillermo del Toro, Spike Lee, Paul Haggis, Alejandro González Ináritu, and Alfonso Cuarón. See Paul Schrader, *Transcendental Style in Film: Ozu, Bresson, Dreyer* (Berkeley: University of California Press, 1972).
16. Levinas repeatedly uses *mise-en-scène*—the theatrical term for setting of the scene that cinema has adapted for setting, lighting, composition, costume, and acting—to describe his positions. In "Proximity of the Other," in *Alterity and Transcendence*, trans. Michael B.

Smith (New York: Columbia University Press, 1999), Levinas uses the term figuratively to describe "the '*mise-en-scène*' of the infinite, an inexhaustible, concrete responsibility" (105). In this usage *mise-en-scène* serves as a kind of metaphor to help make the unfathomable idea of infinite responsibility to the other concrete and understandable. In "Violence of the Face" the notion of mise-en-scène also helps Levinas explain how to think and to see philosophically and phenomenologically. Here *mise-en-scène* becomes crucial to describe "the mental procedure" that renders "concrete meaning" to "datum" that has become "but an *abstraction*" (*Alterity and Transcendence*, 174–75). Similarly, in "Transcendence and Intelligibility" he says that "to do phenomenology" that escapes "abstraction," it helps to do the "'staging'" or "'*mise-en-scène*'" that avoids such "abstractions" (*Emmanuel Levinas*, 158). In *In the Time of the Nations*, trans. Michael B. Smith (Bloomington: Indiana University Press, 1994) Levinas uses *mise-en-scène* to describe "the reconstitution of any object or notion" (180–81). In an interview with Francois Poirié he says that to achieve "the true thinking and the thinking of the true," it becomes necessary to "move from the object to its mise-en-scène" (Jill Robbins, ed., *Is It Righteous to Be? Interviews with Emmanuel Levinas* [Stanford, CA: Stanford University Press, 2001], 32). In a later interview with Christoph von Wolzogen, however, Levinas perhaps makes his most direct statement about the linkage between phenomenology and mise-en-scène. Before noting that "consciousness is precisely this staging," he says, "phenomenology is the search for a mise-en-scène." In the same interview, he emphasizes the importance of "*time*" in making the "mise-en-scène" in the "synthesis" of Kant's schema "sensible." Just as in film, therefore, time and mise-en-scène, make "such a thing concrete" (Robbins, *Is It Righteous to Be?* 151–52).

Levinas's language suggests that thinking philosophically and phenomenologically literally compares to thinking cinematically, that seeing and understanding an object clearly involves a process that relates to cinematic mise-en-scène. Thus, mise-en-scène becomes an exchangeable idea between Levinas's phenomenology of the clarity of the mind's consciousness of an object and the setting up and understanding of film.

17. See, e.g., Vivian Sobchack, *The Address of the Eye: A Phenomenology of Film Experience* (Princeton, NJ: Princeton University Press, 1992); and Richard Allen and Murray Smith, eds., *Film Theory and Philosophy* (Oxford: Oxford University Press, 1997).

18. See Sarah Cooper, ed., "The Occluded Relation: Levinas and Cinema," special issue, *Film-Philosophy* 11, no. 2 (Aug. 2007); and Sarah Cooper, *Selfless Cinema? Ethics and French Documentary* (London: Legenda, 2006).

19. Brian K. Bergen-Aurand, "Regarding Anna: Levinas, Antonioni and the Ethics of Film Absence," *New Review of Film and Television Studies* 4 (Aug. 2006): 107–29, 109.

20. See Thomas Doherty, *Hollywood's Censor: Joseph I. Breen and the Production Code Administration* (New York: Columbia University Press, 2007); and Thomas Doherty,

Pre-Code Hollywood: Sex, Immorality, and Insurrection in American Cinema, 1930–1934 (New York: Columbia University Press, 1999). See also Lea Jacobs, *The Wages of Sin: Censorship and the Fallen Woman Film, 1928–1942* (Berkeley: University of California Press, 1997); and Jon Lewis, *Hollywood v. Hard Core: How the Struggle over Censorship Saved the Modern Film Industry* (New York: New York University Press, 2000).

21. Obviously film works as a temporal medium, an art form that operates through time. Jean-Luc Godard's frequently quoted notion that "the cinema is the truth, twenty-four times a second" still applies to film today. See Gilberto Perez, *The Material Ghost: Films and Their Medium* (Baltimore: Johns Hopkins University Press, 1998), 345. I discuss this a bit more in Sam B. Girgus, *America on Film: Modernism, Documentary, and a Changing America* (Cambridge, UK: Cambridge University Press, 2002), 9–10. For a more recent discussion of Godard's idea and time in film see Laura Mulvey, *Death 24x a Second: Stillness and the Moving Image* (London: Reaktion, 2006).

22. Mediating between Levinasian transcendence and Deleuzian immanence, Ricoeur and Wood develop complex interactions of time, narrative, and being. In the relationship of time to ethics in film, the hermeneutics of Ricoeur, the phenomenological deconstruction of Wood, and the poststructuralism of Deleuze suggest an alternative temporality for film of diachronic disjuncture that opens a new dimension for ethics. See Paul Ricoeur, *Time and Narrative*, vol. 3, trans. Kathleen Blamey and David Pellauer (Chicago: University of Chicago Press, 1988), 208; David Wood, *Time After Time* (Bloomington: Indiana University Press, 2007); Gilles Deleuze, *Cinema 1: The Movement-Image*, trans. Hugh Tomlinson and Barbara Habberjam (Minneapolis: University of Minnesota Press, 1986); Gilles Deleuze, *Cinema 2: The Time-Image*, trans. Hugh Tomlinson and Robert Galeta (Minneapolis: University of Minnesota Press, 1989); and D. N. Rodowick, *Gilles Deleuze's Time Machine* (Durham, NC: Duke University Press, 1997).

23. As a possible assist in this effort for film, Wood proposes a conceptual apparatus he calls "time-shelters," which provide "a framework for the way in which time enters the constitution of beings—not just Being—of things, events, complexes of relationships, institutions, persons" (*Time After Time*, 26). Wood's method involves his original construction and deconstruction of "the temporal that Heidegger frames in terms of the transcendental horizon for the question of Being" (ibid., 59). Wood's approach resonates, as well, with Ricoeur's notion of the horizon in relation to time and narrative. Accordingly, the time-shelter structures Wood's conjecture "that Being might, in the end, be nothing other than Time" (62). He says, "Be*ing* would be nothing but a way of tim*ing*" (62). For Wood, time, as constituted by the time-shelter and the horizon of being, subverts "representational thinking" (86). He says, "thinking of Being is modally different from representational thinking" (87).

Wood's time-shelter and its relation to the horizon of being can transfer to a new way of thinking about film in terms of an intellectual and artistic construct that can be termed a time-frame. As a cinematic version of Wood's time-shelter and horizon, the time-frame develops classic mobile framing, a basic term of film art for the moving of the film frame in its presentation of the scene being shot. The model of the time-frame and horizon of being advances Wood's antirepresentational position by reconsidering the relationship of time, space, and movement in the film frame and by emphasizing thinking of being as opposed to representing time spatially in film. The time-frame transforms mobile framing by concentrating on time even in scenes and sequences built primarily on movement and spatial relations.

While contrasting in many ways to these other philosophers, Deleuze, in *Cinema 1: The Movement-Image*, advances elements that can help in applying Levinasian theory to film. Deleuze reconsiders the relationship of time and movement in film in a way that theorizes freeing time from the domination of movement and space. Deleuze's theoretical imagination avers the importance of a discordant temporal order for new ethical discourse. Deleuze contrasts "movement-images which are mobile sections of duration" with "time-images, that is duration-images, change-images, relation-images, volume-images which are beyond movement itself" (*Cinema 1*, 11). The movement-image, based on "the interval between two movements or two actions," can be viewed as an "indirect image of time" that "originates from montage, or from the composition of movement-images" (32). Deleuze constructs a cinema of moving parts that becomes a vehicle for the transition toward freeing the imagination from closed boundaries of thought. Lacking "a centre of anchorage and of horizon," the destabilizing movement of film creates a volatile world of image and movement. This process of linked movement enables "closed systems, finite sets" to become part of "an infinite set" (58–59). Deleuze suggests sets, movement, and assemblage become "relations of great value between philosophy and the cinema" that in turn lead to relations of ethical significance (116).

24. As part of his response to the ethical challenge, Levinas insists on a diachronic time that connects each individual to infinity, a concession to a force greater than being that makes each one more than a number in a group or on a calendar. "Dia-chrony," he writes, "is a structure that no thematizing and interested movement of consciousness—memory or hope—can either resolve or recuperate in the simultaneities it constitutes" (*Time and the Other*, 137). Such a notion of diachronic time opens time to the opportunity for redemption.

In Levinasian thought synchronic and diachronic time extends to such concepts as alterity, transcendence, the same and the other, the face, and proximity. Synchronic time—the regular, abstract time of the clock and the calendar—paradoxically contrasts with and complements diachronicity, the time of disruption. The diachronic offers a different, distanced perspective on ordinary synchronicity that enables the construction of an ethical challenge. The synchronic and diachronic define each other.

In his preface to *Time and the Other* Levinas acknowledges the indispensability of the "thread" and the *"always"* of synchronic time, while in "Diachrony and Representation," he emphasizes that synchronicity "congeals into the abstraction of the synchronous" (*Time and the Other*, 32, 103). The synchronic becomes deadened forms of ontological accounting that "constitute the rationality of an already derived order" (*Time and the Other*, 104). Synchronicity, therefore, connotes sameness, unexamined values and ideas, and ethical conformity. Synchronicity also functions for Levinas, however, as a springboard for diachronic temporality, the time that surges toward transcendence, infinity, and originality, the very opposite of synchronous deadness. Thus, synchronicity serves the creativity of the diachronic.

As a countermovement to the sameness, linearity, and continuity of everyday synchronicity, the diachronic, Levinas argues, makes ethical thinking possible, transcendence tenable, and infinity comprehensible. In "Essence and Disinterestedness" Levinas describes this time of transcendence and ethics as "recuperable temporalization," a signal for "a lapse of time that does not return, a diachrony refractory to all synchronization, a transcending diachrony" (*Emmanuel Levinas*, 116). In this ungovernable, irascible temporal dimension the diachronic approaches infinity. Levinas says in "The Old and the New" that his "profoundest thought, which bears all thought, my thought of the infinite older than the thought of the finite, is the very diachrony of time, non-coincidence, dispossession itself" (*Time and the Other*, 137).

For Levinas, diachronic time also establishes the "solitude" to sustain the otherness that he believes ethics demands. As he says, time "in its dia-chrony would signify a relationship that does not compromise the other's alterity" (*Time and the Other*, 31). Through diachronic time the other resists incorporation into another's being. The pluralism that diachronic time helps create imposes separation from the other so "that the other is in no way another myself, participating with me in a common existence" (*Time and the Other*, 75).

25. See my *Hollywood Renaissance: The Cinema of Democracy in the Era of Ford, Capra, and Kazan* (Cambridge, UK: Cambridge University Press, 1998), 25–55.

26. David Ross Fryer, *The Intervention of the Other: Ethical Subjectivity in Levinas and Lacan* (New York: Other Press, 2004), 32.

27. Kelly Oliver, "Paternal Election and the Absent Father," in *Feminist Interpretations of Emmanuel Levinas*, ed. Tina Chanter (University Park: Pennsylvania State University Press, 2001), 224–40, 226.

28. See Levinas, *Totality and Infinity: An Essay on Exteriority*, trans. Alphonso Lingis (Pittsburgh: Duquesne University Press, 1969), 257–59, on the caress. Subsequent references to this work will be cited parenthetically in the text.

29. The scene gains further intensity when we consider it in the light of Ricoeur's theories on narrative, ethical identity, the interweaving of fiction and documentary, and space and time. Ricoeur's studies of aporetic temporality help explain how film in general and *The Grapes of Wrath* in particular operate in several temporal dimensions—the seasonal time of agriculture and sharecropping, the journey to California, the metaphorical biblical journey, basic narrative structuring. *The Grapes of Wrath* enacts Ricoeur's argument for "a poetics of narrative" that interweaves fiction and history with a "third time" that "mediates between lived and cosmic time" to become "historical" time. In film Ricoeur's theories of multiple temporalities can inform the Levinasian impulse to suggest a time of ethical renewal. Thus, *The Grapes of Wrath* also dramatizes Tom's time of transformation and redemption from a rebel and outlaw to a prophetic, ethical voice for social and political change, a process comparable to Ricoeur's idea of changing identity from sameness to selfhood. In this sense time and narrative as described by Ricoeur anticipate a Levinasian argument for ethical transcendence and redemption. See Ricoeur, *Time and Narrative*, 3:99, 102, 142, 188, 241, 242, 243, 250.

30. For a classic study and history of documentary during this period see William Stott, *Documentary Expression and Thirties America* (London: Oxford, 1973).

31. See Ricoeur, *Time and Narrative*, 3:192.

32. See Emmanuel Levinas, "Reality and Its Shadow," in *The Levinas Reader*, ed. Seán Hand (Malden, MA: Blackwell, 1989). The power of such scenes constitutes a response to Levinas's argument in "Reality and Its Shadow" against representation. This position on art stems significantly from Levinas's ethical, religious, and aesthetic concerns with images and idolatry. He writes that "a represented object, by the simple fact of becoming an image, is converted into a non-object; the image as such enters into categories proper to it which we would like to bring out here. The disincarnation of reality by an image is not equivalent to a simple diminution in degree. It belongs to an ontological dimension that does not extend between us and a reality to be captured, a dimension where commerce with reality is a rhythm" (134). Indeed, Levinas's concern with art and the image as a "disincarnation of reality" remains a critical issue in his work. His belief that "the picturesque is always to some extent a caricature" (135) entails a problem throughout his writings with his relationship to art.

33. Levinasian scholars and critics naturally question the consistency of Levinas's position on art and the image in relation to his overall philosophy. As Bergen-Aurand says, "Unlike so much of his work, dedicated to an infinite response to the other and toward the

very pluralism at the heart of a difficult religion and ethics, his terms are absolutist here." He says that for Levinas, "Aesthetics stands outside ethics" (Bergen-Aurand, "Regarding Anna," 112–13).

34. See, e.g., Derrida, *Specters of Marx*; see also Derrida's classic essay "Violence and Metaphysics: An Essay on the Thought of Emmanuel Levinas," in Jacques Derrida, *Writing and Difference*, trans. Alan Bates (Chicago: University of Chicago Press, 1978), 79–153; and Jacques Derrida, *Adieu to Emmanuel Levinas*, trans. Pascale-Anne Brault and Michael Naas (Stanford, CA: Stanford University Press, 1999).

35. See Critchley, *Ethics-Politics-Subjectivity*; and Critchley, *Infinitely Demanding*.

36. Alison Ainley, "Levinas and Kant: Maternal Morality and Illegitimate Offspring," in *Feminist Interpretations of Emmanuel Levinas*, ed. Tina Chanter (University Park: Pennsylvania State University Press, 2001), 203–23, 219.

37. Tina Chanter, introduction to *Feminist Interpretations of Emmanuel Levinas*, ed. Tina Chanter (University Park: Pennsylvania State University Press, 2001), 1–27, 16.

38. Diane Perpich, "From the Caress to the Word: Transcendence and the Feminine in the Philosophy of Emmanuel Levinas," in *Feminist Interpretations of Emmanuel Levinas*, ed. Tina Chanter (University Park: Pennsylvania State University Press, 2001), 28–52, 31.

39. Ewa Płonowska Ziarek, *An Ethics of Dissensus: Postmodernity, Feminism, and the Politics of Radical Democracy* (Stanford, CA: Stanford University Press, 2001), 58–59. Ziarek argues that one of the "two forms" this process of purification takes in Levinas involves "ethical masochism." This aspect of the process entails a "surplus of obscene enjoyment" in the harshness of the law that "can be compared to the sadism of the superego." The second way "Levinas avoids an ethics of eros," according to Ziarek, involves the "process of sublimation associated in his work with the idea of divine creation and paternal love." She accepts Critchley's argument of the importance of sublimation in dealing with the trauma that occurs with the extremism of Levinas's ethical argument. Yet she sees in Levinas an "idealizing sublimation" and says its connection to "paternal love and asexual motherhood" helps sustain "a certain hostility" toward "the nonsublimated form of eros represented by feminine sexuality."

40. John Llewelyn, *The HypoCritical Imagination: Between Kant and Levinas* (London: Routledge, 2000), 129, 205.

41. See Girgus, *Hollywood Renaissance*.

1. AMERICAN TRANSCENDENCE

1. Lawrence Buell, *Emerson* (Cambridge, MA: Harvard University Press, 2003), 213, 227.
2. Ibid., 227, 158–59. See also Perry Miller's introduction to *The Transcendentalists: An Anthology*, ed. Perry Miller (Cambridge, MA: Harvard University Press, 1950), 3–15. Miller

points out that the "inherently religious character of New England Transcendentalism has not been widely appreciated, mainly because most students are not acquainted with all the writings, and so fall into the habit of judging the whole by the more familiar, but not always typical, works of Emerson and Thoreau. But also, the misapprehension gains credence because all the insurgents strove, like Emerson and Thoreau, to put their cause into the language of philosophy and literature rather than theology" (8–9).

3. Perry Miller, *The New England Mind: The Seventeenth Century* (Boston: Beacon, 1961), 21. Subsequent references to this work will be cited parenthetically in the text.

4. Perry Miller, "From Edwards to Emerson," in *Errand into the Wilderness* (New York: Harper, 1956), 184–203, 184–85.

5. Emmanuel Levinas, "Transcendence and Height," in *Emmanuel Levinas: Basic Philosophical Writings*, ed. Adriaan T. Peperzak, Simon Critchley, and Robert Bernasconi (Bloomington: Indiana University Press, 1996), 19. Subsequent references to works in this collection will be cited parenthetically in the text.

6. Emmanuel Levinas, "Ethical Subjectivity," in *God, Death, and Time*, trans. Bettina Bergo, ed. Jacques Rolland (Stanford, CA: Stanford University Press, 2000), 160–62, 161. Subsequent references to this source will be cited parenthetically in the text.

7. Ralph Waldo Emerson, "The Poet," in *Ralph Waldo Emerson: Selected Prose and Poetry*, ed. Reginald Cook, 2nd ed. (New York: Holt, Rinehart and Winston, 1969), 121–40, 125. Subsequent references to this essay or other essays in this collection will be cited parenthetically in the text.

8. Ralph Waldo Emerson, "The Transcendentalist," in *The Essential Writings of Ralph Waldo Emerson*, ed. Brooks Atkinson (New York: Modern Library, 2000), 81–95, 89.

9. Emerson says, "This way of thinking, falling on Roman times, made Stoic philosophers; falling on despotic times, made patriot Catos and Brutuses; falling on superstitious times, made prophets and apostles; on popish times, made protestants and ascetic monks, preachers of Faith against the preachers of Works; on prelatical times, made Puritans and Quakers; and falling on Unitarian and commercial times, makes the peculiar shades of Idealism which we know" (*The Essential Writings of Ralph Waldo Emerson*, 86).

10. Sacvan Bercovitch, "Emerson, Individualism, and Liberal Dissent," in *The Rites of Assent: Transformations in the Symbolic Construction of America* (New York: Routledge, 1993), 319.

11. Emmanuel Levinas, *Beyond the Verse: Talmudic Readings and Lectures*, trans. Gary D. Mole (Bloomington: Indiana University Press, 1994), 37, 39.

12. Slavoj Žižek, "Neighbors and Other Monsters: A Plea for Ethical Violence," in *The Neighbor: Three Inquiries in Political Theology*, by Slavoj Žižek, Eric L. Santner, and Kenneth Reinhard (Chicago: University of Chicago Press, 2005), 134–90, 157.

13. See Tina Chanter, "Prohibiting Miscegenation and Homosexuality: *The Birth of a Nation, Casablanca*, and *American History X*," in *The Picture of Abjection: Film, Fetish, and the Nature of Difference* (Bloomington: Indiana University Press, 2008), 180–215.
14. Emmanuel Levinas, *Time and the Other*, trans. Richard A. Cohen (Pittsburgh: Duquesne University Press, 1987), 33.
15. See Paul Ricoeur, *Oneself as Another*, trans. Kathleen Blamey (Chicago: University of Chicago Press, 1992), 337.
16. For a discussion of this and other aspects of Wayne's character in *The Searchers* see my *Hollywood Renaissance: The Cinema of Democracy in the Era of Ford, Capra, and Kazan* (Cambridge, UK: Cambridge University Press, 1998), 25–55.
17. Simon Critchley, *Infinitely Demanding: Ethics of Commitment, Politics of Resistance* (London: Verso, 2007), 120. Subsequent references to this book will be cited parenthetically in the text.
18. On "spiritual optics" see John Llewelyn, *The HypoCritical Imagination: Between Kant and Levinas* (London: Routledge, 2000), 205.
19. See Critchley on Derrida's *Specters of Marx* in Simon Critchley, *Ethics-Politics-Subjectivity: Essays on Derrida, Levinas and Contemporary French Thought* (London: Verso, 1999), 143–82, esp. 154.
20. Critchley, *Ethics-Politics-Subjectivity*, 109. See also Richard Rorty, *Achieving Our Country: Leftist Thought in Twentieth-Century America* (Cambridge, MA: Harvard University Press, 1998); and Simon Critchley, Jacques Derrida, Ernesto Laclau, and Richard Rorty, *Deconstruction and Pragmatism*, ed. Chantal Mouffe (London: Routledge, 1996).
21. See Ewa Płonowska Ziarek, *An Ethics of Dissensus: Postmodernity, Feminism, and the Politics of Radical Democracy* (Stanford, CA: Stanford University Press, 2001), 62–63.
22. Sacvan Bercovitch, "Introduction: The Music of America," in *The Rites of Assent*, 22; and Sacvan Bercovitch, "The Ritual of Consensus," in *The Rites of Assent*, 29–67.
23. Sacvan Bercovitch, "The Problem of Ideology in a Time of Dissensus," in *The Rites of Assent*, 367, 368.
24. Hector St. John de Crèvecœur, *Letters from an American Farmer; and Sketches of Eighteenth-Century America: More Letters from an American Farmer* (New York: Signet, 1963), 62–63.
25. Thomas Jefferson to John Cartwright, Monticello, June 5, 1824, in *The Political Writings of Thomas Jefferson: Representative Selections*, ed. Edward Dumbauld (Indianapolis: Bobbs-Merrill American Heritage Series, 1955), 126. He also famously wrote to William S. Smith in the same year: "The tree of liberty must be refreshed from time to time with the blood of patriots and tyrants. It is its natural manure" (ibid.).
26. See Jefferson to Madison, January 30, 1787; and Jefferson to Smith, November 13, 1787; both in *The Political Writings of Thomas Jefferson*, 67, 69.

27. Emmanuel Levinas, *The Levinas Reader*, ed. Seán Hand (Malden, MA: Blackwell, 1989), 242.
28. See Hand's prefatory remarks for "Ideology and Idealism," in *The Levinas Reader*, ed. Seán Hand (Malden, MA: Blackwell, 1989), 235–36.
29. Emmanuel Levinas, *Outside the Subject*, trans. Michael B. Smith (Stanford, CA: Stanford University Press, 1993), 120.
30. See John Winthrop, "A Modell of Christian Charity," in *The Puritans: A Source of Their Writings*, ed. Perry Miller and Thomas H. Johnson, vol. 1 (New York: Harper Torchbook, 1963), 195–99; Jefferson to James Madison, April 27, 1809, quoted in Wai-chee Dimock, *Melville and the Politics of Individualism* (Princeton, NJ: Princeton University Press, 1989), 9; Emerson is quoted in "Emerson, Individualism, Liberal Dissent," in Bercovitch, *The Rites of Assent*, 340; Lincoln, "Annual Message to Congress, December 1, 1862, in *Abraham Lincoln: Great Speeches* (New York: Dover, 1991), 97.
31. See Jackson Lears, *Rebirth of a Nation: The Making of Modern America, 1877–1920* (New York: HarperCollins, 2009).
32. Sarah Cooper, *Selfless Cinema? Ethics and French Documentary* (London: Legenda, 2006), 23.

2. FRANK CAPRA AND JAMES STEWART

1. Emmanuel Levinas, *Totality and Infinity: An Essay on Exteriority*, trans. Alphonso Lingis (Pittsburgh: Duquesne University Press, 1969), 21.
2. See "A Disparate Inventory," in *The Cambridge Companion to Levinas*, ed. Simon Critchley and Robert Bernasconi (Cambridge, UK: Cambridge University Press, 2002), xxix. See also Richard J. Bernstein, *Radical Evil: A Philosophical Investigation* (Cambridge: Polity, 2002), 166–83, and Derrida, *Adieu to Emmanuel Levinas*, trans. Pascale-Anne Brault and Michael Naas (Stanford, CA: Stanford University Press, 1999).
3. See Joseph McBride, *Frank Capra: The Catastrophe of Success* (New York: Touchstone, 1992); Raymond Carney, *American Vision: The Films of Frank Capra* (Cambridge, UK: Cambridge University Press, 1986); Richard Glatzer and John Raeburn, eds., *Frank Capra: The Man and His Films* (Ann Arbor: University of Michigan Press, 1975); Charles J. Maland, *Frank Capra* (Boston: Twayne, 1980); Leland Poague, *Another Frank Capra* (Cambridge, UK: Cambridge University Press, 1994); Robert Ray, *A Certain Tendency of the Hollywood Cinema, 1930–1980* (Princeton, NJ: Princeton University Press, 1985); Robert Sklar, "God and Man in Bedford Falls: Frank Capra's *It's a Wonderful Life*," in *The American Self: Myth, Ideology, and Popular Culture*, ed. Sam B. Girgus (Albuquerque: University of New Mexico Press, 1981), 211–20.
4. Not always as recognized or appreciated as this domestic dialogue in his works is the awareness in his films of the connection between the United States and Europe. Europe as an artistic force, as a history of cultural greatness, and as a center of modern crisis

figured prominently in many of his films. A dark consciousness of the ominous contrast between the democratic modernism of America and the deepening antidemocratic and totalitarian forces of Europe pervades them. Capra knew refugee directors from Europe, such as Ernst Lubitsch, and the America of his films stood as a counterstatement to the growing danger overseas. In America modernism to Capra often meant opportunity, the challenge to tradition and authority, the advance of freedom. Modernism in Europe could mean dehumanization, restriction, the power of the state to repress and control. Thus, as an indication of the artistic and intellectual complexity of Capra's work, as well as his sensitivity to European artistic trends and movements, some have discussed how his films include the European influence of a bleaker vision of life and experience as expressed in film noir. See Robin Wood, quoted in Maland, *Frank Capra*, 146. See also James Naremore, *More Than Night: Film Noir in Its Contexts* (Berkeley: University of California Press, 1998).

5. The artistic and cultural significance of these films helped give Capra a major role in the construction of a "Hollywood Renaissance," a creative culmination of films and directors that helped both describe and form American culture in the mid-twentieth century. Along with Capra, such directors as John Ford, Howard Hawks, George Stevens, and Elia Kazan, among others, were part of a much broader national consensus of creative figures and thinkers who were engaged in a dialogue with the American idea. See Sam B. Girgus, *Hollywood Renaissance: The Cinema of Democracy in the Era of Ford, Capra, and Kazan* (Cambridge, UK: Cambridge University Press, 1998).

6. For specific details and explanations of his theory see Gilles Deleuze, *Cinema 1: The Movement-Image*, trans. Hugh Tomlinson and Barbara Habberjam (Minneapolis: University of Minnesota Press, 1986), 11, 32, 55, 58–59, 114–17. Subsequent references to this work will be cited parenthetically in the text.

7. For a discussion of these terms and concepts see Paul Ricoeur, *Time and Narrative*, vol. 3, trans. Kathleen Blamey and David Pellauer (Chicago: University of Chicago Press, 1988), 26, 41, 101–4, 118, 123, 144, 192, 208, 242–43, 250, 258, 271. See also Paul Ricoeur, *Oneself as Another*, trans. Kathleen Blamey (Chicago: University of Chicago Press, 1992), 2, 124–25, 165, 167, 318. Subsequent references to these books will be cited parenthetically in the text.

8. See my *Hollywood Renaissance*, 56–86, and the accompanying footnotes for additional details and descriptions of secondary sources and the work of critics and scholars.

9. See D. N. Rodowick, *Gilles Deleuze's Time Machine* (Durham, NC: Duke University Press, 1997). All subsequent references to Rodowick's book will be cited parenthetically in the text. See also Gilles Deleuze, *Cinema 2: The Time-Image*, trans. Hugh Tomlinson and Robert Galeta (Minneapolis: University of Minnesota Press, 1989).

10. Derrida, *Adieu to Emmanuel Levinas*, 151n130.
11. Emmanuel Levinas, "Inside Heidegger: Bergson," in *God, Death, and Time*, trans. Bettina Bergo, ed. Jacques Rolland (Stanford, CA: Stanford University Press, 2000), 54. Subsequent references to essays in this collection will be cited parenthetically in the text.
12. Tina Chanter, *Time, Death, and the Feminine: Levinas with Heidegger* (Stanford, CA: Stanford University Press, 2001), 146.
13. T. S. Eliot, *The Complete Poems and Plays, 1909–1950* (New York: Harcourt, Brace and World, 1971), 48. For an original and stimulating discussion of this theme see Rob White, *The Third Man* (London: BFI, 2003), 53–54.
14. See essays in *Emmanuel Levinas: Basic Philosophical Writings*, ed. Adriaan T. Peperzak, Simon Critchley, and Robert Bernasconi (Bloomington: Indiana University Press, 1996), 61–62, 75, 94–95, 122–23, 163, 170–71. Subsequent references to works in this book will be cited parenthetically in the text.
15. See Stella Sandford, *The Metaphysics of Love: Gender and Transcendence in Levinas* (London: Athlone, 2000), 77, 78.
16. For an excellent psychoanalytical discussion of Smith's martyrdom and male hysteria see Dennis Bingham, *Acting Male: Masculinities in the Films of James Stewart, Jack Nicholson, and Clint Eastwood* (New Brunswick, NJ: Rutgers University Press, 1994), 1–96; Charles Wolfe, "*Mr. Smith Goes to Washington*: Democratic Forums and Representational Forms," in *Close Viewings: An Anthology of New Film Criticism*, ed. Peter Lehman (Tallahassee: Florida State University Press, 1990), 318.
17. Jill Robbins, ed. *Is It Righteous to Be? Interviews with Emmanuel Levinas* (Stanford, CA: Stanford University Press, 2001), 118.
18. John Llewelyn, *Emmanuel Levinas: The Genealogy of Ethics* (London: Routledge, 1995), 132.
19. "Pirkei Avoth," in *The Traditional Prayer Book*, ed. David De Sola Pool (New York: Behrman House, 1960), 1.12.666.
20. See Simon Critchley, *Infinitely Demanding: Ethics of Commitment, Politics of Resistance* (London: Verso, 2007).
21. See John Wild, introduction to *Totality and Infinity: An Essay on Exteriority*, by Emmanuel Levinas, trans. Alphonso Lingis (Pittsburgh: Duquesne University Press, 1969), 11–20.
22. See Perry Miller, "The Rhetoric of Sensation," in *Errand into the Wilderness* (New York: Harper, 1956), 167–84, 181.
23. Sklar, "God and Man in Bedford Falls," 212.
24. "Pirkei Avoth," in *The Traditional Prayer Book*, 3.17.678.

25. Ewa Płonowska Ziarek, *An Ethics of Dissensus: Postmodernity, Feminism, and the Politics of Radical Democracy* (Stanford, CA: Stanford University Press, 2001), 55.
26. For a detailed discussion of the controversy and debate over the meaning of the end of the film see my *Hollywood Renaissance*, 86–107.
27. Luce Irigaray, *An Ethics of Sexual Difference*, trans. Carolyn Burke and Gillian C. Gill (Ithaca, NY: Cornell University Press, 1993), 73, 75, 82.

3. THE CHANGING FACE OF AMERICAN REDEMPTION

1. Originally quoted in *Cahiers du cinéma* (October 1959); cited in Gilles Deleuze, *Cinema 1: The Movement-Image*, trans. Hugh Tomlinson and Barbara Habberjam (Minneapolis: University of Minnesota Press, 1986), 99.
2. Emmanuel Levinas, "Reality and Its Shadow," in *The Levinas Reader*, ed. Seán Hand (Malden, MA: Blackwell, 1989), 134, 135.
3. Libby Saxton, "Fragile Faces: Levinas and Lanzmann," in "The Occluded Relation: Levinas and Cinema," ed. Sarah Cooper, special issue, *Film-Philosophy* 11, no. 2 (2007): 1–14, 4, 5. www.film-philosophy.com/2007v11n2/saxton.pdf (accessed June 1, 2009). See also Saxton, *Haunted Images: Film, Ethics, Testimony and the Holocaust* (New York: Wallflower Press, 2008).
4. Sarah Cooper, *Selfless Cinema? Ethics and French Documentary* (London: Legenda, 2006), 17.
5. Judith Butler, *Precarious Life: The Powers of Mourning and Violence* (London: Verso, 2004), 144.
6. Emmanuel Levinas, *Existence and Existents*, trans. Alphonso Lingis (Pittsburgh: Duquesne University Press, 2001), 48–49.
7. See Sam B. Girgus, *America on Film: Modernism, Documentary, and a Changing America* (Cambridge, UK: Cambridge University Press, 2002), 9–10; and Gilberto Perez, *The Material Ghost: Films and Their Medium* (Baltimore: Johns Hopkins University Press, 1998), 345.
8. Woody Allen, "Through a Life Darkly," review of *The Magic Lantern: An Autobiography*, by Ingmar Bergman, *New York Times*, Sunday, Sept. 18, 1988, Books sec., 30.
9. David Mamet, "Hard Lessons Learned in the Ring," *New York Times*, Sunday, April 27, 2008, Arts & Leisure sec., 19.
10. Béla Balázs, "The Close-Up," in *Film Theory and Criticism: Introductory Readings*, ed. Gerald Mast, Marshall Cohen, and Leo Braudy, 4th ed. (Oxford: Oxford University Press, 1992), 261.
11. On aura and Perez, see Sam B. Girgus, *The Films of Woody Allen*, 2nd. ed. (Cambridge, UK: Cambridge University Press, 2002), 9–16; see also Theodor W. Adorno, *Aesthetic*

Theory, ed. Gretel Adorno and Rolf Tiedemann, trans. Robert Hullot-Kentor (Minneapolis: University of Minnesota Press. 1996), 274, 310–11.

12. For a discussion of the recent trend of putting stars and celebrities in a negative light "under the media microscope," see Virginia Heffernan, "The Beautiful People: The Uglier the Better," *New York Times*, Sunday, July 15, 2007, Arts & Leisure sec., 1, 29.

13. John Llewelyn, *Emmanuel Levinas: The Genealogy of Ethics* (London: Routledge, 1995), 66.

14. Emmanuel Levinas, *Outside the Subject*, trans. Michael B. Smith (Stanford, CA: Stanford University Press, 1993), 94. Subsequent references to this work will be cited parenthetically in the text.

15. Llewelyn, *The HypoCritical Imagination: Between Kant and Levinas* (London: Routledge, 2000), 172.

16. Simon Critchley, *Infinitely Demanding: Ethics of Commitment, Politics of Resistance* (London: Verso, 2007), 40.

17. Levinas, *Totality and Infinity: An Essay on Interiority*, trans. Alphonso Lingis (Pittsburgh: Duquesne University Press, 1969), 291.

18. Susan Griffin, *Pornography and Silence: Culture's Revenge Against Nature* (New York: Harper Colophon, 1981), 208, 217. The calendar photograph can be found in Norman Mailer, *Marilyn: A Biography*, produced by Lawrence Schiller (New York: Grosset and Dunlap, 1973), 80. Subsequent references to this work will be cited parenthetically in the text.

19. Ibid., 213; and S. Paige Baty, *American Monroe: The Making of a Body Politic* (Berkeley: University of California Press, 1995), 78.

20. Barbara Leaming, *Marilyn Monroe* (New York: Three Rivers, 1998), 375.

21. James Naremore, *Acting in the Cinema* (Berkeley: University of California Press, 1990), 15.

22. Emmanuel Levinas, *Otherwise Than Being or Beyond Essence*, trans. Alphonso Lingis (Pittsburgh: Duquesne University Press, 1998), 158.

23. Quoted in Salomon Malka, *Emmanuel Levinas: His Life and Legacy*, trans. Michael Kigel and Sonja M. Embree (Pittsburgh: Duquesne University Press, 2002), 75.

24. See Paul Buhle and David Wagner, *Radical Hollywood: The Untold Story Behind America's Favorite Movies* (New York: New Press, 2002).

25. See Paul Ricoeur, *Time and Narrative*, vol. 3, trans. Kathleen Blamey and David Pellauer (Chicago: University of Chicago Press, 1988), 208; and David Wood, *Time After Time* (Bloomington: Indiana University Press, 2007), 26.

26. See Gilles Deleuze, *Cinema 1: The Movement-Image*, trans. Hugh Tomlinson and Barbara Habberjam (Minneapolis: University of Minnesota Press, 1986), 226, 117.

27. Cindy Lucia, *Framing Female Lawyers: Women on Trial in Film* (Austin: University of Texas Press, 2005), 42, 37.

28. See chapter 8, "Spike Lee, Denzel Washington, and the Rebirth of Malcolm X: Cinetext for a Black American Dream," in Girgus, *America on Film*, 174–201.
29. Cooper, *Selfless Cinema?* 28. While choosing not "to anchor" her own work on Levinas and documentary on racial difference, Cooper underscores Félix Guattari and Gilles Deleuze's argument that "racism proceeds in terms of measuring deviation from the face of the white man."

4. SEX, ART, AND OEDIPUS

1. Emmanuel Levinas, "Ethical Subjectivity," in *God, Death, and Time*, trans. Bettina Bergo (Stanford, CA: Stanford University Press, 1993), 160–62, 160.
2. Emmanuel Levinas, "From Consciousness to Prophetism," in *God, Death, and Time*, 202–6, 205; and "Transcendence and Intelligibility," in *Emmanuel Levinas: Basic Philosophical Writings*, ed. Adriaan T. Peperzak, Simon Critchley, and Robert Bernasconi (Bloomington: Indiana University Press, 1996), 149–60, 158. See also Levinas, "God and Philosophy," in ibid., 129–48, where he says, "Philosophy is not merely the knowledge of immanence; it is immanence itself" (134).
3. Simon Critchley, *Ethics-Politics-Subjectivity: Essays on Derrida, Levinas and Contemporary French Thought* (London: Verso, 1999), 203.
4. Rachel Donadio, "Report Says That as Young Man, Czech Writer Informed on a Supposed Spy," *New York Times*, Oct. 14, 2008, A5: "The allegations would diminish Mr. Kundera's moral stature as a spokesman, however enigmatic, against totalitarianism's corrosion of daily life. In a statement, the reclusive Mr. Kundera vehemently denied the account. 'I object in the strongest manner to these accusations, which are pure lies,' he said in a statement released by his French publisher, Gallimard."
5. See Emmanuel Levinas, *Totality and Infinity: An Essay on Exteriority*, trans. Alphonso Lingis (Pittsburgh: Duquesne University Press, 1969), 291.
6. See Tina Chanter, *The Picture of Abjection: Film, Fetish, and the Nature of Difference* (Bloomington: Indiana University Press, 2008). Subsequent references to this work will be cited parenthetically in the text.
7. See David Wood, *Time After Time* (Bloomington: Indiana University Press, 2007).
8. See Matthew Arnold, "Dover Beach" and "The Grand Chartreuse," in *The Poetry and Criticism of Matthew Arnold*, ed. A. Dwight Culler (Boston: Houghton Mifflin, 1961), 162, 187.
9. See Chanter, *The Picture of Abjection*; and Simon Critchley, *Infinitely Demanding: Ethics of Commitment, Politics of Resistance* (London: Verso, 2007).

10. Luce Irigaray, *Sexes and Genealogies*, trans. Gillian C. Gill (New York: Columbia University Press, 1993), 121.
11. Rob White, *The Third Man* (London: BFI, 2003), 68, 64.
12. Pauline Kael, "Take Off Your Clothes," *New Yorker*, Feb. 8, 1988, 70.
13. See Jiri Pehe, "A Spring Awakening for Human Rights," *New York Times*, Sunday, Aug. 24, 2008, Week in Review sec., 10.
14. Terrence Rafferty, "Llastooks," *Sight and Sound* (summer 1988): 206–9, 207. Other Kaufman films of note include his remake of *Invasion of the Body Snatchers* (1978); *Henry and June* (1990), about the relationship of Henry Miller and Anaïs Nin, the controversial and celebrated avant-garde figures of modernist and popular culture; and *Rising Sun* (1993), a crime thriller set in Japan.
15. Vincent Canby, "Film: 'Lightness of Being,' from Novel by Kundera," *New York Times*, Feb. 5, 1988, B1. Kaufman also comments on the film as a "fairy tale" on the DVD discussion and elsewhere.
16. See my "*Raging Bull*: Revisioning the Body, Soul, and Cinema," in Sam B. Girgus, *America on Film: Modernism, Documentary, and a Changing America* (Cambridge, UK: Cambridge University Press, 2002), 67–86.
17. Quoted in David Ehrenstein, *The Scorsese Picture: The Art and Life of Martin Scorsese* (New York: Birch Lane, 1992), 155.
18. Patrick Cattrysse, "*The Unbearable Lightness of Being*: Film Adaptation Seen from a Different Perspective," *Literature/Film Quarterly* 25 (1997): 222–30, 228.
19. Sigmund Freud, *Three Essays on the Theory of Sexuality*, trans. James Strachey (New York: Basic Books, 1962), 19, 20.
20. See Luce Irigaray, *Speculum of the Other Woman*, trans. Gillian C. Gill (Ithaca, NY: Cornell University Press, 1985), 114.
21. Luce Irigaray, *This Sex Which Is Not One*, trans. Catherine Porter (Ithaca, NY: Cornell University Press, 1985), 154.
22. See Jacques Derrida, *Adieu to Emmanuel Levinas*, trans. Pascale-Anne Brault and Michael Naas (Stanford, CA: Stanford University Press, 1999), 76, 99.
23. Ewa Płonowska Ziarek, *An Ethics of Dissensus: Postmodernity, Feminism, and the Politics of Radical Democracy* (Stanford, CA: Stanford University Press, 2001), 53, 51.
24. Milan Kundera, *The Unbearable Lightness of Being*, trans. Michael Henry Heim (New York: Harper Colophon, 1984), 248. Subsequent references to this work will be cited parenthetically in the text.
25. Diane Perpich, "From the Caress to the Word: Transcendence and the Feminine in the Philosophy of Emmanuel Levinas," in *Feminist Interpretations of Emmanuel Levinas*, ed.

Tina Chanter (University Park: Pennsylvania State University Press, 2001), 28–52. Perpich says:

> It is a seeking that is not satisfied by the presence of the other, but only renewed at a deeper level; it is a flight toward the other that does not involve a return to the self. The seeking of the caress, he says, does not degenerate into contact that would represent the ego's hold upon the other, a way of having her in his grasp. In effect, the caress is a relationship to the other in which the relationship does not diminish the distance between the terms and the distance does not prevent the possibility of a relationship. As such, it seems to offer a perfect model of transcendence. (42)

26. "The erotic no longer represents a pure possibility of pure transcendence; rather it shows with striking clarity just how every break with immanence is recuperable, capable of being reabsorbed within the structures of consciousness and being, or as Levinas will later say, within 'the Same'" (Perpich, "From the Caress to the Word," 45).
27. See Cattrysse, "*The Unbearable Lightness of Being*," 229, for a discussion of this documentary aspect of the film. For an interesting discussion and retrospective of the photography and documentary of this time and place based on a recent exhibit see Robert Smith, "Joseph Koudelka: Invasion 68 Prague," *New York Times*, Oct. 3, 2008, B33.
28. See Herbert Marcuse, *One-Dimensional Man: Studies in the Ideology of Advanced Industrial Society* (Boston: Beacon, 1964), 56, 74.
29. See Norman O. Brown, *Life Against Death: The Psychoanalytical Meaning of History* (New York: Vintage, 1959); and Herbert Marcuse, *Eros and Civilization: A Philosophical Inquiry into Freud* (New York: Vintage, 1962).

5. FELLINI AND *LA DOLCE VITA*

1. Peter Bondanella, *The Films of Federico Fellini* (Cambridge, UK: Cambridge University Press, 2002), 65. Subsequent references to this work will be cited parenthetically in the text.
2. Frank Burke, "Federico Fellini: Realism/Representation/Signification," in *Federico Fellini: Contemporary Perspectives*, ed. Frank Burke and Marguerite R. Waller (Toronto: University of Toronto Press, 2002), 26–46, 35.
3. See for example Bondanella, *The Films of Federico Fellini*, 80–81.
4. Frank Burke, *Fellini's Film* (New York: Twayne, 1996), 104.
5. Peter Bondanella, *The Cinema of Federico Fellini*, foreword by Federico Fellini (Princeton, NJ: Princeton University Press, 1992), 139. Subsequent references to this work will be cited parenthetically in the text.

6. Emmanuel Levinas, *Totality and Infinity: An Essay on Exteriority*, trans. Alphonso Lingis (Pittsburgh: Duquesne University Press, 1969), 254.
7. See, e.g., Marguerite R. Waller, "Whose *Dolce vita* Is This Anyway? The Language of Fellini's Cinema," in *Federico Fellini: Contemporary Perspectives*, ed. Frank Burke and Marguerite R. Waller (Toronto: University of Toronto Press, 2002), 107–20. For Waller, "The kind of cinematic movement I have been describing creates a never before seen or experienced time and space—a time and space in which the fundamental activity is not representation, or even signification per se, but rather a perpetual production and confrontation of different systems and logics" (114–15). For sure, Fellini progresses in *La dolce vita* in moving toward a dramatically new cinematic vision that involves an original use of images to create a new kind of visual rhythm for film. Waller and other critics suggest, however, that he comes closer to achieving the kind of transformation that Waller describes in subsequent films of fantasy and interior psychic imagination, beginning with $8\frac{1}{2}$ (1963).
8. See Tullio Kezich, *Federico Fellini: His Life and Work*, trans. Minna Proctor, with Viviana Mazza (New York: Faber and Faber, 2006).
9. Tullio Kezich, "Federico Fellini and the Making of *La Dolce Vita*," *Cineaste* 8 (winter 2005): 8–14, 8.
10. See, e.g., Vincent Canby, "Warm Memories and Hot Nightmares Are Etched in Fellini's Singular Vision," *New York Times*, Oct. 29, 1993, B1; and Amy M. Spindler, "Fashion's Affair with the Paparazzi," *New York Times*, Sept. 9, 1997, B6.
11. Alessia Ricciardi, "The Spleen of Rome: Mourning Modernism in Fellini's *La Dolce Vita*," *MODERNISM/modernity* 7 (2000): 201–19, 205.
12. Federico Fellini, *Comments on Film*, ed. Giovanni Grazzi, trans. Joseph Henry (Fresno: California State University, 1988), 136.
13. See David Wood, *Time After Time* (Bloomington: Indiana University Press, 2007), 26–28, 59–62, 86–97. Wood's time-shelter proposes flexible borders that operate as an open event-horizon. The time-shelter and horizon help structure the relationship between time and being. His theory suggests the possibility of an interpretation of such time-shelters as time-frames for film. The time-frame, as I conceive it, reimagines the usual mobile framing of film to emphasize temporality as opposed to spatial organization and movement. The time-frame invites thinking about film as a means for undermining conventional temporality to open a new temporal order that will concentrate on the relationship of time, being, and the other. Wood's concern involves overcoming rigid representational thinking through the renegotiation of the interaction between time and being. The concept of the time-frame, then, can initiate new thinking about how time in film relates to ethics, being, and representation.
14. See Ricciardi, "The Spleen of Rome," 217n11.

15. Emmanuel Levinas, "Reality and Its Shadow," in *The Levinas Reader*, ed. Seán Hand (Malden, MA: Blackwell, 1989), 137–38.
16. See Paul Ricoeur, *Time and Narrative*, vol. 3, trans. Kathleen Blamey and David Pellauer (Chicago: University of Chicago Press, 1988), 101, 102, 192, 104, 208.
17. Ibid., 242–50. Such aporetics involve, for example, the paradox of the "initial great aporia, the aporia of a double perspective" of individual and social or historic time in human experience or, to give another example, the compression into one time of the "three ecstasies of time—the future, the past, and the present."
18. See Ricciardi, "The Spleen of Rome," 206; Ricciardi also comments on the architecture of the church and the music Steiner will play.
19. Emmanuel Levinas, *Outside the Subject*, trans. Michael B. Smith (Stanford, CA: Stanford University Press, 1993), 2, 1.
20. Emmanuel Levinas, "Transcendence and Intelligibility," in *Emmanuel Levinas: Basic Philosophical Writings*, ed. Adriaan T. Peperzak, Simon Critchley, and Robert Bernasconi (Bloomington: Indiana University Press, 1996), 149–59, 155.
21. Emmanuel Levinas, "God and Philosophy," in *The Levinas Reader*, ed. Seán Hand (Malden, MA: Blackwell, 1989), 166–89, 176–79.
22. See Levinas, "Time and the Other," in *The Levinas Reader*, ed. Seán Hand (Malden, MA: Blackwell, 1989), 37–58, 52.
23. Kelly Oliver, "Paternal Election and the Absent Father," in *Feminist Interpretations of Emmanuel Levinas*, ed. Tina Chanter (University Park: Pennsylvania State University Press, 2001), 224–40, 239.

6. ANTONIONI AND *L'AVVENTURA*

1. See Seymour Chatman, "All the Adventures," in *L'Avventura: Michelangelo Antonioni, Director*, ed. Seymour Chatman and Guido Fink (New Brunswick, NJ: Rutgers University Press, 1989), 3–15, 5, 4, 3.
2. Peter Brunette, *The Films of Michelangelo Antonioni* (Cambridge, UK: Cambridge University Press, 1998), 44.
3. Brian K. Bergen-Aurand, "Regarding Anna: Levinas, Antonioni, and the Ethics of Film Absence," *New Review of Film and Television Studies* (August 2006): 107–29, 109.
4. Geoffrey Nowell-Smith, *L'Avventura* (London: BFI, 2002), 12.
5. John Llewelyn, *The HypoCritical Imagination: Between Kant and Levinas* (London: Routledge, 2000), 205.
6. Bergen-Aurand, "Regarding Anna," 109. For other valuable articles with similar and relevant philosophical and theoretical themes and approaches see Jack Turner, "Anto-

nioni's *The Passenger* as Lacanian Text," *Other Voices: The (e)Journal of Cultural Criticism* 1, no. 3 (Jan. 1999): www.othervoices.org/1.3/jturner/passenger.html (accessed June 4, 2009); and Hamish Ford, "Antonioni's *L'avventura* and Deleuze's Time-Image," *Senses of Cinema*, no. 28 (Sept.-Oct. 2003): http://archive.sensesofcinema.com/contents/03/28/l_avventura_deleuze.html (accessed June 4, 2009).

7. Quoted in Sam Rohdie, *Antonioni* (London: BFI, 1990), epigraph.
8. Marcia Landy, *Italian Film* (Cambridge, UK: Cambridge University Press, 2000), 298.
9. All of these well-known arguments by Levinas, proffered in such works as *Time and the Other*, *Totality and Infinity*, and *Otherwise Than Being or Beyond Essence*, are discussed and delineated, as well as refuted, in detail in *Feminist Interpretations of Emmanuel Levinas*, ed. Tina Chanter (University Park: Pennsylvania State University Press, 2001).
10. Tina Chanter, introduction to *Feminist Interpretations of Emmanuel Levinas*, ed. Tina Chanter (University Park: Pennsylvania State University Press, 2001), 1–27, 3, 2.
11. Alison Ainley, "Levinas and Kant: Maternal Morality and Illegitimate Offspring," in *Feminist Interpretations of Emmanuel Levinas*, ed. Tina Chanter (University Park: Pennsylvania State University Press, 2001), 203–23, 219.
12. Emmanuel Levinas, *Totality and Infinity: An Essay on Exteriority*, trans. Alphonso Lingis (Pittsburgh: Duquesne University Press, 1969), 263.
13. See Claire Elise Katz, "Reinhabiting the House of Ruth: Exceeding the Limits of the Feminine in Levinas," in *Feminist Interpretations of Emmanuel Levinas*, ed. Tina Chanter (University Park: Pennsylvania State University Press, 2001), 145–70, 146.
14. Ewa Płonowska Ziarek, *An Ethics of Dissensus: Postmodernity, Feminism, and the Politics of Radical Democracy* (Stanford, CA: Stanford University Press, 2001), 54–59.
15. Luce Irigaray, "Questions to Emmanuel Levinas: On the Divinity of Love," in *Re-reading Levinas*, ed. Robert Bernasconi and Simon Critchley (Bloomington: Indiana University Press, 1991), 109–18, 110.
16. William Arrowsmith, *Antonioni: The Poet of Images*, ed. Ted Perry (New York: Oxford University Press, 1995), 31.
17. Michelangelo Antonioni, "Cannes Statement," in *L'Avventura: Michelangelo Antonioni, Director*, ed. Seymour Chatman and Guido Fink (New Brunswick, NJ: Rutgers University Press, 1989), 177–79, 178. Subsequent references to this statement will be cited parenthetically in the text.
18. Sigmund Freud, *Three Essays on the Theory of Sexuality*, trans James Strachey (New York: Basic Books, 1975), 15.
19. Freud, "The Most Prevalent Form of Degradation in Erotic Life," in "Contributions to the Psychology of Love," in *Sexuality and the Psychology of Love: Sigmund Freud*, ed. Philip Rieff (New York: Collier, 1963), 58.

20. See Simon Critchley, *Infinitely Demanding: Ethics of Commitment, Politics of Resistance* (London: Verso, 2007), 60–87.
21. Michelangelo Antonioni, *The Architecture of Vision: Writings and Interviews on Cinema*, ed. Carlo di Carlo, Giorgio Tinazzi, and Marga Cottino-Jones (New York: Marsilio, 1996), 229, 58.
22. See Gilberto Perez, *The Material Ghost: Films and Their Medium* (Baltimore: Johns Hopkins University Press, 1998), 379.
23. See Rohdie, *Antonioni*, 149, where Rohdie says, "An aspect of the documentary tradition is not that it presumes to tell the truth, nor seeks to be objective, but that fundamentally it doesn't fully know and in that sense is not in complete possession of its narrative; the sense of such documentaries is not the presentation of a known, but the investigation of a not-known and part of the technique of that investigation, given the uncertainty of the camera, and of the narrator, is to remain both reticent and external in relation to the events, often coming upon [them] as they take shape, and for that reason not dominating them."
24. See Paul Ricoeur, *Time and Narrative*, vol. 3, trans. Kathleen Blamey and David Pellauer (Chicago: University of Chicago Press, 1988), 142–44.
25. See Nowell-Smith, *L'Avventura*, 14–19; and Rohdie, *Antonioni*, 7–24; see also Guido Fink, "Michelangelo Antonioni: A Biographical Sketch," in *L'Avventura: Michelangelo Antonioni, Director*, ed. Seymour Chatman and Guido Fink (New Brunswick, NJ: Rutgers University Press, 1989), 17–28.
26. Luce Irigaray, "The Fecundity of the Caress: A Reading of Levinas, *Totality and Infinity*, 'Phenomenology of Eros,'" in *An Ethics of Sexual Difference*, by Luce Irigaray, trans. Carolyn Burke and Gillian C. Gill (Ithaca, NY: Cornell University Press, 1993), 185–217, 185. Subsequent references to other essays in this work will be cited parenthetically in the text under the volume title *An Ethics of Sexual Difference*).
27. On Antonioni and temps mort see Seymour Chatman, *Antonioni, or, The Surface of the World* (Berkeley: University of California Press, 1985), esp. 126.
28. Kelly Oliver, "Paternal Election and the Absent Father," in *Feminist Interpretations of Emmanuel Levinas*, ed. Tina Chanter (University Park: Pennsylvania State University Press, 2001), 224–40, 228, 230.
29. See Irigaray, "Questions to Emmanuel Levinas," 113; Stella Sandford, *The Metaphysics of Love: Gender and Transcendence in Levinas* (London: Athlone, 2000).
30. Emmanuel Levinas, *Otherwise Than Being or Beyond Essence*, trans. Alphonso Lingis (Pittsburgh: Duquesne University Press, 1998), 74.
31. Irigaray, "Questions to Emmanuel Levinas," 110.

32. Roland Barthes, "Dear Antonioni," in Geoffrey Nowell-Smith, *L'Avventura* (London: BFI, 2002), 63–68, 66, 67.
33. See Oliver, "Paternal Election and the Absent Father," 231; and Emmanuel Levinas, *Existence and Existents*, trans. Alphonso Lingis (Pittsburgh: Duquesne University Press, 2001), 57–58, 56, 60.
34. Brunette, *The Films of Michelangelo Antonioni*, 31, 160n9. Paul Bonitzer, "The Disappearance (On Antonioni)," is reprinted in *L'Avventura: Michelangelo Antonioni, Director*, ed. Seymour Chatman and Guido Fink (New Brunswick, NJ: Rutgers University Press, 1989), 215–19.
35. See Arrowsmith, *Antonioni*, 36, 148, 152.
36. See Antonioni, *The Architecture of Vision*, 5–68.
37. See Irigaray, "Questions to Emmanuel Levinas," 110, 117.
38. See Nowell-Smith, *L'Avventura*, 38; and Arrowsmith, *Antonioni*, 32.
39. F. Scott Fitzgerald, *Tender Is the Night* (New York: Charles Scribner's Sons, 1933), 201.
40. See Antonioni, *The Architecture of Vision*, 7, 89, 166, 214, 233.
41. See Sam B. Girgus, "Beyond the Diver Complex: The Dynamics of Modern Individualism in F. Scott Fitzgerald," in *The Law of the Heart: Individualism and the Modern Self in American Literature* (Austin: University of Texas Press, 1979), 108–28.
42. Brunette, *The Films of Michelangelo Antonioni*, 40. See also Rohdie, *Antonioni*, 54. Rohdie develops Noël Burch's explanation of a somewhat similar use of the camera by Antonio for a "double and doubling" effect that brings attention to origins and copies of shots and perspectives and dramatizes the idea of "death and nothingness" in the film *Cronaca di un amore* (1950; Story of a Love Affair). See Noël Burch, *Theory of Film Practice* (New York: Praeger, 1973), 78–79.
43. Slavoj Žižek, "Neighbors and Other Monsters: A Plea for Ethical Violence," in *The Neighbor: Three Inquiries in Political Theology*, by Slavoj Žižek, Eric L. Santner, and Kenneth Reinhard (Chicago: University of Chicago Press, 2005), 134–90, 189. See also Stella Sandford, *The Metaphysics of Love: Gender and Transcendence in Levinas* (London: Athlone, 2000).

INDEX

abjection: art and, 130; of father, 186–91; logic of, 125–26
abstract cinema, 171–72
Achieving Our Country (Rorty), 42
"Adieu" (Derrida), 49
Adorno, Theodor W., 83
adventurism, 39–40
aesthetic screen, 113
Ainley, Alison, 17–18, 173
Allen, Woody, 82–83, 151
alterity: the body and, 183; elevation of, 173; of the feminine, 12, 164n5, 173, 175, 194; time and, 3; transcendent, 19, 20. *See also* the other
American cinema of redemption: actors of classic, 81; classic films, 6, 25–26; documentation of actors, 92; vs. European, 144; messianism in, 14; moral visions, 38–40. *See also specific films*
American culture: cinematic articulations of ambiguity in, 50; democratic hero, 73; Monroe as symbol, 90; pornography in, 89
American ideology: anarchy and, 41; biblical symbolism, 33–34; the disempowered and, 44–45; dissensus and, 42–44, 46, 47; exceptionalism, 39, 42, 46, 48; exuberant, 119; frontier and, 54, 116; myth of national identity, 53; reaffirmation of, 26
"American Scholar" (Emerson), 31, 32
anarchism, 40–41
angel of sex, 90–91
Anouilh, Jean, 117
Antigone (Anouilh), 117
Antonioni, Michelangelo: abstract cinema, 171–72; background of, 182; Cannes Statement, 177–79, 181, 189, 191; on characteristics of women, 211–12; on concluding scenes of *L'avventura*, 213–14; documentary and, 171–72, 181–82, 240n23; feminism in films, 189. *See also L'avventura*
aporetic temporality, 225n29
aporia of double perspective, 238n17
Arnold, Matthew, 116
Arrowsmith, William, 177–78, 203
art: abjection and, 130; as caricature, 156–57; coherence with ideology, 147; documentary and, 151–52; ethics and, 154–55, 225–26n33; idolatry of, 17, 156–57, 225n32; sexuality fused with, 126
aura of photographic image, 83

Auschwitz, 56
L'avventura: absence of dialogue, 201; close-ups, 196, 202, 204–205, 209; concluding scenes, 212–15; dead time, 184; documentary aspects, 180–82, 197–98; eroticism as social illness, 178; the female body as home, 192–93, 196–97; feminism and, 183; foreshadowing in, 198–99; importance of, 170; long takes, 202; opening scene, 168–69, 183–85, 189–90, 197; premiere, 176–77; sexual ethics, 176, 177; as study of psychical impotence, 180; themes, 191, 204–205; time in, 170, 171; understatement in, 208

Balázs, Béla, 83
Barthes, Roland, 197
Basic Philosophical Writings, 59
Beauvoir, Simone de, 172–73
being and not being, 202
belonging, sense of: ethical commitment and, 108; individual distinction within, 109; newness of, 107; use of music and, 107
the beloved, 174
Benjamin, Walter, 83
Bercovitch, Sacvan, 33, 42–44, 46
Bergen-Aurand, Brian K., 9, 169–70, 225–26n33
Bergman, Ingmar, 77–82, 80, 82–83
Bernstein, Richard J., 49
Beyond the Verse, 33, 34, 47–48
Il bidone, 148
blackness, power of, 106–112
Bobby (dog), 2
the body: alterity and, 183; architecture of, 205–208; borders of, 211; conflict with the soul, 200–203; ethics and, 136, 191; the eyes as separate from, 74; mapping of, 126, 130; power of, 192; relation to the other and, 129; sexuality and, 206; sexualized, 86, 128; temporal displacement and, 70–71; transcendence and, 175. *See also* the female body
Body and Soul, 35–38, 102, 104
Bogart, Humphrey, 34–35
Bondanella, Peter, on *La dolce vita*: in body of Fellini works, 149; coherence of film art and ideology, 147; importance of, 144, 151, 153–54; transcendence in, 149–50; as transition, 150
—on trilogies of Fellini, 148–49
Bonitzer, Pascal, 203
bowler hat symbol, 123–24, 130
Brando, Marlon, 38, 39
Brunette, Peter, on Cannes Statement, 177; on feminism and Antonioni's films, 189
—on *L'avventura*: close-up, 209; on disappearance of Anna, 203; on eroticism as illness, 198; on redemption, 200; on train, 210; on women, 169
Buell, Lawrence J., 27–28
Burch, Noël, 241n42
Burke, Frank, 150
Butler, Judith, 79

camera: as agent of misogyny, 167; as change agent, 137–39, 161
Campbell, Joseph, 7
Canby, Vincent, 120
Cannes Statement (Antonioni), 177–79, 181, 189, 191
Capra, Frank, 50; European influence on, 229–30n4; personal crisis, 74; theme of

morality, 49–50. *See also It's a Wonderful Life; Mr. Smith Goes to Washington*
Capracorn, 50, 71, 76
the caress, 13, 19–20, 136–37, 235–36n25
Carney, Ray, 50
Carrière, Jean-Claude, 119
Casablanca, 34–35
Cattrysse, Patrick, 122
Cavell, Stanley, 27–28
change: emphasized by use of montage, 51; proclivity for, 45–46, 228n25
Chanter, Tina: on *Casablanca*, 34–35; on effect of World War II on Levinas, 1; on face-to-face, 220n11; on the feminine, 18; on feminist participation in philosophy of Levinas, 172–74; on fetishes, 125; on mapping of the body, 126; on otherness of women, 18–19; on passage from the saying to the said, 58–59
Chatman, Seymour, 169
Childress, Sarah, 94, 95
chosenness, 65–66
cinema of the body, 62–63
cinema of the invisible/of interstices, 168–71, 197, 203
cinema of minimalism, 169
cinema of moving parts, 223n23
cinema of redemption: American vs. European, 144; approach of, 5–6; classics, 6; diversity, 8, 220n15; *La dolce vita* as transitional work, 148, 149, 150, 237n7; quest for redemption, 7–8; role of time, 6; transcendence, 6–7. *See also* American cinema of redemption

cinematography: absence of dialogue, 201; creating disjuncture, 209–210, 241n42; of group action, 161; of the invisible, 168–71, 197, 203; long takes, 202; montage, 51, 53–56, 156; of moral ambiguity, 145; music and, 54, 100, 107, 118, 121–22; of nihilism, 116, 117–18; point-of-view shots, 15–17; repeated pattern of shots, 10; representation of values through, 156; sound and, 109; use of understatement, 208. *See also* close-ups; concluding scenes; documentary techniques; opening scenes
civil disobedience, 47
Clift, Montgomery. *See The Misfits*
close-ups: battle of good and evil, 103, 104–105; to change organization of time and space, 12–13; for contrast, 196; directors associated with, 82; disconnection and, 202; empowerment and, 209; holiness and, 86–87; independence and, 204–205; interiorization and, 94–95; martyrdom and, 60; meaning of the face, 80; modern art and, 82; the soul and, 82–83; space of responsibility and, 139
Common Sense (Paine), 41
concluding scenes: death not as end, 141–43; forms of redemption, 11–12; Hollywood happy ending, 72–73; possibility of transcendence, 147; rejection of regeneration, 13–14; role of the feminine, 11; uncertainty in, 212–15
consensus: dissensus and, 43, 44; ethics and, 41
continuing majorities, 45

Cooper, Sarah: on the face and racism, 234n29; on the face and visage, 110; on space of responsibility, 48, 78–79, 80, 81, 139; works of, on Levinas and cinema, 8–9

Crèvecœur, Hector St. John de, 44–45

Critchley, Simon: on aesthetic screen, 113; on asymmetry of responsibility to the other, 3, 85–86, 99–100; on dissensus, 41, 42–43; on ethics and politics, 40–42; on new language for civil disobedience, 47; on radical immanentism, 7; on subject as object, 15; on sublimation and trauma, 226n39; on trauma, 99

Cronaca di un amore, 241n42

crucifixion image, 60, 61

cultural continuities, 29

culture and the face, 81

curvature of intersubjective space, 85–86, 114

Czechoslovakia under Communism, 119–20, 131–32, 138–39

daughters: alienation and, 184–85, 188–89; as future, 188, 189; in patriarchy, 185, 186; as subhuman, 165

Dead End Kids, 26

death: ethical responsibility to the other and, 36; ethics overcomes, 5; immanence and, 167; living and, 208; not as end, 64, 72, 141–43; time and, 62, 63

de Beauvoir, Simone, 172

defecation, 131, 132–33

Deleuze, Gilles: on the meaning of the face in close-ups, 80; on montage and, 55, 56; on movement-images, 223n23; on racism and the face, 234n29; on time and movement in film, 51, 55

democracy: American cathedral of, 54, 56; anarchy and, 41; dissensus and, 40–41, 42–44, 47; ethics and politics and, 40–42; as religion, 54, 56

Derrida, Jacques, 17; on democracy, 41; on disjuncture of time, 3; funeral oration for Levinas, 49; on responsibility to the other, 48; on time in Judaism, 56; on transcendence within immanence, 72, 128

Descartes, René, 8, 30, 211

despair, 14

Dewey, John, 41

diachronic time: infinity and, 202–203; in montage, 56; to overcome tyranny of ordinary time, 61–62; redemption and, 223n24; of the soul, 32; synchronic time and, 223–24n24; transcendence and, 56–57

the disempowered: American ideology and, 44–45; empowering, 110–11, 112

disjuncture of time: in cinema of redemption, 6; Derrida on, 3; ethical and psychological disjuncture and, 104; perspective and position in cinematography and, 209

dissensus: democracy and, 40–41, 42–44, 47; regeneration and, 45, 228n25; revolution and, 45–46

divine paternity, 21, 22

documentary techniques: Antonioni, 171–72, 180–82; art blended with, 151–52; eroticism as illness and, 181, 197–98; fiction and, 182, 183; filming the invisible, 181; hopelessness, 15; reality and, 181–82, 240n23; to refigure time, 15–16; voice-overs, 67

La dolce vita: close-ups, 12–13; concluding scene, 11–12, 13–14, 147; dehumanization of women in, 165, 166–67; documentary vision, 144–46, 151–52; Fellini's moral distance, 153–54; opening scene, 152–53, 155–58, 169; redemption in, 12; relationship between time and space, 150, 237n7; temporal order, 163–64; transcendence in, 12–14; as transitional work, 148, 149, 150, 237n7

"Dover Beach" (Arnold), 116

duration, 57

earthly city, 38–39

Edwards, Jonathan, 66

Eliot, T. S., 59

embodiment: abject paternity and, 186–89; the female body and, 175; importance of, 174–75; structure of, 71–72

Emerson, Ralph Waldo: achievement of transcendence and, 32, 227n9; American exceptionalism and, 46; civil disobedience and, 47; Levinas and, 30–31, 32–33; Puritans and, 27, 28, 30

eroticism as illness: documentary techniques and, 181, 197–98; in modern society, 178, 179

"Essence and Disinterestedness," 224n24

ethical face, invisibility of, 84

ethical responsibility to the other: all-powerful Deity and, 68; asymmetry of, 3–4, 15–16, 62, 85–86, 99–100; awakening to, 37–38; the body and, 129; death and, 36; exposure and vulnerability, 139; hostage to, 114; as illusion, 118; in Judaism, 63; language of, and American ideology, 35; parental relationship and, 164–66; politics and, 47–48, 88; proximity and, 192; religious witness to, 59–60; reward and, 76; seeing self in eyes and place of the other, 73; the soul and, 36; time and, 3; total understanding and, 87; violence and, 98

ethical subjectivity: asymmetry of, 114; challenge to create new, 12; defenselessness and, 101; modernity and, 113, 114, 115–18; requirements, 114

"Ethical Subjectivity," 30

ethics: art and, 154–55, 225–26n33; the body and, 191; consensus and, 41; death and, 5; the female body as initiator, 183; human attempts to cheat, 49–50; knowledge and, 98; love and, 5, 117, 217, 220n11; politics and, 14–17, 40–43, 133–34; as primary in philosophy, 3–4, 27; solitude and, 224n24; traditional film approach, 9; transcendence and, 4, 197–200; violence and, 97–98

ethics of response, 170

ethics of sexual difference, 194

ethics of sexuality, 129, 174–75

Existence and Existents, 1, 3, 18, 202

existentialism, 2

the eyes: seeing self in, of the other, 73; seeing world through another's, 119; as separate from the body, 74

the face: ambiguity and, 105; aura and, 83–84; authenticity of character, 94; defenseless, 85; of evil, 102; as

the face (*continued*)
    expression of ultimate responsibility to the other, 220n11; as focus of ethical demand, 93; holiness and, 79, 86–87, 160; impossibility of achieving ethical representation, 77–78, 79; interaction with culture, 81; invisibility of ethical, 84; Judaism and, 77; racism and, 234n29; redemption and, 80–82, 86–89, 93, 99, 100–101, 110; as reflection of the other, 111–12; as reflection of soul, 108–109; transcendence and, 84, 95–96, 220n11; as ultimate sign of the human, 60; visage and, 78–79, 80, 81, 89, 110

face to face: Chanter on, 220n11; nature of responsibility, 85; the other and, 11; Puritanism, 30

fathers. *See* paternity

"The Fecundity of the Caress" (Irigaray), 176, 182–83, 194, 206

fecundity vs. virility, 186

Fellini, Federico: 144–45; background of, 151; directorial style, 154; Rossellini and, 150; trilogy of salvation/grace, 148–49. *See also La dolce vita*

the female body: embodiment and, 175; as home, 192–93, 196–97; as initiator of ethics, 183; mystery of femininity in, 172; potential power of, 130; as prison, 183; transcendence and sexualized, 191

the feminine: alterity and, 12, 164–65, 173, 175, 194; the caress and, 19–20; crisis of, 183–85; as distinguished from women, 18; as home, 11, 196–97; immanence and, 19–20; overcoming sexism and, 135; sons as substitution for, 175–76; as source of redemption, 172; subjectivity of, 176; subordinated, 19, 22, 220n11; transcendence of male through, 172

feminism/feminists: Antonioni and, 189; common ground with Levinas, 173; engaging Levinas for, 17–20; ethics of dissensus, 42. *See also specific philosophers*

fetishes, 123–26, 130

fiction woven with history, 17, 52, 54, 119, 138, 182

film: as blend of art and documentary, 151–52; as documentary about actors, 92, 152; face and, 77; problem of the face, 80; representational codes, 182; representation of time, 223n23; temporal nature, 222n21; traditional approach of ethics, 9; as truth, 82, 138; as visual opera, 121–22

film noir, 230n4

films of character, 148

film-within-film mechanism, 67, 69, 121

Fitzgerald, F. Scott, 207

the flesh. *See* the body

Fonda, Henry. *See The Grapes of Wrath*

Ford, John. *See The Grapes of Wrath; The Searchers*

"The Fortune of the Republic" (Emerson), 46

freedom, 107–108, 138

Freud, Sigmund, 124, 179–80, 186, 187

Fryer, David Ross, 11

Gable, Clark. *See The Misfits*

Garfield, John, 26, 35–39

Gilman, Richard, 169

God. *See* religion

God, Death and Time, 57, 63, 73, 74

"God and Philosophy," 5, 31, 32, 37, 65–66, 164

Godard, Jean-Luc, 222n21
"The Grand Chartreuse" (Arnold), 116
The Grapes of Wrath: close-ups, 86–88; documentary techniques, 15; ethics and politics in, 14–17; the face and redemption, 86–89; religious imagery, 87
Greene, Graham, 115
Griffin, Susan, 89
Guattari, Félix, 234n29

Hancock, John, 56
Hand, Seán, 46
Heidegger, Martin, 2, 8, 49, 63, 204, 222n23
Hillel (Rabbi), 63, 68
history: connections to, 157; empowerment of the disempowered, 110–11, 112; fiction woven with, 17, 52, 54, 119, 138, 182; reenactments, 56
holiness of the face, 79, 86–87
Hollywood Renaissance, 22, 230n5
Holocaust, 1, 99
home: the body as, 206; male domination of, 210; role of, 192; significance of, 205; women and, 11, 192–93, 196–97, 203–204
homoeroticism, 198–99
hope, realm of, 64
horizon of being and time-shelters, 222–23n23
horizon of expectation, 61
human rights and rights of the other, 46
Husserl, Edmund, 2, 49
The Hustler, 102–106

identity: changing, 225n29; crisis of, 25; of male in Hollywood, 52; redemption as renewal of, 96. *See also* nonidentity
identity of nonsense, 72

"Ideology and Idealism," 45–46
idolatry: of art, 17, 156–57, 225n32; of fellow humans, 58; image of the face and, 77
illeity, 59–60
images: aura of, 83; movement-images, 54–56, 223n23; reality and, 77; shallowness of, 156–57; time, 55, 57–58; use of mirrors and, 126, 127–28, 129, 198–99. *See also* art
imagination and movement-images, 55
immanence: the feminine and, 19–20; murder and, 167; redemption and, 146, 147; transcendence and, 128, 158–59, 163, 164, 201
immanent subjectivity, 154
infinite asymmetry, 3
infinity: access to, 57, 186; child as relationship to, 166; diachronic time and, 202–203, 224n24; individual connection, 223n24; love and, 143, 164; spirituality and, 29–30, 31; time and, 10, 11, 36
"Inside Heidegger: Bergson," 57
institutionalized desublimation, 139
internal exile, 194
In the Time of the Nations, 33
Irigaray, Luce: on Antigone, 117; on architecture of the body, 206; on borders of the body, 211; on dichotomy between sexual impulse and object, 187–88; on embodiment, 175; on ethics of sexual difference, 194; on female sexuality, 20; on fetishization of women, 125; on jouissance, 206, 208; on mirror metaphor, 127–28; on sexual difference in the other, 174; on sexuality

Irigaray (continued)
and spirituality, 188; on sexuality and transcendence, 182–83; on spiritual love, 201; on subjectivity of the feminine, 176; on subversion of otherness of the other, 175; on thresholds, 193–94; on time and deployment of space, 210; on women as home, 203–204; on women's multifaceted sexuality, 126–27; on wonder as passion, 75, 211

Israel (nation), 34

It's a Wonderful Life: concluding scene, 72–73; montage, 68; opening scenes, 74; redemption in, 38; themes, 50; time in, 66; tollbooth scene, 69–70

I vitelloni, 148

James, William, 66, 76
Jefferson, Thomas, 45, 46
jouissance, 206, 208
Judaism: American national redemption and, 33–34; divine paternity in, 21; image of the face and, 77; responsibility for the other in, 63; time in, 56; World War II and, 1–2, 99

Kael, Pauline, 119
Kant, Immanuel, 8, 20, 27, 62, 64
Katz, Claire Elise, 174
Kaufman, Philip. See *The Unbearable Lightness of Being*
Kezich, Tullio, 151
kitsch, 130–32, 139, 152–53
knowledge and ethics, 98
knowledge and spirituality, 32
Krasker, Robert, 117–18
Kundera, Milan, 114, 131, 132, 234n4

Landy, Marcia, 172
language: civil disobedience and, 47; of ethical responsibility to the other and American ideology, 35; recuperative power of, 59; sexist, 174
Lanzmann, Claude, 80
the last station for Kundera, 142–43
Leaming, Barbara, 91–92
Lears, Jackson, 47
Letters from an American Farmer (Crèvecœur), 44–45
Levi, Raissa, 2
Levinas, Emmanuel: death, 49; education, 2; overlooked, 8; World War II experiences, 1–2
Lincoln, Abraham, 46, 54, 56
Llewelyn, John: on the face, 84, 85; on messianic time, 21; on regeneration, 62; on spiritual optics, 40, 170
love: ethics and, 5, 117, 217, 220n11; exteriority of the other and, 147; of fathers, 186, 188; fetishes and, 124–25; God in carnal, 206; infinity and, 143, 164; metaphysics of, 191; philosophy and, 216; politics and, 138; redemption through, 119; selfless, 140–41; spiritual, 201; transcendence united with, 206–207
"Love of Self" (Irigaray), 194
Lucia, Cindy, 104
Luci del varietà, 148

Mailer, Norman, 89, 90–91, 92
Maland, Charles, 50
Malcolm X, 106
male identity, 52, 92–93
Mamet, David, 83

Marcuse, Herbert, 139
martyrdom: of individual, 60, 86; moral, 39; the other and, 20–21; for sins of nation, 106–108
McBride, Joseph, 50
media: as agents of misogyny, 167; reality and, 145, 151, 159; responsibilities of, 162
Merleau-Ponty, Maurice, 163
messianic time, 20–22
Miller, Arthur, 89, 90–92, 100
Miller, Perry, 28–29, 30, 66, 227n2
mirrors, use of, 126, 127–28, 129, 198–99
mise-en-scène: of nihilism, 116; time coherence, 157; of transcendence, 38–39; use by Levinas, 8, 220–21n16
The Misfits: background of, 90, 92; characters as actors' alter egos, 95; close-ups, 94–95; as documentary, 92; ethics of responsibility in, 98–99; mustang hunt, 97–98; redemption in, 89, 93, 99, 100–101; use of music, 100; as vehicle for Monroe, 90–92
"A Model of Christian Charity" (Winthrop), 46
modernity: in American vs. European films, 230n4; celebrity culture, 160; challenges to, 32; eroticism and, 178, 179; ethical crisis of, 134; ethical subjectivity and, 113, 114, 115–18; Hamlet as metaphor for, 3; history and, 157; morality and, 49; movement and, 156; nihilism of, 116, 145, 146–47, 150; religion and, 152–53; role of women, 189–90; secularism and, 67; sexuality and, 123, 191; surveillance and, 138
Monroe, Marilyn, 89–101

montage: to compress time frames, 53–54; diachronicity in, 56; to emphasize change, 51; movement as modernity, 156; as movement-image, 54–56
moral ambiguity, cinematography of, 145
moral man, 178–79
moral messengers, 37
"The Most Prevalent Form of Degradation in Erotic Life" (Freud), 179–80
mothers, 172
movement: to disrupt temporalities, 210, 241n42; ethical priorities and, 105; modernity and, 156; time and, 51, 54–55, 67–68, 154
movement-images: in film, 223n23; montage as, 54–56
Mr. Smith Goes to Washington: close-up, 60; Deleuzean time and movement in, 51; filibuster, 60–61, 63–64; montage in, 51, 53–54; redemption in, 38; themes, 50, 60; time in, 35, 57, 62, 67; transcendence in, 56, 57; triumph of good over evil, 52–53; use of history, 54; use of music, 54
Murch, Walter, 119
music: film as visual opera, 121–22; freedom and, 138; nationalism and, 54; nihilism and, 118; in opening scenes, 136; sense of belonging and, 107; sexuality and, 122; uncertainty, 215

Naremore, James, 92
New Jerusalem, America as, 33–34, 46
Newman, Paul, 102–106
the new man (Crèvecœur), 45
New Yorker, 119
nihilism: cinematography of, 116, 117–18; of modernity, 116, 145, 146–47, 150

noema-noesis relationship, 163
nonidentity, 71, 72, 73
Le notte di Cabiria, 148, 150
Nowell-Smith, Geoffrey: on background of Antonioni, 182; on *L'avventura*, 170, 176–77; on sexuality, 198

"The Occluded Relation: Levinas and Cinema" (Cooper), 8–9
Oedipus (Sophocles), 133–34, 136
Oliver, Kelly: on abject father, 186–89; on dehumanization of women, 165; on face to face and the other, 11; on "there is" ("raw being"), 202
On the Waterfront, 38, 160
opening scenes: crisis of the feminine, 183–85; ethical positioning and intrusion, 10; as fairy tale, 120–23; the feminine and, 168–69; infinity and, 74; music, 136; religion as kitsch, 152–53; to reveal the invisible, 197; role of women and, 189–90; use of time, 155–56, 237n13
originary time, 57
the other: actualization of the self and, 11; alienated, 14–15; child as the Same and, 165–66; disjuncture of time and, 3; the face and, 111–12, 220n11; human rights and, 46; inability to be, 211; love and exteriority of, 147; as reflection of the self, 160; role of sexual difference in, 174; sacrifice of the self for, 20–21; seeing self in eyes and place of the other, 73; seeing through the eyes of, 15–16; separation from, 224n24; subversion of otherness of, 175; time and priority of, 170; transcendence through relationship with, 12–14. See also alterity; ethical responsibility to the other
Otherwise Than Being, 42, 128, 216

Paine, Thomas, 41
parental relationships, 164–66, 172, 184–85
The Passenger, 181, 203
paternity: abject, 186–91; disembodied, 186–89; divine, 21, 22; impotence of, 187; love and, 186, 188
"Peace and Proximity", 32
Perez, Gilberto, 83, 181, 185
Perpich, Diane: on the caress, 19, 136–37, 235–36n25; on the feminine, 18
phenomenology, 2, 221n16
"Phenomenology of Eros," 174
philosophy: determinate nature of, 173; ethics as primary in, 3–4, 27; history, 113, 234n2; love and, 216
photography, 137–39, 161
"Pirkei Avoth" ("Sayings of the Fathers"), 63, 68
pluralism and diachronic time, 224n24
"The Poet" (Emerson), 31, 32
poetics of narrative, 157, 225n29
point-of-view shots, 15–17
politics: ethics and, 14–17, 40–43, 133–34; love and, 138; responsibility to the other and, 47–48, 88
prophecy, 31
psychical impotence, 180
Puritanism, 27, 28–29, 30, 32–34, 39

"Questions to Emmanuel Levinas: On the Divinity of Love" (Irigaray), 175, 176, 183

racial inclusion, 54
racism, 39–40, 234n29
radical immanentism, 7
Raeburn, John, 50
Rafferty, Terrence, 119, 126, 127
Raging Bull, 120
Ray, Robert, 50
reality: capturing on film, 181–82, 240n23; image and, 77; invisibility of, 170–71; media and, 145, 151, 159
"Reality and Its Shadow," 77
recuperable temporalization, 224n24
redemption: ambiguities of, 102; American national, 33–34; diachronic time and, 223n24; earthly city and, 38–39; the face and, 80–82, 86–89, 93, 99, 100–101, 110; the feminine as source, 172; immanence and, 146, 147; martyrdom for national, 106–108; politics of, 14–17; protagonist as enemy of, 102; renewal of identity as, 96; search for miracle and, 161–63; sexism and racism in, 39–40; through love, 119; time and, 35–36; universal narratives of, 7; without finality, 101
Reed, Carol, 115–18
"Regarding Anna: Levinas, Antonioni and the Ethics of Film Abuse" (Bergen-Aurand), 9
regeneration: of the disempowered, 44; dissensus and, 45, 228n25; life without, 13–14; opportunities, 4; as principal event of time, 62; Puritan, 28–29; state and, 33–34
religion: America as New Jerusalem, 33–34; democracy as, 54, 56; as kitsch, 152–53; nonsectarian, in films, 26; patriarchy and, 185, 186, 215; Transcendentalism and, 28
—God: in carnal love, 206; curvature of space and, 86; defecation and, 131; as film director, 67, 68, 69
—use of imagery of crucifixion, 60, 61; by Fellini in salvation trilogy, 148–49; Jesus, 75, 87, 152–53; Madonna, 215. *See also* spirituality
Renoir, Jean, 83
representational thinking, 222n23
repressive desublimation, 139
responsibility: election and, 65–66; face to face, nature of, 85; rights and, 42
revolution, arguments for, 45–46, 228n25
Ricciardi, Alessia, 152, 159
Ricoeur, Paul: on asymmetry of ethical responsibility to the other and, 62; on history and fiction, 182; on horizon of expectation, 61; on multiple temporalities, 52, 54, 74, 225n29; on reenactments, 56; on relationship between time and narrative, 52, 157
rights and responsibility, 42
The Right Stuff, 119
Rodowick, D. N.: on cinema of the body, 62; on movement-image, 55–56; on time and nonidentity, 71, 72
Rohdie, Sam: on Antonioni and documentary, 181–82, 240n23; on movement to disrupt temporalities, 241n42
Rorty, Richard, 41–42
Rosenzweig, Franz, 8, 163
Rossellini, Roberto, 150
Rossen, Robert, 35–38, 102–106

the Same, 165–166, 236n26
"The Same and the Other," 31
Sandford, Stella: on illeity, 60; on love, 19, 191, 220n11
Sarte, Jean-Paul, 2, 49
Saxton, Libby, 77–78
the saying and the said, 58–59, 87
"Sayings of the Fathers," 63, 68
Lo sceicco bianco, 148
scientific man, 178–79
Scorsese, Martin, 120
The Searchers: concluding scene, 11, 13; opening scene, 10–11; the other in, 10; racism and sexism in, 39–40; redemption in, 12, 38; transformation of time in, 10
the self: asymmetrical ethical priority and, 4, 5, 20–21, 37–38; as Messiah, 21; the other and actualization of, 11; the other as reflection of, 160; as seen in eyes and place of the other, 73
Selfless Cinema? Ethics and French Documentary (Cooper), 9
selfless love, 140–141
sexism: linguistic, 174; overcoming, 135, 193–94; redemption for men only, 39
"Sexual Differences" (Irigaray), 194, 210, 211
sexuality: art fused with, 126; the body and, 206; dichotomy between impulse and object, 187–88; ethics of, 129, 174–75; female, 20, 126–27, 191; fetishes and, 123–26; male, 123, 128, 158–59; modernity and, 123, 191; music and, 122; as pathology, 178, 179, 180, 181, 197–98; as self-centered exploitation, 115; spirituality and, 188; transcendence and, 137, 182–83, 236n26; transcendence and ethics of, 197–200; uncontrollable nature, 179
Shoah, 80
signification, 192
Sklar, Robert, 67, 69, 75
solitude, 224n24
sons: as future, 172, 189; paternal election of, 164–65; paternal power and, 186; as substitution for the feminine, 175–76
Sophocles, 133–34, 136
the soul: close-ups and, 82–83; conflict with the body, 200–203; Emerson on, 31; ethical relationship to the other, 36; exteriority of search for, 83; the face as reflection of, 108–109
space and time, 55, 150, 210, 237n7
space of responsibility: Cooper on, 48, 78–79, 80, 81; in *The Grapes of Wrath*, 86; in *The Hustler*, 106; in *The Unbearable Lightness of Being*, 139
spirituality: blackness as, 110; infinity and, 29–30, 31; knowledge and, 32; love and, 201; sexuality and, 188; in transcendence, 5; Transcendentalism and, 28; trivialized, 152–53. *See also* religion
spiritual optics, 40, 170
the state, 33–34
Stewart, James, 25–26, 38–39. *See also It's a Wonderful Life*; *Mr. Smith Goes to Washington*
La strada, 148, 149
sublimation, 139, 226n39
"Substitution," 5
suicide, 68–69
synchronic time and diachronic time, 223–24n24

technology, triumph over religion of, 152–53
Tender Is the Night (Fitzgerald), 207
They Made Me a Criminal, 26
The Third Man, 115–18
the third man/person/way, 59–60
Thoreau, Henry David, 47
Three Essays in the Theory of Sexuality (Freud), 124, 179
thresholds, 193–94, 195, 196
time: alterity and, 3; aporetics of, 157, 238n17; behind ordinary, 57, 71; in cinema of redemption, 6; cinematic representation, 223n23; compression by montage, 53–54; crucifixion of ordinary, 61; dead, 184; death and, 62, 63; dimensions, 51–52, 53–54, 225n29; disjuncture of, 3, 6, 104, 209; infinity and, 10, 11, 36; linear as male, 212; messianic, 20–22; mise-en-scène and, 221n16; movement and, 51, 54–55, 67–68, 154; multiple, 52, 73, 103–104; nonidentity in, 71, 72; priority of the other and, 170; reality beyond ordinary, 88; redemption and, 35–36; redeployment, 210–11; refiguration of, 17, 52, 54, 119, 138, 182; regeneration as principal event, 62; space and, 55, 150, 210, 237n7; temporal nature of film, 222n21; tyranny of ordinary, 61; unhinged, 1, 2–3, 4, 62. *See also* diachronic time
Time and the Other, 11, 18
time-frames: as challenges to spectator subjectivity, 155–56, 157; compression of, 53–54; time-shelters and, 237n13
time-images, 55, 57–58
time-shelters: horizon of being and, 222–23n23; temporality emphasis, 155, 237n13

Toland, Gregg, 16–17. *See also The Grapes of Wrath*
Totality and Infinity, 42, 49, 62, 128, 166, 174, 183, 192, 216–17
train symbol, 209–210
transcendence: alterity requirements, 19; the body and, 175; the caress and, 136–37, 235–36n25; diachronic time and, 56–57; Emerson and achievement of, 32, 227n9; exteriority of, 134; the face and, 84, 95–96, 220n11; finite, 220n11; frustrated, 7; immanence and, 128, 158–59, 163, 164, 201; love united with, 206–207; of male through the feminine, 172; mise-en-scène of, 38–39; near impossibility of achievement, 149–50; possibility of temporal, 158; sacrifice of women, 216; sexism and, 193–94; sexual ethics and, 197–200; sexuality and, 137, 182–83, 236n26; sexualized female body and, 191; third man and, 59–60; through relationship with the other, 12–14
"Transcendence and Height," 29–30, 33, 65
"Transcendence and Intelligibility," 30, 221n16
transcendental ideal, 64
transcendental impulse, 203
Transcendentalism, 26, 27–28, 30–31, 39, 227n2
"The Transcendentalist" (Emerson), 31, 32
The Transcendentalists: An Anthology (Miller), 28
trauma, 99, 100
truth: documentary and, 181–82, 240n23; film as, 82, 138; perceptions of, 158; search for, 162, 163; seized indirectly, 197

"Truth of Disclosure and Truth of Testimony," 31

The Unbearable Lightness of Being: American cinema of redemption and, 144; close-up, 139; concluding scene, 141–43; difficulties of filming, 119–20; linear time in, 115; modernity and formation of ethical subjectivity, 114; opening scene, 120–23, 135–36; redemption in, 144; title, 143; use of music, 121–22

"Violence of the Face," 221n16
virility vs. fecundity, 186
visage: the face and, 78–79, 80, 81, 89, 110; space between the face and, 80
visual minimalism, 169
Vorkapich, Slavko, 53

Waller, Marguerite R., 126–27n7
The Wanderers, 119
Washington, Denzel, 106–112
The Waste Land (Eliot), 59
Wayne, John, 10–11, 38–40. See also *The Searchers*
Welles, Orson, 116–17
whore-goddess syndrome, 90
whore-Madonna syndrome, 93
Wild, John, 66
Williams, Patricia, 42, 44
Winthrop, John, 46
women: as aesthetic objects, 169; characteristics ascribed by Antonioni to, 211–12; dehumanization of, 165; as distinguished from the feminine, 18; as enablers of men's access to infinity, 186; entrapment of, 185; in ethics of sexuality, 129; fetishization of, 125; home and, 11, 192–93, 196–97, 203–204; independence and, 204–205, 207; misogyny and, 165, 166–67; in modern society, 189–90; as mothers, 172; otherness of, 18–19; potential power of the body, 130; as reflection of man, 127; sacrifice of, for transcendence, 216; sexuality of, 20, 126–27, 191. See also daughters; the female body; the feminine
wonder, passion of, 74–75, 211
Wood, David: on being and time, 222–23n23; on horizon of being and time-shelters, 52, 222–23n23; on time and film, 9, 27; on time-frame, 52, 155–56, 157, 222–23n23, 237n13; on time-shelter, 222–23n23, 237n13
World War II, 1–2

Zaentz, Saul, 119–20
Ziarek, Eva Plonowska: on disempowered, 44; on embodiment, 71–72, 174–75; on ethics in politics, 42–43; on ethics of sexuality, 129; on female sexuality, 20; on idealization of sublimation, 226n39; on identity of nonsense, 72; on immanence and the feminine, 20; on permanent revolution, 46; on transcendence within immanence, 128; on transcendence without sacrifice, 216
Žižek, Slavoj, 5, 34, 216

Melodrama and Modernity: Early Sensational Cinema and Its Contexts
BEN SINGER

Wondrous Difference: Cinema, Anthropology, and Turn-of-the-Century Visual Culture
ALISON GRIFFITHS

Hearst Over Hollywood: Power, Passion, and Propaganda in the Movies
LOUIS PIZZITOLA

Masculine Interests: Homoerotics in Hollywood Film
ROBERT LANG

Special Effects: Still in Search of Wonder
MICHELE PIERSON

Designing Women: Cinema, Art Deco, and the Female Form
LUCY FISCHER

Cold War, Cool Medium: Television, McCarthyism, and American Culture
THOMAS DOHERTY

Katharine Hepburn: Star as Feminist
ANDREW BRITTON

Silent Film Sound
RICK ALTMAN

Home in Hollywood: The Imaginary Geography of Hollywood
ELISABETH BRONFEN

Hollywood and the Culture Elite: How the Movies Became American
PETER DECHERNEY

Taiwan Film Directors: A Treasure Island
EMILIE YUEH-YU YEH AND DARRELL WILLIAM DAVIS

Shocking Representation: Historical Trauma, National Cinema, and the Modern Horror Film
ADAM LOWENSTEIN

China on Screen: Cinema and Nation
CHRIS BERRY AND MARY FARQUHAR

The New European Cinema: Redrawing the Map
ROSALIND GALT

George Gallup in Hollywood
SUSAN OHMER

Electric Sounds: Technological Change and the Rise of Corporate Mass Media
STEVE J. WURTZLER

The Impossible David Lynch
TODD MCGOWAN

Sentimental Fabulations, Contemporary Chinese Films: Attachment in the Age of Global Visibility
REY CHOW

Hitchcock's Romantic Irony
RICHARD ALLEN

Intelligence Work: The Politics of American Documentary
JONATHAN KAHANA

Eye of the Century: Film, Experience, Modernity
FRANCESCO CASETTI

Shivers Down Your Spine: Cinema, Museums, and the Immersive View
ALISON GRIFFITHS

Weimar Cinema: An Essential Guide to Classic Films of the Era
NOAH ISENBERG

African Film and Literature: Adapting Violence to the Screen
LINDIWE DOVEY

Film, A Sound Art
MICHEL CHION

Film Studies: An Introduction
ED SIKOV

Hollywood Lighting from the Silent Era to Film Noir
PATRICK KEATING

GPSR Authorized Representative: Easy Access System Europe, Mustamäe tee
50, 10621 Tallinn, Estonia, gpsr.requests@easproject.com

www.ingramcontent.com/pod-product-compliance
Lightning Source LLC
Chambersburg PA
CBHW050901300426
44111CB00010B/1326